The BUSINESS **Shrink** | **Understanding the Strategy and Psychology of Business**

THE
disgruntled
EMPLOYEE

Manage challenging staff
without losing your mind

Peter Morris, Radio's Business Shrink
Introduction by Peter Laufer

A
BUSINESS

avon, massachusetts

Published by Adams Business, an imprint of
Adams Media, an F+W Publications Company
57 Littlefield Street, Avon, MA 02322
www.adamsmedia.com

ISBN-10: 1-59869-414-6
ISBN-13: 978-1-59869-414-7

Printed in Canada.

J I H G F E D C B A

Library of Congress Cataloging-in-Publication
Data is available from the publisher.

This publication is designed to provide accurate
and authoritative information with regard to the
subject matter covered. It is sold with the understanding that the publisher is not engaged in
rendering legal, accounting, or other professional
advice. If legal advice or other expert assistance is
required, the services of a competent professional
person should be sought.
—From a *Declaration of Principles* jointly
adopted by a Committee of the American
Bar Association and a Committee of
Publishers and Associations

Many of the designations used by manufactur-
ers and sellers to distinguish their product are
claimed as trademarks. Where those designations
appear in this book and Adams Media was aware
of a trademark claim, the designations have been
printed with initial capital letters.

This book is available at quantity discounts for
bulk purchases. For information, please call
1-800-289-0963.

contents

acknowledgments

The list is long of those I need to acknowledge for the successes of the *Business Shrink* radio show, Web site, blog, and—of course—this book.

Mindy Schulte was the show's founding producer; she was followed by Dan Zoll and Katrina Rill. Together, my producers have been tenacious and skillful at securing the extraordinary guest list for the radio show, stars reflected in the sources you find in this book.

James Vontayes and Michelle Wiersema have been by my side since the launch of the show as associate producers. It is James Vontayes who keeps me focused in our Chicago studio—especially on the dictatorial requirements of the clock. Radio and its coconspirator time are severe taskmasters, and James makes sure I do not forget that the conversations I enjoy with guests and the audience must not linger endlessly, no matter how enjoyable and informative they may be.

Our technical director, Ken Bryant, keeps us on the air, with help from our audio engineers Jada White and Andrew Roth.

Ned Robertson is the Business Shrink art director and Chris Slattery our design director.

I've been ably assisted by writers and researchers Randy Lyman, Jeff Kamen, Julie Mitchell, and Marc Polonsky.

James Harris is our Web developer and Joel Mackey our Webmaster.

The Business Shrink marketing director is Shane Hackett. Coordinating the brand is Kurt Iverson.

My thanks to our fine transcribers Kathy Talbert and Barbara Skow.

And finally, of course, I want to thank my guests for participating in the interviews and conversations from which we learn so much, and my listeners—especially those who choose to call the show and who add just the dose of reality we need to make sure the Business Shrink is taking care of business.

Peter Morris
Chicago

about The BUSINESS Shrink series

Peter Laufer » Welcome to the Business Shrink series, books designed to help you navigate the often-treacherous seas of the business world. Business Shrink Peter Morris is your cocaptain on your business journey. So relax. He's been across these waters dozens of times, and he's here to help make sure you make it safely to your business ports of call.

For several years now I've been privileged to work directly with Peter Morris as he's developed his nationwide radio show, launched his interactive Web site, and dipped his quill in the inkwell to put his words on paper for the Business Shrink books. I've been paying close attention as he's sparred on the air with an extraordinary cast of characters from the pantheon of business players: CEOs and entrepreneurs, business school deans, business book authors, and business news reporters. Add to that list the spectacular business questions and business stories that come from the callers and e-mailers in the radio show audience, and you can understand what a stimulating work environment it is for me to roll up my sleeves and labor in the Business Shrink's world.

It is a nonstop learning experience, and there is absolutely no question in my mind that after all those hours in the studio with Peter Morris—the two of us interpreting, pontificating, joking, and analyzing business—I've earned my MBA equivalent from the virtual Business Shrink Institute of Advanced Business Affairs. The books in this series are filled with the kind of advice and information that will provide you with the same sort of education I've enjoyed.

As the Business Shrink, Peter Morris explores the so-often-ignored reality that successful business relies on psychology and strategy. He knows successful business means problem solving. Too many people consider that business is based solely on power and logic and that it's absent feeling. At the same time they dismiss feeling as not logical and not businesslike.

In fact, this three-way intersection of business, psychology, and strategy is critical for people solving thorny problems in their business lives. The Business Shrink helps his "patients" find solutions to business problems based on this formula. From his years of experience on the frontlines of the business wars, entrepreneur Peter Morris knows how to help others find that critical balance point between logic and feeling. And he knows how and when to add an appropriate dose of power.

Brash, blunt, and loath to suffer fools gladly or otherwise, Peter Morris combines his academic and professional background (Princeton, Harvard, thirty-plus years of international real-estate adventures) with the street-smarts of a cigar-chomping Chicago success story. The result is these scrappy guides to solving daily business problems.

Every week Peter Morris is on the air across America with his radio show dealing with the business-world problems of his audience members. He brings his radio problem-solving techniques to these books, teaching readers how to manage workplace problems on a daily basis, before those problems become crises. And he defines *business* in the broadest possible manner: Just about everything we do every day involves business.

Because of his years of entrepreneurial experience, Peter Morris knows the needs of the small business owner and the small business employee. He can offer effective solutions to most business problems because he's seen and dealt with most of the symptoms that plague business owners and employees. Over and over again his listeners respond to his personalized answers to their questions by thanking him and saying, "That's a great idea. I never thought of that. I'm going to try that." When he hears back from them, for follow-up treatments, more often than not his ideas worked. The Business Shrink's personality cuts through the fog of jargon and offers a straight path to solutions. Peter Morris has a clear view of the business world and of how to develop win-win scenarios. His advice is long lasting—and in these books he offers readers templates for solving future problems.

Think you have too little time and not enough money? Those concerns are usually just excuses, according to the Business Shrink, who counsels readers to step outside normal expectations and categories, and adopt his worldview. Perhaps most important, this Chicagoan has a low tolerance for self-pity. His advice is as merciless as it is productive.

Peter Morris has multiple degrees from the School of Hard Knocks, along with an undergraduate degree from Princeton University in Public Affairs and East Asian Studies, and a law degree from Harvard Law School. Over the past thirty-odd years of doing business worldwide, he has made and lost fortunes. He knows the systems. Today his primary work is as a real-estate investor and as a financial adviser for funding and merger acquisition activities. He currently owns and controls real-estate assets worldwide with a development value in excess of $1 billion. His other interests include investing in and establishing biotech and health-care companies in conjunction with Harvard University and its affiliated hospitals.

As the Business Shrink, Peter Morris enjoys the opportunity to share his expertise with the radio audience, answering questions from novices in business and analyzing the state of the business world with business experts. Peter Morris leads newcomers to business by the hand, helping them figure out their paths to success while he engages as a peer with the captains of industry, analyzing capitalism's successes and failures. Peter Morris insists that a successful business and a happy businessperson must combine right-brain and left-brain activities. He knows successful business means problem solving.

These are opinion-driven business books, but these opinions have been tested in those thirty years of real-world successful experience. Life requires some tough choices; it requires facing reality. "Get real and make sense," says the Business Shrink, "and you can solve your business problems." He teaches his readers how to get past the things that stymie and consume them, and then how to get on with the business of business. These are problem-solving books, designed for you to write in, dog-ear, and spill your lunch on—in other words, for you to refer to repeatedly, as problems and challenges arise within your work life.

The Business Shrink series helps readers do what Peter Morris does: reduce a crisis to a yawn. Anywhere in the business world where a reader may be mired, Peter's been during his long career, so his view helps the reader get past the obstacles and obtain business success.

Bon voyage!

the disgruntled employee and you

You Can't Please 'Em All You may be the best boss in the world, but you still can't please everyone. Disgruntled and unhappy employees are everywhere. Some of them just don't like to work. Some don't like to *have to* work (a slightly different dilemma). Some of them are angry at life; some are angry at their mothers; some are angry at you.

If you're a nice person, you probably want everyone to be happy. There are indeed many things you can do to make your employees' lives pleasant, and to a certain extent their comfort on the job is your responsibility. But this is not your main responsibility. Your primary responsibility is to maintain an efficient workplace. A fair, well-run workplace will make most employees happy, but not all.

As you no doubt are aware, the unhappy employee can cause many problems, for you and the rest of your team.

It's Really Not about You Unless you're a monster of a boss, your disgruntled employee's unhappiness is probably not about you or your managing style. It *could* be about you, but it could also be about low wages, coworker dynamics, or the person's psychological disposition and personal life.

Many people are chronically dissatisfied. They feel destined for bigger and better things. They have a sense of entitlement and believe that life owes them things. They don't really want to work for anyone else at all.

Regardless of why an employee is disgruntled, you have to employ *logic, emotion,* and *strategy* in dealing with the employee and the problems he or she causes.

The Logical Side

Start with logic. What precisely is going on? How does the employee show that he or she is disgruntled?

Some discontented employees take a passive-aggressive approach. Rather than directly stating what they're unhappy about, they show their displeasure by coming in late, turning in sloppy work, dressing too casually, or making verbal digs at coworkers.

Other unhappy employees let their tempers show. They are easily annoyed. They complain about the workload or about the company itself or about working conditions. They are chronically difficult to get along with, and they create headaches for everyone.

So your first job is simply to identify the habits and behaviors that mark a particular employee as disgruntled.

Next, look at the consequences. How is this employee's behavior affecting the workplace? How is it affecting *you*? If you allow a disgruntled employee to broadcast his attitude for too long, he could become a role model for others, who may unconsciously assume that his manner is appropriate. If you feel you can tolerate the disgruntled employee, and if his work is good despite his attitude, and nobody else seems bothered by him, and you don't think he is compromising your department's mission in any way, then fine. Sometimes it's okay to let an unhappy employee maintain his state of dissatisfaction. The key is to look carefully and make sure that there are no hidden consequences to the employee's behavior. It's one thing if the rest of your office can laugh off the dissatisfied employee; it is quite another if some of your other workers feel intimidated or stressed out by him.

Next, consider your options. What courses of action are available to you, as a manager? And what are the likely

results of each course of action? Among other consider-
ations, think about how whatever you do will "go over"
with the rest of your team, and whether you might be
vulnerable to a grievance. It isn't easy being at the top.
You have to be very careful not only to *be* fair but also to
appear fair.

In a nutshell, these are the logical steps you should
take to fix the situation:

- Identify the employee's behavior
- Consider the consequences of the employee's
  behavior
- Decide on options for dealing with the employee's
  behavior

The Emotional Dimension

Emotions pervade everything. Everyone is a walking stew
of emotions. Some emotions are closer to the surface than
others. Some people keep their emotions hidden more
deeply than others, but you can be absolutely certain that
emotions are the prime motivator in every phase of our
lives. Even when we are trying to be "businesslike," we
are driven by emotions, including desire, insecurity, pride,
and perhaps fear and greed.

This is really not a bad thing. Emotions are the juice
of life. They are the fundamental force behind all our
striving and ambition, and positive emotions are the ultimate payoff.

You have to identify what kinds of emotions determine the words and behavior of the disgruntled employee
and what is her payoff?

This may not be easy to figure out, but if you can
glean even a little bit of emotional insight into your discontented employee, you will have a firmer handle on
the situation, because you will understand what types of
rewards and sanctions will best motivate her to behave in
an acceptable fashion.

This isn't easy. People are complex, and their internal emotional lives are extremely complicated. Just when you think a particular employee really needs a lot of praise, you might find her sullen with resentment because she feels you're being condescending. Or when you've figured out that another employee feels too much pressure and you lighten his workload for a while, you may discover that he becomes angry and suspicious of you for "undermining" his aspirations in the company. Just when you decide that a particular worker has become too arrogant and insolent and needs a strong scolding (in private of course), he might burst into tears and run out of your office. Yikes!

So you have to tread very, very carefully in the realm of emotions. Understand also that emotions change all the time and that contradictory emotions can coexist in the same person *at the same time.*

Have you ever loved *and* hated someone? Of course you have. Many of the people we love the most—including parents, children, and spouses—are also people who've inspired (admit it) hatred at times. But love and hate are the extreme examples of conflicting emotions. There are many far more ordinary, everyday varieties. Have you ever been excited, but also very nervous, about giving a presentation to your superiors or to a prospective major client? Pride and insecurity coexist all the time. (In fact, some people maintain that they are never separate.) Like and dislike also occur simultaneously. Far less dramatic than love and hate, like and dislike are much more common in the workplace. Some people might phrase it this way: "There are some things I like about him, and some things I dislike about him." An academic psychologist might put it like this: "You feel simultaneously attracted and averse to this individual."

Moods descend and pass more rapidly than the weather. Emotional disposition is affected by everything from body chemistry to room temperature to personal history to last night's sleep—not to mention other people's moods!

One employee might be impossibly irritable before she's had her first cup of coffee; another might get insanely hyperactive and nervous if he unwittingly imbibes regular coffee instead of decaf. Some people get restless after lunch; others feel more relaxed after the midday break. A wayward glance, a thoughtless word, or a simple smile can make or break an employee's mood for the day.

Don't imagine that you can control all this, or any of it. You, too, go through a world of different feelings every day. Just watch. See how often you feel content, annoyed, miserable, or elated in a twenty-four-hour period.

With disgruntled employees, there is a recurring emotional weather pattern, usually a storm. Unfortunately, that storm tends to rain indiscriminately on everyone in the vicinity. So how do you change the weather?

If you can find out what the disgruntled employee *really* needs, you just might be able to alter the general climate. Then again, some unhappy employees do not want to change, and they do not care to be understood. Some people find emotional satisfaction in being unhappy, and nothing you can do is going to turn that around. That is another thing you'll just have to figure out.

But in the meantime, you must be aware of how the disgruntled employee's behavior impacts the emotions of everyone else. You need to mitigate that effect wherever possible. As the boss, you are a referee on the field of emotion. You cannot control the action or interaction of all the players, but it is up to you to set proper limits. It is your job to enforce penalties and consequences when someone's behavior or speech is clearly "out of bounds."

- Use the words and behavior of the disgruntled employee to help you analyze her emotional status vis-à-vis the job. Her words—from casual conversation to formal work-related responses—can help you determine what she really wants from the job and the organization.

- Once you find out what the disgruntled employee *really* needs, you will be in a much better position to work with him to change his behavior or actions.
- Remember, you cannot control all the actions or interactions of your employees, but you can set limits and boundaries.

Strategy Strategy puts it all together. You take logic and emotion, and then you work out a systematic approach, a plan of some kind. On a long-term (or, in some cases, a short-term) basis, how will you deal with your disgruntled employee? What types of actions will you take? How many chances will you give this person to change? What are you willing to do to make her happy?

Peer pressure is a powerful force. One effective strategy is to enlist the help of other workers who perceive that there is a problem and who are mature enough to try to help in a way that will not exacerbate the problem or cause the disgruntled one to feel yet more resentful. You can talk to your trusted team members privately, individually, or in small groups about how best to handle and address the complaints of the dissatisfied worker. You can encourage your team members not to tolerate her unpleasant behavior. You can even bring the issue up in a team meeting—again, depending on your very careful reading of the emotional weather. This approach may be justified if different coworkers have been complaining to you about the disgruntled person.

Or you may choose a staggered strategy of escalating consequences over time, being very explicit with your worker as to what she can expect if she doesn't shape up and behave well. Consequences may include incidence reports, unfavorable evaluations, revocation of privileges or responsibilities, canceled bonuses, demotion, and suspension or firing.

If you choose this course, be sure to schedule regular meetings with the disgruntled employee to talk about her progress and to hear her feedback.

You may seek advice from team members or from managers in other departments. In these circumstances, always be discrete. You may take a long-term approach of mollifying the disgruntled employee and finding ways to make her more comfortable and less nervous, if you decide that's all that's needed. Or you may decide on a more disciplinary strategy or even a wait-and-see approach. Perhaps the employee involved is fairly new to your company or your team, and you don't altogether know what to expect from her or understand what her underlying issue is.

In any event, when you strategize, you subordinate your moment-by-moment reactions in favor of an over-arching scheme. You don't "shoot from the hip"—or merely follow the whims of your own moods—as you deal with a troublesome employee. You keep the big picture in mind, and you have a goal in view. Remember that you have an abiding responsibility to yourself and your company and your team members and that all you do for and with the disgruntled employee is in the service of those responsibilities. What you want, ultimately, is for the person to fit in and express her talents and skills happily in the environment that you provide for your team. And if that is impossible, sound strategy dictates that the person will probably have to go, either to another company or another department.

We All Get Out of Sorts Sometimes

It is important to distinguish between a chronically disgruntled employee and an occasionally unhappy employee.

Sometimes family problems and other off-the-job stressors can turn a normally delightful coworker into a morose, irritable curmudgeon. Especially if you have known this person for a long time, you should not be quick to pigeonhole him as someone with an attitude problem. We all go through times like this.

Becoming disaffected and irritable now and then is a natural part of life. Any work environment that demands a consistently sunny demeanor from its employees is a tyranny. It's one thing if your employees are interfacing with the public or with clients; then you have a right to expect that they will keep their grumpy moods to themselves. But apart from that, the best way to handle occasional disgruntlement is with a little humor and acceptance. You probably expect the same from others.

In fact, the most disgruntled employee is often the boss. Many office workers report that they are at the mercy each day of their boss's unpredictable disposition. If the boss got a good night's sleep and is feeling cheery, the sun shines on everyone. But if the boss is in an unpleasant frame of mind, then nothing is good enough, nobody else is allowed to be lighthearted, and the emotional atmosphere is stifling.

I certainly hope the previous paragraph does not describe *your* workplace.

In any event, remember to cut people some slack. One or two bad moods, or even one or two *weeks* of bad moods, do not a disgruntled employee make. An important distinguishing characteristic of a truly disgruntled employee is that their unhappiness goes on and on, seldom abating for long.

An employee's bad mood is unfortunate.

A disgruntled employee is a *problem*.

Or Is It Always a Problem?

Actually, a disgruntled employee need not necessarily be viewed as a problem. Sometimes there are systemic troubles in the work environment, and the employee in question is the canary in the coal mine. Other employees may be more tolerant of inefficient or archaic procedures, inadequate

working conditions, poor interoffice communication systems, and other types of unacceptable circumstances that
in fact are not only bad for employees but also for business.
Sometimes the unhappy employee is the voice of discontent for others who are more fearful to speak.

Unfortunately, even when this is the case, the disgruntled employee may not be willing or able to directly state
the problem. Like a small child who throws a tantrum when
something is bothering him but is incapable of verbalizing
his feelings, a discontented employee is often responding
to genuine irritants and obstacles at work but may not be
capable of clearly articulating what's making him so mad.
He just knows that work seems harder and more cum-
bersome than it should. He feels a sense of injustice and
oppression. He is miserable and doesn't know why.

This is where you, as the boss, have to be very sensitive
and emotionally attuned to the dynamics of the office.
You have to look and listen carefully and refrain from
snap judgments. Usually, in a situation like this, you've
already had some clues that all is not as it should be. One
of the best indicators as to whether the problem is with
the person or with something else in the environment is
the way coworkers respond to his expressions of irrita-
tion. If they seem vaguely gratified, or at least not upset,
it's possible they implicitly share some of the disgruntled
one's sentiments.

This could be an occasion for serious re-evaluation of
the workplace and its routines. But you need a strategy
to get to the bottom of what's going on. You might ask
probing questions of those who are closest to the affected
employee. Or you might take a more direct approach:
Call the disgruntled employee into your office and ask
him if he has any suggestions to improve the workplace.
Even if he doesn't know offhand what's been bothering
him, he'll at least have to think about it.

Of course, most of the time, it's not about the workplace. If only one employee is acting out of sorts, chances

are that the source of the disgruntlement lies within that person. Nevertheless, it is important to remember that not all upset or disaffected employees are destructive or disruptive.

You could even think of a disgruntled employee as a good challenge to your patience. This is no joke. Why should things always have to be easy? Shouldn't there be room for people who are a little prickly, as long as they perform their jobs honorably and dependably?

There is a story about the spiritual teacher G. I. Gurdjieff. At Gurdjieff's spiritual community in France, one old man annoyed everyone with his messy habits and cantankerous personality. Nobody liked him. One day the man decided to leave the community, but Gurdjieff followed him and talked him into coming back. The other members of the community were horrified. Here they were finally rid of this disgruntled old guy, and then the leader of the community goes out and brings him back! Gurdjieff explained, "This man is like yeast for bread. Without him you would never learn about anger, irritability, patience, and compassion."

Now it is certainly not your job to teach your workers how to be saints or to aspire to sainthood yourself. But if you have a difficult person in your office, why not take Gurdjieff's lesson to heart and try to develop a little patience and compassion? If you can look upon your disgruntled employee with some measure of acceptance and calm, it might make it that much easier to deal with some of the other difficulties in your life. And your other employees might respect you for it.

So don't always assume that the dissatisfied employee is the one who has to be "cured"—or the one who has to go. Often this is the case, but not always.

The Measure of an Effective Boss How you deal with a disgruntled employee will reflect definitively on the quality of your leadership. It will greatly determine how your workers perceive you, and how you perceive yourself.

This is why the most important element of the situation is not how the employee behaves but how *you* behave. You should never accept rude, distracting, or disrespectful behavior from an employee, but there is *never* an excuse for you to be rude or disrespectful either. Being firm and clear is important, but disrespectful words and tones of voice are demeaning to you as well as to your employee.

Be clear. If there is some behavior you need to criticize, say precisely what that behavior is. If, for example, you need to talk to an employee about her "attitude," have at least two or three examples in mind so you can be sure she knows what you mean. If there is a behavior that is unacceptable, be clear about what the acceptable alternative to that behavior would be.

In dealing with disgruntled employees, you must be consistent. The employee's behavior may be unpredictable, but yours should not be. You are in charge, and all your employees need to know what they can expect of you. Therefore, after you decide on a strategy and an approach—particularly if you have explicitly delineated a series of consequences for certain types of behavior—stick with that approach, at least until you are faced with compelling reasons to alter it.

Most of all you have to be fair; and that is the hardest, most complicated thing. In an imperfect world, it is impossible to be perfectly fair. "That would mean taking into account every factor, including your employee's upbringing and psychological constitution. You cannot do that. But you can make an effort to treat all your employees equally, spreading the message that if certain behaviors are not tolerated from one employee, they will not be tolerated from any other employees either. You must also make sure that your own attitudes and actions are motivated by what is best for the entire workplace, not by your personal likes and dislikes.

Let go of resentments. When a disgruntled employee shapes up, you need to forgive (if not forget) past transgressions in order to move forward together as a team.

Remember, it's not about you. Unless you're a terrible boss (and if you *are* a terrible boss, you probably wouldn't be interested in reading this book), the unhappy employee's underlying issue is not related to you or even to your department. It is hard not to take disrespectful or disruptive behavior personally when you are trying to run a tight ship and create a pleasant, efficient atmosphere for everyone. Yet, one of the keys to being a wise and mature manager is *never* to take aberrant behavior personally. This is an ideal goal, and you won't achieve it, but it's something to keep in mind when you face irritated employees.

Unhappy workers come in all shapes and sizes. Some of these employees present more of a challenge than others. If you are a supervisor for any length of time, your patience and managing skills will be tested in many different ways by disgruntled employees.

1 the phenomenon of the disgruntled employee

Who Is
Disgruntled? How do you recognize a disgruntled employee?

A lot of people like to look at the clock and count the minutes before they get to go home. Or they think, "Gosh, only ten more years until I get to retire." Although this is certainly an unfortunate and unhappy state of mind for the employee, it does not mean that the employee is, strictly speaking, *disgruntled* in the sense that we are tackling here. There is an inner, emotional dimension at work when people are disgruntled, but to keep things simple and avoid getting lost in psychoanalysis, let's start by defining a "disgruntled employee" strictly in terms of *behavior*. In the broadest terms:

- He is not fully engaged in his work most of the time.
- Her performance is spotty or erratic.
- He is unreliable.
- She doesn't socialize well with peers or superiors.
- He regularly expresses annoyance and irritability around the workplace.
- She provokes anger from others.

A disgruntled employee may also stir up workplace discontent among coworkers and habitually speak cynically about the job, the company, and perhaps about you.

Intuitively, everyone knows who the discontented employee is. But observing this person's behavior is the foundation for beginning to deal with it.

A Plague of Disgruntlement? Some social scientists believe that there are more disgruntled employees in the work force today than ever before. Some of them point to the "good old days" after World War II. Soldiers came back from the war happy to be alive, thrilled that their entire universe was no longer threatened, and grateful to Rosie the Riveter for relinquishing her job to the returning men. They would never have dreamed of letting minor dissatisfactions or a need for "more challenge" or "more meaning" ruin their day at work. These men knew they were lucky to have livelihoods! And the country had only recently emerged from the Great Depression, so these workers knew how bad things could get. But even the end of the Depression and the Allied victory in World War II didn't guarantee a happy work force. Wages had been frozen during the war, and 1946 was a year of strikes across America as workers sought to improve their status on the job.

Today, we live in more bountiful times. Despite the wars America has been involved with abroad, and even in spite of September 11, most of us take peace within our own borders for granted. Today's worker has grown up in a culture of instant gratification unimaginable to the laborer of fifty or sixty years ago. The baby boomers, Generation Xers, and Generation Yers have been coddled and flattered by advertisers, mass media, and well-intentioned educators and psychologists who talk about the "basic human need" for "self-actualization" and "achieving full potential." Not to mention, the cacophony of popular social philosophers and academics who decry the "dehumanization" of the workplace and have coined terms like *corporate drone* and *cogs in the gears of industry*.

Baby boomers, Gen Xers, and Gen Yers are increasingly mobile; they change jobs often. Changes occur for a variety of factors not prevalent in the 1950s and earlier, and the increasing number of women in the work force fuels that revolving door. Some workers make a horizontal, not vertical, leap to take a similar job within the same industry because the new company offers a more appealing work environment. Others change jobs to follow a relocated spouse. Still others choose to work part-time in order to spend more time at home raising children. The kind of loyalty that made it common to work for the same company for an entire career rarely exists now. Employees relish moving from job to job or even from career to career.

With massive changes taking place in the definition of work, rapid reconfiguration of many different working roles and careers, and all the remarkable emerging forms of twenty-first-century technology, people in the work force seem to have more choices than ever before. But, ironically, the very number of choices creates an underlying sense of anxiety and unease. It can breed a new kind of fear—the fear of not getting the goodies you deserve.

Therefore, today, it is much easier than ever to think you're getting a raw deal in life, no matter how many amenities you enjoy or what salary you draw. It's even become something of a fashion, a badge of sophistication, to be a bit of complainer and a cynic and never to admit you like your job.

On the other hand, now as ever, people want to get along with their coworkers, and many of us form deep, lasting friendships with associates from work. But when coworkers are cranky, self-centered, and hard to get along with, it can make an otherwise pleasant job into a misery. In the words of Katherine Crowley, the author of *Working with You Is Killing Me* and a guest on my radio show, "The actual activity of doing one's job is often relatively simple. The far more challenging thing about work is the relationships; the people you have to work with, the people who may invade your boundaries, the difficult boss, an unruly employee, a peer that doesn't carry his or her own weight."

A disgruntled employee is a kind of blight in the office, causing emotional and physical distress to supervisors and coworkers. Katherine Crowley likens the disgruntled employee to an elephant in the room, something you can try to ignore but that commands the bulk of your attention all the same. She says, "When you're under stress [from having to deal with a difficult person], it reduces your immune system. . . . Individuals go to work every day with a knot in their stomach or literally a pain in their neck, or their blood pressure begins to rise as they approach. . . . People often feel trapped at work. I'm trapped by my incompetent coworker or by this demanding customer, and I don't know how to get out."

An unhappy coworker can be downright scary. Even if the person never becomes physically violent, the threat of violence is often perceived to be there (especially if the disgruntled one is a drinker or drug user); verbal assaults and sarcasm also take their toll. The angry worker frays everyone's nerves, and turns the office into an unsafe, unwelcoming place for coworkers.

It's Even Worse for You

For you as a supervisor, the disgruntled worker presents a triple whammy. On the one hand, you have to endure the same negativity that everyone else does, which is wearing on the spirit. But it is also your designated role to set limits on what is and is not allowable, in terms of expressions of anger and discontent. So you have to be very careful; many disgruntled employees are extremely skilled at "toeing the line"—that is, going just so far but not far enough to clearly warrant disciplinary action. Furthermore, in many situations, you have to be extra careful not to be nasty or negative to the angry employee because that behavior, coming from you as a supervisor, could be construed as harassment or discrimination. So you have to suppress your natural human responses to these employees in many situations.

But most complicated of all, you're also responsible for the safety and well-being of *all* your subordinates, and therefore you're also called upon to *protect* the rest of the office from psychological and, in some cases, physical abuse by the disgruntled employee. If an employee is "acting out" in some fashion, and you stand by and let it happen, or fail to take prompt action, she can wreak havoc in a short time. She may hurt someone else on the job or hack into the company computer or verbally explode in some way that affects the company's customers and other relationships. Managers are often found liable, both legally and within the confines of a company, for the excesses of a disgruntled employee. Terry Bacon, the author of *What People Want: A Manager's Guide to Building Relationships That Work*, spoke to the safety and security issues when he was a guest on my radio show. "You have a responsibility to ensure safety in the workplace," he told us, "and that's why there's no substitute for very swift action if you see someone's reaching the brink. You just have to pull them aside and you have to take them off the line and deal with the situation very quickly."

At a certain point, in your role as manager you're no longer simply dealing with *just* a disgruntled employee, and whether or not to fire this person, or work with him to change his behavior. You're also making important decisions (pertaining to the disgruntled employee) that will greatly affect the lives of other workers, the company itself, customers, and even other third parties.

As manager, you're responsible for doing all you can to protect corporate property, as well as the personal property of people in the office, if there is a known threat to such property. Disgruntled employees have a horrific talent for "sucking the oxygen out of the room," drawing exclusive attention to themselves, and leaving managers with very little emotional energy to devote to the needs of other employees who are *not* unhappy. As a result, other workers may wind up feeling neglected and underappreciated, until they too become disgruntled. In this way, discontent can easily spread like the plague.

Poisoning the
Atmosphere

In short, disgruntled employees can poison the workplace atmosphere for everyone, and spread their discontent like a malignant virus.

They can do so in a variety of ways. Some of these employees are very articulate and skilled at generating sympathy for their point of view. They infect other workers with their distrust and scorn for company policy, until these sentiments start to spread throughout an organization or a department. Two or three unhappy people start "organizing" the rest of the workplace into a type of "emotional labor union," and then everyone digs into a bunker mentality that says, "I hate this place. I feel exploited and unhappy. So I'm just going to do the bare minimum from now on. I'm just going to do what I have to, and look for a way out of here, or take an early retirement." No one gives the job their best effort anymore, productivity suffers, and morale plummets. It is remark-

 Advice for employees: See life from your boss's POV.

As an employee, you'll make your life a lot more comfortable if you periodically think about your workplace from your boss's perspective. She works for a boss, too, remember. You're both in the soup together, and if you consider her stresses and strains once in a while, perhaps your own complaints will be assuaged. In a February 2007 report, The Conference Board (a prominent business research organization) reported that Americans are increasingly unhappy with their jobs. Less than half of all Americans say they are satisfied with their jobs, down from 61 percent only twenty years ago. And this decline in job satisfaction, while highest among the newest entrants to the work force—those under the age of twenty-five—is rampant among all workers no matter what their age, race, income, and residence. Those are scary and sobering statistics for both workers and their bosses. With some work and a little luck, you can mitigate dissatisfaction in your own workplace, and considering what the boss faces each day may ease your sense of burden and burnout.

able how quickly this can occur and how often disgruntled employees consider it their divinely appointed mission to foment dissatisfaction.

Of course, unhappy employees do not have magic powers, and they cannot actually hypnotize formerly satisfied, well-performing workers into imagining that they are unhappy. But many do have a talent for exploiting intrinsic problems in the workplace, making mountains out of molehills, and emphasizing the negative. Sometimes, a negligent company or manager *gives* the discontented employee power by ignoring small problems that grow into bigger problems and cause disaffection among employees. When the boss is not willing or able to address the "little issues" that affect quality of life in the workplace, it is easy for workers to grow cynical, and for the truly disgruntled employee to fan the flames of resentment and distrust.

Therefore, as a smart manager, make sure you don't give your employees any valid reasons to become disgruntled and disaffected. Keep your ear to the ground, investigate the earliest rumblings of general restlessness or displeasure in the workplace, and get to the bottom of it and root it out before it becomes entrenched.

The Insidious Dangers of Leniency

Another way that disgruntled workers can poison a workplace atmosphere is by getting away with their disagreeable behavior. When other employees see that the person is allowed to behave inconsiderately and push limits but doesn't suffer any tangible consequences, they may get disgruntled about *that*. Worse yet, when an unhappy employee gets "kicked upstairs"—that is, promoted or recommended for promotion by a supervisor who simply wants her out of his own department—this can inspire enormous, justified resentment on the part of employees who have been laboring diligently and are far more deserving of reward than the discontented one.

No More Ms. Nice Gal

Now, let's say I get a call from Joanne, the manager of a local retail chain store.

JOANNE: I don't know what to do. There's this employee I really like. She's been with me for over a year, and she used to be cheerful, productive—one of my best salespeople. But she just went through a really ugly breakup. At first I tried to understand, gave her some time off, looked the other way if she came in a little late or didn't look her best. But now it's been over a month, and she's late almost every day; she comes in full of excuses. And sometimes it looks like she hasn't washed her hair for days!

ME: So she used to be a great employee, and you think the breakup is affecting her work?

JOANNE: Yes, and now I'm not even sure I can keep her. The rest of my staff is talking about her, and she's setting a bad example.

ME: It's totally understandable that when your employee was going through her breakup, you gave her some personal time. But, as a manager, when you see an employee starting to bring her personal, emotional baggage to work in a way that affects her performance and infects your staff, you have to get involved, and fast. If you are too lenient and let things such as chronic tardiness slide, your problems are only going to get worse. It sounds like you need to sit her down and talk about what's going on.

JOANNE: I tried talking to her about the lateness, but she started to cry.

ME: Well, that does make it difficult. People often bring their emotions to work; it's only human. But you need to have another conversation with her. Make sure she knows you understand what a tough time she's been through. Then you need to be firm and tell your employee that if she can't start arriving on time and maintaining her personal hygiene, you might need to let her go.

JOANNE: I really don't want to do that.

ME: No, of course you don't. So remind her of how successful she's been in the past. Let her know you respect and value her as a person. You might plant the idea that if she focuses on her job, the memory of the ex-boyfriend might recede a little bit; work might be the perfect distraction. And Joanne, she might just come around.

• • •

It's difficult to deal with emotions in the workplace, no matter who you are and especially when you're the boss. But supervisors need to learn the difference between handling a delicate situation with respect and humanity and becoming the kind of manager that people can walk all over because they are too lenient or "soft."

FOLLOW-UP

A few days later, Joanne calls back.

ME: Does your heartbroken employee still work for you, Joanne?

JOANNE: Yes, thank goodness. But it was so hard to deal with.

ME: I know it must have been difficult. What did you do?

JOANNE: Well, I took your advice, and I called her in and told her I missed the "old" her. And that I had always considered her one of my top people.

ME: What was her response?

JOANNE: Well, she cried again, and I thought maybe she was going to quit!

ME: But she didn't?

JOANNE: No, I let her get it out and offered her a tissue. And then I said that even though things were hard right now, I needed her to start coming in on time and looking professional the way she did before. I did tell her that maybe if she started focusing on her job she wouldn't think so much about the breakup.

ME: And so?

JOANNE: She said she totally understood. And she said that she was sorry for the way she'd been acting. And the next day she came in when she was supposed to, wearing a cute new outfit. I know it was difficult for her, but she really tried to stay positive for her whole shift. I think it did make her feel better.

ME: Great! So, what would you do differently in the same situation?

JOANNE: I would not be as easy on an employee with personal problems for as long a time. I'd stop being so nice, I guess.

ME: Sounds like the right solution, even though I'm sure you are a very nice person. And maybe you could get together with your entire staff and explain that while you understand they will all have personal problems that interfere with their work from time to time, consistently underperforming won't be tolerated. ■

Then there is the role model factor, which you should never underestimate if you are a manager. If you allow a disgruntled employee to come to work dressed in a slovenly, unprofessional manner, pretty soon the rest of your office may begin "dressing down" as well, and you will have an undesirable trend on your hands.

Leniency, when motivated by compassion, may be a humane and commendable strategy—up to a point. Some disgruntled people are, quite frankly, damaged goods from the get-go. They may be so emotionally hurt, so injured inside, that they cannot help but be mad at the world. They may do a decent job anyway, so you might want to cut them some slack. You might take pity on them. You might perceive (correctly) that when they get unreasonably irate or irritable or even petulant, they're not really making a statement about the job. They're crying out for help, even though they don't know it. Their self-esteem is so low that they don't even care about how they are perceived by other people. They don't expect to be liked anyway. So you try to help them by giving them credit for what they do right, and communicating implicitly that you accept them as they are. That is very nice of you.

However, your kindness toward the "wounded" employee may be viewed as unfair by his coworkers, who know they could never get away with the same type of behavior. They may think you're showing favoritism. They may wonder why you like him so much. Chances are they may not see what you see, particularly if the disgruntled employee only reports to you. Coworkers won't necessarily understand what the disgruntled employee's contribution is to the team.

Of course, you could tell them. You might discreetly explain the rationale for your tolerant policy, so they understand how you feel and so they know that you're not overlooking them while you're being kind to the wounded soul on staff.

Still in all, this may not be enough to alleviate the bile and jealousy caused by a lenient policy toward a troublesome worker. It can still be demoralizing to the rest of the office, if they think you are being "too nice." While you may see the disgruntled employee as merely pathetic, to everyone else, he may be blatantly offensive.

The Disgruntled Employee as an Outcast

Sometimes a discontented employee will be isolated by her peers as somebody who's kooky and who doesn't appreciate what she has. She may sit alone at lunch and never be invited to outside social events. She may be the object of denigrating humor, to her face or, more commonly, behind her back. In short, the disgruntled employee may become the office pariah. This happens often, and it's an ugly thing.

Even if the disgruntled one "deserves" it, scapegoating is never healthy for the culture of a workplace. When one person becomes an object of habitual blame or ridicule, everyone else is also debased. When it becomes routine to express a lack of respect for any given individual, people lose respect for themselves as well, even if at first they don't realize it.

The best, most efficient workplaces possess a team spirit. On a healthy team, everyone is included, and everyone is valued. When someone is having a problem, the rest of the team gets behind that person and helps him or her to solve the problem and feel better, and—not incidentally—to perform better. A good team strongly supports all its team members, in good times and in challenging times.

One person who is chronically the weak link in this chain of camaraderie and support drags down the morale of the entire team. Ill will toward even one person in the office fosters an atmosphere of tension and meanness. Once it has been established that it is okay to treat a particular individual with something less than kindness and consideration, the character of the entire workplace becomes far less admirable—even if the case can be made that the person doesn't deserve the same respect and thoughtfulness as everyone else.

Therefore, as manager, it is important that you never tolerate acts or words of abuse, either *from* the disgruntled employee or *to* the disgruntled employee from others. Eventually, the unhappy employee may have to leave the team, but unless and until he does, you must insist that he be treated with the same civility and regard as anyone else. That treatment is something everyone should have a right to expect from each other in a collegial environment.

It can be very difficult to ask your subordinates to behave well toward someone who has not behaved well toward them. The disgruntled employee may habitually act or speak out in ways that violate basic principles of etiquette and consideration. It is hard for others not to get angry and vindictive when they feel intruded on or abused. Assure them that their complaints are important to you. You must take action to protect them and to hold the offending employee accountable, privately and perhaps even publicly. But you must absolutely insist that your otherwise well-behaved employees do not retaliate in kind. "An eye for an eye makes everyone blind." Do *not* let your workplace degenerate into a war zone. Keep your antennae tuned to the emotional ambiance of your department, and take steps early to mitigate the stress and aggravation caused by a maladjusted employee.

Emotional Baggage

Everyone brings a freight train of emotions with them into the workplace, whether those emotions are expressed or not. Emotions, as I said before, are the sap of life, and it is not a bad thing that they are present in every interchange, either on the surface or just below. But it is important that they don't take over when they get too strong.

Most workers have enough control over their emotions that they do not get in the way of doing a good job. In fact, many workers err too far in the direction of control—they may have a seriously ill child or spouse but don't want to mention it at work because they consider it "personal business" that should be kept out of the office. When people try to keep too tight a lid on their emotions, they can explode or become paralyzed, either of which is bad for productivity.

So, as a manager, it is proper and appropriate to create a culture that allows the free expression of some emotion and even personal business. Staff meetings, for example, are often a good time for each team member to briefly state how they're doing. If everyone in the office knows, for example, that Sam is in the middle of a wrenching divorce, there are ways of showing support and bucking up Sam's spirits, by buying him lunch, for example. Offering gestures of support as a group is more powerful than a gift or statement of sympathy from an individual; this type of group compassion also serves to cement the team spirit.

Sometimes two people in an office setting have what we shrinks like to call "interlocking vulnerabilities." That is, they have psychological issues that play against each other. For example, one guy might be insecure or easily hurt, always perceiving signs of rejection, because he was rejected a lot as a kid. If he's unlucky, he might share an office with another guy who has "space issues." He needs a lot of privacy; he grew up in a big family and couldn't stand it, and he's a natural introvert. So the first guy, who's looking for approval and for indications that people like him, always starts small talk to turn a routine hello into an occasion for a joke or a little story. The second guy just wants to quietly do his work; he tries to be polite but inside he's bristling. Why can't the other guy just leave him alone and get to work? Why can't he find someone else to fascinate?

After a while, the first guy picks up on the second guy's lack of enthusiasm and feels rejected and disliked, while the second guy feels more and more annoyed and encroached upon. It grows worse over time, until they start to dislike and resent each other.

This is an example of how two people can exacerbate each other's emotional issues. If each had the capacity to understand the other, maybe they could step back a bit and be more accommodating and less reactive. But unfortunately (or perhaps fortunately), not everyone is a psychologist, and most offices don't have resident psychologists on staff to sort these things out for everyone. So coworkers have to muddle through these situations as best they can.

If you, as a manager, recognize the intricate and dysfunctional dance two such employees are involved in, there may be an easy fix. First, try to separate the two so they don't have to work cheek to jowl. Consider assigning each employee to report to a different supervisor. In the best case, move one employee to a different department or work group.

A disgruntled employee usually has a heavier load of emotional baggage than most people and a more difficult time keeping that baggage from spilling out of the freight car and onto the office floor. She often has more points of vulnerability and insecurity than the average worker, so it doesn't take that much to activate her emotional issues. Some people might call this *immaturity*, because, like a child, the discontented employee has problems with self-control and expresses herself in ways that are often inappropriate to the work environment.

But *immaturity* is a funny word, because it often applies to any behavior that adults deem childlike. People say, "Oh, I only show my immature side when I'm with my close friends." People might call it "immature" to laugh at certain kinds of silly jokes, or to giggle too much. Sometimes "immaturity" refers to letting the emotional, untamed side of your personality hang out a little bit, exposing your unrefined, unbuttoned-up self. A little immaturity, in this sense of the word, is a healthful and necessary thing. We're all a little immature sometimes, thank goodness.

One of the problems with the disgruntled employee's brand of immaturity is that, often, it stimulates not only the latent immaturity in coworkers but often the worst kinds of immaturity. This employee literally acts like a child when she doesn't get her own way, pouting and sulking, even lashing out at coworkers. Such negative behavior can trigger equally juvenile and counterproductive responses in other employees. The disgruntled worker's stock-in-trade is often the uncanny ability to get a fix on the ways in which other people are vulnerable, and then push those vulnerability buttons for all they're worth. The result for the workplace is at best squabbling and at worst physical violence.

Certain types of emotional baggage are common. For example, we've all experienced people being rude or inconsiderate to us or even dismissing our needs and our interests. So when a disgruntled employee does that, even if we know we're not being singled out because we see her doing it to everyone else as well, she triggers an emotional response, and we react from a very "immature" place; we want to protect ourselves and hit back.

But it gets even worse, because some disgruntled employees are so self-destructive that they unconsciously seek to irritate everyone in the most discomfiting ways possible. If you're someone, for example, who likes to keep to himself and doesn't like to be touched or even spoken to that often, the disgruntled employee might be the one who greets you each day with a booming "How ya doin'!" and a mighty slap on the back or a squeeze on the arm. If you're someone who really cares about keeping her office neat, the disgruntled employee might carelessly leave a stack of papers on your desk or "accidentally" drip something gooey from his sandwich onto the floor by your chair.

This type of behavior is known as *passive aggression*. Passive-aggressive people habitually do things that embarrass, irritate, or inconvenience other people, and they do so in ways that look innocent on the surface. Many disgruntled employees have a strongly developed passive-aggressive side to their personalities. They know how to trigger people, and when that happens, the other person's emotional baggage comes into play in ways that are counterproductive to the mission of the workplace.

One bad apple can spoil the whole bunch, and a discontented employee's immaturity *can* negatively impact the decorum of an office. An unhappy employee can wear down other people's self-possession and self-control over time; common courtesies may become less common, and slowly but surely, careless and offensive speech may become a norm rather than an exception. People get more "raw." They start to feel as if they, too, have a license to act out some of the feelings that they have simmering inside. They may even become less tolerant of each other, not just less accepting of the disgruntled employee.

An unhappy employee can slowly, almost imperceptibly, reduce a smoothly functioning office to a psychodrama set. People start to magnify their little squabbles and dissatisfactions, and their relationships take center stage; their petty conflicts become more important than getting the work done. The emotional side of life takes over, like some kind of unruly monster.

Emotions are an important component of work life, but emotions should not be allowed to wield a dictator's power. When the office becomes "loaded" with everyone's combined emotional freight, it's time for the supervisor to reassert the logical purpose for everyone being there in the first place. What are we here to accomplish? What's getting in the way of the work flow these days?

Don't forget to be strategic, too. *Why* is everybody on pins and needles, and *how* can we improve the situation *right now* so that we can get back on track as a team? What interventions are needed? Which of these psychodramas truly need attention, and which can be ignored for the time being? What rules of conduct need to be instituted or re-emphasized?

The Manager as Psychologist

The difficulty with getting to the bottom of an emotional morass is that people often don't have a handle on what's bothering them. Disgruntled employees, in particular, don't walk in like well-behaved schoolchildren with an essay about what's wrong and how to make it right, and "if you do this, I'll do that, and we'll be fine."

So you, as the manager, have to make *inferences*. You have to look at the data at hand, and take your best guess as to how to resolve an emotionally charged atmosphere in the workplace. You can solicit input from your team, but it's up to you to be above the fray. You're not looking to solve everyone's problems either. What you're looking for is the best possible way to mollify people so that they'll cool out and start focusing again on their work in a way that's consistent and undistracted. You need to strike the right chord, find the right theme, and evoke the most effective incentives. You have to re-establish control of your departmental culture.

66 99 | **Advice for employees:** Accept your own errors.

Amazing but true: Some of us become disgruntled because we make mistakes and just cannot get past them. We foul something up on the job and then consider ourselves failures. We do not forgive ourselves. Our coworkers and bosses forget the misstep, but it plagues us. When you make a mistake, take responsibility and do all you can to correct it. Then get on with the show. Learn whatever lessons you can from the incident. Then forget about what you did wrong and concentrate on doing things right. I guarantee you that nine times out of ten, when you are still beating yourself up about an error in judgment, your colleagues have long since forgotten all about it.

It may be impossible to do this if the disgruntled employee remains on your staff. You may not be able to summon up enough of a counterbalancing influence to his destructive impact. No matter how hard you try, you may not be able to improve morale as long as the disgruntled employee continues to sow negativity. You must find a way to defuse him, but how?

If you can't fire him, you have to understand him. You have to find *his* triggers. You have to find ways to get him under control, to motivate him to rein in his damaging behavior, so that you can begin to reassert your authority over the mores of the workplace. The strategy will vary from employee to employee, but you absolutely cannot allow him to continue to sabotage the workplace environment. Win him over if you can, scare him if you have to, keep him on edge, or meet some of his irrational needs—but restrain him you must.

Remember, you have one advantage over the disgruntled employee. You at least know what you are feeling and why. A discontented worker generally lacks this type of self-knowledge. Unfortunately, so do most people. We are not trained as children to be introspective or self-aware.

When people understand themselves and how they feel, not just what they think, and are able to manage their emotions and their relationships, they're better able to make business decisions, form more enduring business relationships, and be happier and healthier and more effective in the workplace. But such people are rare. Understanding yourself is a skill. Managing emotions is another skill, and handling relationships well is yet another. Elementary schools do not offer courses in these skills, although perhaps in more enlightened times, they eventually will.

Self-understanding is a lifelong endeavor. It takes discipline and fearlessness, and rigorous self-honesty. We are all complicated beings, and our motives and desires are just as complex as we are. To know where we're coming from at any given time is of immeasurable value.

Managing emotions is different from simply repressing them, or keeping them at bay. Managing emotions also means knowing how to tend to your feelings, give them their proper due, help yourself feel better, and get your emotional needs met. Managing emotions means knowing when and where it is "safe" and appropriate to express emotions, and when they should be set aside. (Remarkably most people are able to do this fairly well most of the time, despite never having been given any guidance or training.)

There have been tens of thousands of books published on the subject of human relationships and how best to conduct them. For the purposes of the workplace, an ideal relationship is one in which people enjoy each other's company but don't distract each other from the tasks at hand. As a supervisor, those are the types of relationships you want to nurture. If you have a dash of amateur psychological skill, it may help you figure out which employees to pair as project teammates, or as office mates, and which employees may be best suited to interface with the disgruntled person in the office and not be too affected.

You don't have to study psychology textbooks. All it really takes is a little effort and willingness to pay attention and try and be sensitive. And remember, whether or not it's in your formal job description, it *is* a part of your job to wear the psychologist's hat, if you are responsible for the performance of a group of people.

Extending the Honeymoon

Most employees come into a job feeling as if they're on a kind of honeymoon. They're willing to work hard, they feel energized, and they're excited about their new responsibilities and relationships. Of course, some of that enthusiasm diminishes over time as work becomes more routine, and if the employee fits in, she begins to take her job a bit for granted.

One of your tasks, as manager, is to try to extend that honeymoon, to keep the energy and excitement level high. There are lots of ways to do this, including praise, incentives, public recognition for work well done, challenging assignments, bonuses, and so forth.

At the very least, if you are paying attention to a new employee's emotional moods, you probably won't grind down her enthusiasm with thoughtless remarks or deeds.

But with the disgruntled employee, rather than a honeymoon phase, there may be an "anti-honeymoon," because the employee often brings an antagonistic mentality to the job from the outset. Sometimes you can avoid such persons by sniffing them out during the interviewing and hiring process (if you're involved in these decisions), but they often slip through those filters, presenting themselves well and affecting a positive attitude while they're trying to land work, then showing their true colors once they're on the job. (If they weren't good at doing this, there'd probably be no need for this book!)

So with a discontented employee, your challenge is not so much to try and keep alive her initial eagerness to perform well in the job, but rather to establish limits and ensure that she follows office protocol, and meets performance standards in her job.

It may be helpful to remind the disgruntled employee that the first six months are a trial period on the job. You don't want to make her nervous, but it may not be a bad idea to keep her on her guard, and not let her take her position for granted any time soon. Gentle reminders are the best. "Since you're still pretty new here . . ." "Over time, I would expect you to . . ." These kinds of reminders, made in public, are also reassurances to the rest of your staff. They send an implicit signal that if the disgruntled employee does not shape up, she might disappear, which is what many of her coworkers may be secretly hoping.

The period when she feels unsure in the job but really wants to keep it, is *your* honeymoon in a sense, because even if the disgruntled one has an intrinsically poor attitude, she hasn't lost sight yet of the fact that she has to please you. This is a honeymoon you should extend as long as possible. You don't want to be manipulative about it; just be prudent. Don't let your own guard down too soon. Don't let a potentially troublesome employee feel too quickly that she is securely "in the fold." This doesn't mean you should be rude or menacing, but it does mean that you remain measured in your positive regard, very precise in your feedback, and extra clear about what your expectations will be over time. Many a disgruntled employee has used this honeymoon phase as an opportunity to adjust his or her attitude, which is the optimal outcome for everyone concerned.

"Reforming" a disgruntled employee during the honeymoon phase has rippling beneficial effects on the rest of your department as well. It elevates your employees' esteem for you and strengthens their feelings of being crew members on a well-run ship. It reinforces all the healthiest facets of office culture and teamwork.

Disgruntled Employees and Sabotage

There are many ways that the disgruntled employee can hurt you and your company, including fomenting interpersonal havoc, dragging down team morale, and setting a bad example. But many unhappy employees do as much or more damage to a company *after* they are laid off or fired. I'll deal in detail with these in a later chapter, but now I want to mention some of the most common of them.

One of the most common forms of revenge that terminated angry employees take is trying to ruin a company's reputation by spreading false rumors about the organization, through the Internet, the media, and by word of mouth. It is very difficult to protect against slanderous gossip in this day and age, and since the disgruntled employee was once inside your company, unknowing people may afford him a measure of credibility when he holds forth about you. The Internet in particular is impossible to police. There are hundreds of thousands of message boards and blogs where people can post anything at all, with little or no consequence to themselves but potentially devastating effects for the organization or individual that is the object of their wrath.

Several years ago, for example, a man lost his job with a newspaper in Connecticut. He and the paper had a disagreement when he left over whether he was owed overtime pay. This man eventually won $3,000 from the paper, after filing a complaint with the Department of Labor. But more significantly, he became a relentless presence on the Internet message board devoted to the newspaper, where he constantly derided his former employer and its parent company.

Another way in which a former "insider" can damage a company is by leaking sensitive information to a competitor or to the public. At times, information can be a company's most important asset, whether it has to do with a product in the development phase, plans for expansion into new areas, or even an advertising campaign. When this information is leaked, it gives competitors leverage to foil the plans and aspirations of the company. Many a disgruntled former employee will divulge classified company information to a competitor out of sheer spite; others may find a way to get paid to do so.

Computer hacking and electronic sabotage is another danger. When discontented employees have access to a company's computer files and passwords, there is no end to the malicious mischief they can perpetrate, both while they're on the job and after they leave (if they can hack into the computer system from outside, which is something many a computer-savvy person can do). They can falsify data. They can delete critical files. They can download sensitive information and spread it around the Internet. They can damage software or the operating system itself by introducing a virus into the company network.

Finally, disgruntled former employees can also pose a physical danger to the health and well-being of former supervisors and coworkers. Sadly, it is not unheard of for former employees to come storming back into their old places of employment with guns blazing or fists swinging. One famous example was the murder of San Francisco mayor George Moscone and Supervisor Harvey Milk, at the hands of former San Francisco supervisor Dan White in 1978. White had resigned his position as supervisor but had changed his mind and had been petitioning Moscone to give him back his old job. When Moscone refused, White took the ultimate revenge. Sad to say, White was not the first or the last employee to go insane with rage at his former employer.

So what can be done to protect against these types of behavior by a disgruntled employee? First and foremost, every company needs some type of physical workplace security. Even in a small company, people should wear employee IDs, and there should be sign-in sheets and security procedures at the door. When a person leaves the company, he or she should surrender the ID badge. None of this is a guarantee against a mentally imbalanced person bent on violent revenge, but at least it is a deterrent and often an effective one.

To prevent computer hacking, companies should change computer codes and important passwords regularly, at intervals of at least once every few months. Also any company with an internal network should have the strongest possible virus protection and firewall program, and it should be scrupulously kept up-to-date. Whenever possible, larger companies should also have an onsite information technology team to diagnose and root out computer-related problems before they create extensive damage.

Each employee should also have his or her own individual login and password to the company system. This way, when an individual is terminated, his password and

login can be automatically deactivated. Of course, if a
worker is determined to do damage while she is still in
your employ, this creates a more complex situation, and
this is where you may need IT experts to contain the
damage. Extensive and regularly maintained information
backup systems are also highly recommended.

There is, unfortunately, no foolproof way to control
malicious gossip after a disgruntled employee leaves your
company. However, there are preventive measures that
wise employers can take. Your human resources department should conduct exit interviews and evaluations to
determine if a given individual is unstable or resentful
enough to do something incendiary. At least if you have
fair warning, there may be ways to prepare for possible
retaliation.

The termination process should be executed in a
careful and delicate fashion. When you give an employee
notice, do so in the context of a respectful, private conversation. Discuss possible benefits, severance packages,
unemployment compensation, and outplacement services that your company might be able to help with. You
might also discuss the possibility of offering a reference
for another job, if that is appropriate and you feel you
could do so honestly. Plant the seed in the disgruntled
employee's mind that you can still be of service to him,
as a former employer, and frame your decision to terminate not in terms of the disgruntled employee's personal deficits but rather in terms of what doesn't seem to
be working. "Not a good fit" is an excellent tried-and-
true phrase. Without being obsequious or apologetic, it
is worth making an effort to avoid further alienating the
already dissatisfied soon-to-be-former employee.

Never get into an argument with a worker you're getting ready to fire or have just fired; a debate about your
decision will only raise the level of already uncomfortable emotions to a higher pitch. Make it clear that the
decision has been made and that there is no room for

negotiation. Your job during this conversation is to keep it brief, civil, and to the point. Grace on your part is warranted; be as gentle as possible.

Benign Sabotage?

There are, of course, different levels of "harm" that an employee can do to a company. By the strictest definition, even office workers who steal the occasional paper clip or pen are doing harm. But this kind of petty theft is so widespread, companies are used to it, and it is not considered a major problem. Stealing is still stealing of course, and this is not to say that it's okay. But the financial cost of this type of dishonesty is negligible to most organizations, so it is largely a matter that's between the employee and his or her own conscience.

One employee I know uses a lot of manila folders at home, and so she takes folders from work—but only after they've already been used and labeled, and would be discarded if she didn't save them. This is a reasonable and even admirable way of recycling a company's resources.

There are many shades of gray to this type of phenomenon. (I like to say that gray is my favorite color; seldom are matters black and white, especially if they have to do with ethics, psychology, or business sense.)

Knowing It When You See It

When you have a discontented employee, who presents logistical or psychological problems to the community of your workplace, you know it when you see it. Unfortunately, if you don't notice it soon enough, sometimes it's too late to undo the damage. That's why it's important to be vigilant, to pick up on cues of resentment and discontent, and to be aware of the threat that a disgruntled employee can pose to your office and to your peace of mind.

Never ignore the fact that you have an unhappy employee. Sooner or later, unless you are proactive, that person will cause you serious problems.

Telling, not Tattling, Saves the Bottom Line

The BUSINESS
Shrink

Carl, the senior office manager of a small law practice, has always loved his job. He deals with the payroll and accounting staff, orders supplies, and handles human resources. He genuinely likes his staff and the lawyers who run the firm. Lately, though, he's noticed that one of the junior clerks, Joel, has seemed a little down in the mouth. Joel walks around the office with his shoulders slumped and eyes downcast, and he has stopped going out to lunch and for drinks after work with his peers.

Early one morning, Carl peeks into Joel's cubicle.

"Hey, man, how're you doing?" he asks.

"Fine." Joel doesn't lift his gaze from his computer screen.

"Are you doing okay with the new accounting software?" Carl asks.

"Yeah, it's fine." This time Joel looks up. From his expression, Carl can tell something is really bothering him.

"Do you want to grab a cup of coffee?" Carl asks. "We can just go down to the shop on the corner. My treat."

Joel shrugs. "Sure," he says finally, and reaches for his jacket.

As the two men stand in line at the coffee shop, Joel seems agitated, shifting his weight from side to side and looking around nervously.

"Joel," says Carl. "What's going on?"

Joel pauses. Finally he says, "I don't want to get anyone in trouble."

"Okay. But something is obviously bothering you. Is it about work?"

Joel nods. They get their coffee and sit down. Joel looks around again.

"It's Karen," he says. Karen is the intern the office has hired for the summer. Carl interviewed her and found her to be bright and capable, and she seems to get along with everyone. She has just finished her first year of law school.

"What about Karen?" he asks Joel.

"Well, she, um, she does some stuff I know other people wouldn't like," says Joel.

"Like what?" prompts Carl.

"She takes things."

Carl is surprised. "What kinds of things?" he asks.

Joel hesitates. "Well, you know, at first it was little stuff. Notepads, pens, boxes of staples, some tea from the kitchen. But now it's getting worse."

"Worse how?"

"I've seen her take some blank CDs, and you remember when Robert couldn't find his BlackBerry?"

"Yeah." Carl is having a hard time comprehending what Joel is telling him.

"I swear I saw it on her desk under some papers last week, and then it was gone later," Joel says.

"I even asked her about it, and she told me I was nuts. But then about a week later, she was telling everyone how she got this used BlackBerry off eBay, and she could get e-mail on it and all."

Carl shakes his head. "So you're telling me that Karen stole Robert's BlackBerry?"

"I don't know," says Joel. "But I've seen her take other stuff. And it's a weird coincidence."

Carl stands up. "You were right to tell me, Joel," he says. "I'll check into it."

"But promise me you won't tell her it was me who told you?" Joel says.

"Okay," says Carl, and they return to the office.

The next day, after Carl has had some time to think things over and talk to some of the other clerks, he calls Karen into his office.

"What's going on?" she asks.

Carl, choosing his words carefully, tells her that other employees have seen her taking office property. At first Karen denies everything, but when Carl brings up the BlackBerry, she realizes she can no longer lie, and she tearfully confesses.

Later that day, after Carl has let Karen go, he returns to Joel's office.

"Hey, man," he says. "Thanks for being honest with me. You were right."

"Are you sure she didn't know it was me?" Joel asks.

"Yes," says Carl. "I spoke with other people, and they all confirmed what you told me. You did the right thing by telling me."

Joel's whole countenance brightens, and he smiles for the first time in a long time.

"No problem," he says. ■

The Measure of an Effective Boss

I believe strongly in paying attention to and taking advantage of the intersection between psychology and strategy in business. When you can manage your emotions and also manage your relationships with those around you, you are better able to make good business decisions, form stronger and more enduring relationships, and be more effective in the workplace. For managers, this is critical. As a supervisor, you need to know and understand all the people who report to you. Call them by name; take an interest in their lives. Then, when you see the first signs of dissatisfaction or disenchantment, take the reins and turn the situation around. Know your employees' expectations of what their duties are, and clearly state what you expect of them. Keep an open line of communication. When you confront a disgruntled employee, be aware that you have more than one option available. You need not lose a valuable person; maybe his or her role within the organization needs to change. Never allow the problem to fester; the longer you wait, the worse the problem will get. Often problem employees are completely unaware that their behavior leaves something to be desired. If you can discuss it clearly and openly with your employee, sometimes the situation will be remedied after one brief conversation. As an effective manager, you need to be prepared to cope with personnel problems that inevitably arise in the workplace.

Summary: The Phenomenon of the Disgruntled Employee

- Some employees watch the clock, counting down the time until they can leave for the day. But a disgruntled employee is actively unhappy, disrupting both his peers and the workplace.
- There are more and more disgruntled employees in the workplace than ever before; fewer than half of all Americans say they are satisfied with their jobs.
- Discontented workers can spread their unhappiness throughout the workplace like a virus, contaminating the mood of their colleagues and managers.

- A good manager can recognize the signs of a dissatisfied employee and deal with the problem in a one-
  on-one meeting at the first hint of trouble.
- It is human nature to bring emotions to work;
  employees must learn to separate their personal lives
  from their business lives.
- By being too easy on difficult employees, a supervisor sends mixed messages and may contribute to
  other employees becoming dissatisfied or not doing
  their jobs effectively.
- Everyone gets disgruntled from time to time. No
  one in the workplace is immune, especially bosses.
- Sometimes discontented employees can provide a
  valuable window into a bigger problem affecting
  their coworkers and the organization.

2 warning signs and types of disgruntled employees

Warning Signs In most cases, it is relatively easy for coworkers, peers, subordinates, and supervisors to identify the symptoms and actions of someone who's unhappy at work. Generally speaking, tardiness, low or slow production, careless work product, body language, the expression of annoyance and irritability, a withdrawal from social interactions at work, or any combination constitutes warnings signs that an employee is troubled. Almost any kind of dysfunctional work and social behavior pattern can be a sign of a disgruntled employee.

Subpar Performance When an employee starts turning in shoddy or incomplete work or is consistently late turning in projects, this is a clear indication that she no longer considers the job a priority. This can be especially frustrating when the employee was formerly a high-quality performer. Something in the workplace or at home has changed, and as a result she is not interested in achieving her goals.

Low or Slow Production; Lackluster Work Supervisors should always review expected completion dates of all projects from the outset, as well as any benchmarks along the way. An employee who consistently asks for more time or turns in half-finished or low-grade work is not invested in her position. Managers do not tolerate work that barely meets the criteria established at the start. It's like a student turning in a B– paper when what was clearly expected was an A+.

Sloppy or Careless Work

Again, when the guidelines of a project are clear, most people understand the importance of doing a careful, polished job. Messy handwriting, a typewritten report that has not been checked for spelling and grammar, or math errors on a balance sheet are unacceptable. Sam Gosling, assistant professor of psychology at the University of Texas, gathers clues about employees by looking at their workspaces. "The workspace," Gosling told me and my radio show audience, "is part of a broader idea that the environment that we craft around ourselves is rich with clues about what we're like." A highly conscientious, organized, task-oriented person is likely to have a tidy, organized desk. A sloppy, messy workspace is not always an indicator of an unhappy employee, but combined with a poor work product, it can point to trouble.

Missed Deadlines

Everyone misses deadlines from time to time, but an employee who misses them on a regular basis is a sign that something is wrong. If one of your staff cannot turn in her work when it is due and needs to be constantly reminded of deadlines, that person has most likely disengaged from the workplace.

Moody Behaviors

No one is happy all the time. Even those of us who love our work have bad days, even bad hours, on the job. Sometimes an employee isn't feeling his best, is stressed about completing a project on time, or has had a fight with a spouse or child. As long as the bad mood doesn't last, there isn't an issue. But employees who exhibit unpleasant moods, even downright rudeness at work, are a different story. Sudden moodiness in a once-stable employee can be the result of disenchantment with work or a more serious emotional problem.

Withdrawn and Sullen

Who wants to work with a sourpuss? You may have had a boss or a coworker like this—someone with whom you can't talk, who keeps to himself, and who seems to emit negativity. Odds are you weren't the only one who noticed. Sulky, remote employees are universally disliked and can sully the atmosphere of an entire workplace.

Irrational and Prone to Outbursts

Imagine working with a two-year-old all day. That's what it's like working with an employee who is irrational when he doesn't get his own way. These individuals go off on tirades, scream at peers or subordinates, speak out of turn in meetings or other professional gatherings, or burst into tears. These are the symptoms of an employee who is frustrated or angry but not mature enough to manage his emotions.

Body Language

I know when my significant other is in a bad mood. She won't make eye contact, crosses her arms over her chest while conversing, and tries to steer clear of me, shunning my advances. A disgruntled employee may exhibit the same sort of body language. He may avoid eye contact, use fewer gestures when speaking, and skirt any sort of contact with other workers. Troubled employees may even back away when spoken to directly.

66 99 **Advice for employees:** Accept criticism gracefully.

When your boss chastises you, learn to take it with a smile. Unless the criticism is repeatedly unfair, stand tall and listen. Except in cases of abusive supervisors, your boss is trying to make things work better and trying to improve your performance as an employee. That means she respects and appreciates you. She wants you to develop and become an even more valuable member of her team. Don't allow your feelings to be hurt. Don't be argumentative. Listen respectfully and respond productively. Try to learn from the encounter and try to put her recommendations into practice. The result may be that your next encounter with her is on the receiving end of a compliment.

Acerbic, Negative Talk or Sarcasm

Rather than being malicious, some unhappy employees resort to making sarcastic comments about their peers, subordinates, managers, and the company itself within earshot of their coworkers. Or they may simply make derogatory remarks about any of these subjects while at work. Openly maligning coworkers, products, or company is grounds for dismissal within some organizations. It is both rude and disrespectful, and it poisons the working environment.

Types of Disgruntled Employees

Dissatisfied employees come in many flavors. Just as you might classify one of your top performers as a real go-getter and another as dedicated and conscientious, there are employees who are not living up to their potential. These underperformers can bring down the spirits and the productivity of those with whom they work every day. It is your job to recognize the types of disgruntled employees who might be on your staff right now.

"Negative" Personality

There are several kinds of negative personalities in the workplace. Some employees develop negative behaviors as a result of not feeling appreciated for their efforts. Others are simply born pessimists, looking for things to complain about or for someone else to blame when issues arise.

The Cynic

Some employees will disagree with everything you say. They like to be right all the time, so they find problems with coworkers, how they do their jobs, even the way they dress. Cynics may seem to sit quietly on the sidelines, but in reality, they make cutting, cruel comments about any new project or idea.

The Naysayer

A naysayer experiences the world as an unpleasant place. She feels useless and projects her feelings of powerlessness onto everyone else. A naysayer will be certain to tell you that your plans and ideas are ridiculous and can never be realized. Someone with this kind of negative attitude can crush her colleagues' enthusiasm and creativity and turn coworkers into pessimists as well.

The Sniper   Snipers like to use "verbal assault" weapons. They employ underhanded verbal digs, disparaging remarks, and insults to make others feel bad. Snipers may even stoop so low as to use name-calling and physically make fun of their victims without ever understanding the pain they inflict on their coworkers.

The "Do-Little"   One of the worst kinds of negative employees is the "do-little." This person is chronically deadline challenged, unable to turn in high-quality work, and is disliked by his peers because he tends to place the blame elsewhere.

The Hung-over Underachiever   Every Friday morning all over America, workplaces are filled with employees who started their weekend on Thursday night. Constant partiers and chronically hung-over employees slump about the office, downing Advil and coffee, complaining of their hangovers. Needless to say, they don't get much work done. And sometimes they come in hung-over every day of the week.

"It's Not My Job!"   These employees express their negativity by refusing to do any new task if they decide it's not part of their job description, regardless of how simple the request. Often, this is their way of getting back at supervisors or colleagues because of their dissatisfaction with how they are treated. "Not-my-jobbers" aren't getting to do what they want, so they believe they shouldn't have to do anything else that's asked of them.

Little "Lazinesses"   Like the "not-my-jobbers," these employees are not focused on being team players. Because they hold a grudge against the organization or someone within it, they refuse to go the extra mile in helping out in the workplace. Lazy employees never make coffee after they pour the last cup from the communal pot, don't clean up the conference room after meetings, and will never offer to go on a sandwich run or bring bagels for the staff.

The Agitator/
Conspirer
Some people are born pot-stirrers. They need to share their negative feelings as a way of getting rid of them. Agitators find ways to sabotage or otherwise obstruct the progress of a project at work by distracting their colleagues so that no one gets anything done. These employees actively work to stir up bad feelings, especially against management, fostering an "us-against-them" bunker mentality, actively conspiring with peers against the supervisor or the organization.

The Obstructionist
Rather than focusing on the task at hand, an obstructionist will actively seek to derail a project. These employees can be extremely creative in their efforts to stop workflow, from not finding the tools necessary to complete the job to "losing" critical parts of the project.

Whiners and
Complainers
When someone constantly complains about everything at work, it's a sure bet that person is insecure. These people, deep down, believe nobody likes them and that they will never be promoted or understood, so they whine and kvetch about everything from their personal lives to work projects to anyone who will listen (even if you don't).

The Victim
Employees with low self-esteem will often get upset with themselves and become negative, finding fault with everything they do, from work performance to their social status. They are difficult to work with because they believe they are never right and question all of their own decisions. In the worst-case scenario, this employee also believes he or she is being victimized by coworkers or supervisors for poor performance.

Indifferent or Bored Employees

Of course, someone who does not have enough work to do or finds her job uninteresting or not challenging enough will have a poor attitude. If an employee who is feeling stalled or bored comes forward and expresses these feelings to her supervisor, there is usually an easy solution. But frequently these employees take no such initiative. They remain on the job, bored and underused, wasting the company's time and money.

Disaffected Workers

Sometimes, for a variety of reasons, employees become disenchanted with their colleagues, their bosses, and the organization itself. In these cases, employees may grow disaffected or disloyal to their employer. Disaffected employees often express their unhappiness by spreading rumors about their coworkers and about the organization. They may even leak bad or wrong information about the company to the outside. They are a hazard in any workplace.

Disaffected Middle Managers

Unfortunately, today's middle manager is probably one of the most disgruntled of employees. A 2005 survey conducted by Accenture, a global management consulting firm, found that 52 percent of American middle managers were increasing dissatisfied with their organization. Their biggest complaints centered on compensation and prospects for advancement. Many middle managers either don't think they receive proper compensation, or they don't see the chance to move up within the organization. They're literally stuck in the middle as companies downsize or eliminate layers of management. Often they serve less as managers and more as "worker bees." As a result, they can grow disaffected and hostile toward every aspect of their job.

Gossipers and Rumormongers

Employees who spread rumors throughout the workplace are trying, in a distorted way, to establish control over their environment. Incessant gossiping, spinning lies,

The Grumpy, Cheating Bus Driver

The BUSINESS Shrink

My colleague Peter Laufer told me a story about a grouchy bus driver who was definitely involved in petty thievery. Yet somehow the way this bus driver handled the situation, I was left feeling somewhat amused. See what you think.

"When I worked in Washington, D.C.," says Peter, "I worked for NBC News, and I lived in Glen Echo, just outside of the city. I went to work very early in the morning, and I took a bus to what was then the end of the Metro Red Line.

"There were just a few of us who rode the bus that early, maybe two or three people, "Peter continues. "The bus driver had this curious thing that he would do a couple of times a week, and just for the people who got on at my stop, which was the beginning of his run. The driver would smile, put his hand over the fare box, and say, 'It's free today.' The fare was a dollar. Other days he would say, 'How about fifty cents today? It's half off!' It was most peculiar, yet everyone went along with it, and the driver only did this for us few first passengers. We all knew about it, but no one said anything. I think it must have been the bus driver's way of asserting control over the situation, of giving himself the authority to change the fare as he saw fit. The driver wasn't always smiling, though. When he wasn't interacting directly with his passengers, the bus driver often wore a surly expression, and occasionally grumbled to himself as we drove into the city. 'Too darn early,' I heard him say a few times."

This is an interesting anecdote. Clearly, the bus driver was behaving in an unethical manner. He was stealing money from the bus company. And, because none of his riders ever spoke up, his supervisor may never have known, unless they did a strict calculation of fares and riders, which is unlikely. Clearly the bus driver was unhappy with his position; most likely, it was the early hour he had to be on the job. This is why some disgruntled employees resort to taking advantage of the company, dishonesty, and thievery. They feel as though they are not getting the recognition, respect, or whatever else they need from their bosses or organizations. So they get back at them in subtle or not-so-subtle ways.

If I were that bus driver's supervisor, and I found out that he was giving passengers free or discounted rides, the first thing I would do is ask him why. I would take the time to listen to his answer. If it was a question of his feeling undervalued or bored or the fact that he hated knowing his wife had to get the kids to school every single day because he was already at work, or anything I could remedy as an employer, I would. It sounds as though he was a genuinely nice guy who cared about other people, but at the expense of the bus company. Maybe if he had, say, a change in his hours or route, he'd be able to stop stealing.

This guy loved his work, except for the early hour. He didn't measure it against being a U.S. senator or a world-famous artist. He measured it in an existential way, looking at how it provided him enjoyment in life. He "smelled the roses" on the job and he loved people. He loved driving them safely, he loved caring for them, and he loved to be loved. He created an environment where he was thoroughly professional and empathic, and he bonded with his customers. He obviously enjoyed being a kind of father or uncle figure to some of his passengers.

It is true that he did usurp some power and take some money from the bus company, probably not huge dollars, but still, it was stealing, and I cannot condone stealing. However, he didn't do it out of greed. I imagine he "stole" enough to make some people happy, and in doing so, he risked being faced with disciplinary action or even termination if the company found out—and that made it worth it to him. Since the bus company probably never noticed and its bottom line likely didn't suffer, this bus driver's crime really didn't have any victims.

Even sabotage comes in shades of gray. Sometimes the definition of what constitutes a disgruntled or troublesome employee is highly subjective. Had I been the CEO of that particular bus company, and had I discovered what this bus driver was doing, frankly, I might have just ignored it. But then again, I wouldn't have wanted all my drivers to do it. Every specific situation requires its own judgment call. ∎

and denigrating other people's work is a tremendous time waster, and the negative subject matter of the gossip can quickly demoralize and distract a team or department.

The Passive-
Aggressive
Passive-aggressive people seem to comply with the desires and needs of others, but actually passively resist them, while growing increasingly hostile and angry. They may dress poorly, miss deadlines, or turn in poor work product, but they do it in a way that seems innocent yet is not. An employee who has a passive-aggressive personality resents responsibility and shows it through behavior such as procrastination, inefficiency, and forgetfulness.

Advantage Takers
In every business, large or small, there are employees who habitually take advantage, either of the organization, their boss, or both. Advantage takers are smart; they've figured out a way to get around the system to get what they want, whether material objects that don't belong to them or roles and responsibilities they are not capable of or ready to handle.

Manipulators and
Climbers
Everyone knows the manipulator at work. This is the employee who steamrolls over others to reach his goals. He's on a path to the top, regardless of whether it's in his job description or whether he is ready for the challenge. So he ruthlessly uses his coworkers as pawns, taking out his anger and frustration on them and often lying to speed his way up the ladder. He is a master at twisting the truth to make himself look good.

Excessive Use
of Company
Resources
While not outright criminals, some disgruntled employees take out their dissatisfaction with their jobs on their employers. They use office equipment—from phones, fax machines, copiers, and computers—to excess, and for non-work-related tasks. They use the company computer to type their resume, the office printer to print it, and the

corporate e-mail network to send it. Or they use company time to shop online or chat with friends.

Thieves   Insidious and hard to track, petty thieves in the workplace are skilled at pilfering items such as pens, pencils, staplers, and so forth for their own personal use. Worse, more emboldened workplace thieves aim for the expensive goods, making away with everything from calculators to laptops and cell phones. They're usually careful to cover their tracks, and it can take months to hold them accountable. They may not be unhappy enough to quit— instead they just take advantage of their employer.

The Ranting Ego

Another category of negative personalities in the workplace includes those who think too much of themselves and their work. They may seem like the counterpart of those with low esteem, but too often they're part of the same personality package, often driven by the same things. Egomaniacs are some of the most difficult people to work with because they will try to walk all over you whether you work for them or with them. These dictators tell others how to do their jobs and are constantly making unreasonable demands. (Anybody remember Meryl Streep as Miranda Priestly in *The Devil Wears Prada*?) Insecure underneath, but full of bravado and lofty opinions on the outside, a ranting ego makes everyone in the workplace cringe and run for cover. And sometimes it takes a little digging to figure out whose ego is the problem.

The Workaholic/ Burned-Out Employee

Workaholics and employees suffering from burnout seem to be at the opposite ends of the spectrum. In fact, they're just two different stages of the same personality. Workaholics throw themselves into their jobs all day, every day, disregarding their personal lives. As a result, they can

Poor Me, It's Not My Fault! (Or Is It?)

Suppose a fellow named George calls my show one day, and I can feel the frustration in his tone. He works as a copywriter in a small advertising agency. Right away he starts complaining about his boss, Steve, the creative director.

GEORGE: Man, the guy is always all over me. No matter what I do, he tears apart my work. The copy's not sharp enough, or it's too long, or I didn't get the right tone. And it sucks because I know I'm a really talented writer.

ME: I'm sure you are. And it does take skill to be a good writer. You're saying Steve doesn't like anything you do?

GEORGE: No, sometime he does. But mostly he makes me rewrite stuff. Or he makes me stay late—which I really hate because I've got kids—to finish something. He's just never happy; he's always harping on me. It's enough to make me want to quit!

ME: Let me ask you this: At the outset of a project, does Steve sit down with you and the rest of the team and thoroughly explain what's involved? Do you always understand what's expected of you?

GEORGE: Um, well, yeah, usually. We have a creative meeting, and the copywriters and the art directors are given the project parameters. And then usually we brainstorm about ideas.

ME: Do you like those brainstorming sessions?

GEORGE: No, I hate them. I'd rather work on my own. I don't usually pay attention to what goes on in those things; they're a waste of time.

ME: But sometimes don't valuable ideas come out of those meetings?

GEORGE: I don't know. I guess so.

ME: So, is it fair to say, if you're not really participating in the brainstorming, you might be missing some of what's expected of the project?

GEORGE: Hmmm. Well, maybe. But I just usually figure something out.

ME: Right. And then when you turn it in, Steve criticizes it.

GEORGE: Exactly. He picks it apart. And then I have to start over. What a pain!

ME: I agree, it must be a real pain. But what if, since you're not part of the brainstorming team, and because you're feeling a little vulnerable because you're getting so much criticism, you don't always know what Steve wants?

GEORGE: I thought I did . . .

ME: What about this? The next time your team begins to work on a new project, why don't you try brainstorming with your colleagues? Just once, see if you can work with them, and also, make certain you know what Steve expects before you start writing. And then see if Steve isn't quite so critical.

GEORGE: Okay. I guess I can do that.

• • •

George is sensitive to every comment from his boss, and always construes any critique as negative, even when Steve is just giving him constructive feedback. If George takes the time at the start of a new project to learn exactly what is entailed and how to fulfill Steve's expectations, George may be able to take Steve's comments at face value.

FOLLOW-UP

George calls back about two weeks after our initial conversation.

ME: So, George, how's it going?

GEORGE: A little better, I think. Steve actually paid me a compliment. Although he still complained about some of my work for this new client.

ME: A compliment? That's great! What did he say?

GEORGE: He told me I was spot on with the humor in this radio spot I wrote.

ME: Did you get the idea as a result of the brainstorming session?

GEORGE: No, not directly. But we did talk about humor in the session, and people were throwing around all these crazy ideas. It was kind of silly. But I have to admit, it was also sort of fun.

ME: Did being part of that meeting make you feel more like part of the team?

GEORGE: Yeah, it definitely did.

ME: So what about your boss's criticism? How did that make you feel this time?

GEORGE: Well, it still bothered me. I still think Steve is too much of a perfectionist. But he did like my other radio spot. So it made it easier to go back and work on the first one.

ME: Sounds like being part of the team agrees with you, George. And as Steve continues appreciating your writing, I'll bet he gets less critical. Especially if you check in with him to make sure you know what he wants.

GEORGE: I'm willing to give it a go.

ME: Good.

• • •

Just as it was important for George to check in with Steve to make sure he knew what was expected from him at the outset of a new project, it is of vital importance for managers to be clear about what they need from employees. When you do have to give criticism, or constructive feedback, don't make it personal. Be sure the employee understands your point before you move on. Try to find something positive to say; it can make all the difference in the world to an employee with a fragile ego. ∎

become exhausted, isolated, and myopic, too involved to pull back and take stock of what they're doing. Their work product becomes erratic, even shoddy. Burned-out employees, many of whom were former workaholics, are so tired of what they're doing that they disengage from their responsibilities and only do the minimum. Neither is productive, and both types can bring down the moods of their colleagues.

Appearance and Hygiene Issues

We've all known coworkers whose personal hygiene skills need an overhaul. Body and hair odor, bad breath, stinky feet, the list goes on. Even those who douse themselves with cologne or perfume often offend others in the workplace, especially those with allergies. Inappropriate clothing and jewelry, from odd piercings and tattoos to short shirts and low-slung jeans, are not only distracting, they send the message that the employee is not interested in complying with company rules. Disgruntled employees may use inappropriate dress or poor hygiene as a way of letting everyone in the organization know they've got a problem.

The Mixed Bag

In my own career in business spanning more than thirty years, I have had employees whose performance output is spotty, sometimes good, and sometimes bad, but always inconsistent. In one instance, I had a male employee who did an excellent job on things he was committed to, yet often came in late and left early, and dressed poorly. Because he wasn't completely satisfied with his job, he had leeway in his own mind to be dysfunctional at work. So I had to confront him and say, "Hey, I really like your work, but you need to be consistent, you need to dress the part, and you need to be in on time." Because if one employee gets away with unacceptable behavior or habits, it sends the message that others can be lax.

Psychological Conditions

It used to be that employees who exhibited signs of mental illness were ignored until they either quit or were fired. But today, employees' emotional health is gaining more attention, and for good reason. Mental illness is increasingly prevalent in the workplace, from mood disorders to anxiety and depression, post-traumatic stress syndrome, and bipolar and attention-deficit disorder. According to the National Mental Health Association, a nonprofit organization based in Alexandria, Virginia, untreated mental illness costs the United States more than $1 billion in lost productivity each year. Employees with emotional problems may be prone to excessive mood swings and emotional outbursts, displays of anger, low productivity, and forgetfulness. It is important to differentiate between workers who are simply moody and those who have serious mental health concerns who need the care of a professional.

When an Employee Is Physically Dangerous

Some employees are like powder kegs, ready to explode as soon as things don't go their way. Unfortunately, they go beyond whining and complaining, gossip, carelessness, or any of the other types of disgruntled employees we've discussed so far. Difficult to identify, yet potentially as dangerous in the workplace as a loaded gun, an employee who uses physical force or in any way attacks or coerces others, or places them in danger is an employer's nightmare. A good manager must keep his or her staff safe. A dangerous employee can appear "normal" yet explode when provoked, wreaking havoc in any workplace.

Never ignore high-risk behavior. Sometimes it's easy to justify this behavior by assuming that the person is upset and the situation will resolve itself. This can result in a false sense of security. When talking to the problem employee, stick to discussing specific work-related behaviors and actions. Be willing to hear the person out—the experience can give you insight into how the employee perceives workplace issues, however distorted that view may be. The most common thread among violent employees is that they have demonstrated threatening or aggressive behavior toward coworkers or supervisors *before* their attacks. Never dismiss these threatening remarks as idle comments. If you believe the worker is dangerous, seek safety for yourself and other employees, and call security or the police.

Summary: Types of Disgruntled Employees in the Workplace

FICTION: You can always tell an unhappy employee by his or her actions.

FACT: Almost any kind of dysfunctional social action by an employee can be due to the fact that the employee is disgruntled. But everyone has bad moods and bad days. Supervisors need to know how to identify the different types of disgruntled employees.

FICTION: The worst kind of dissatisfied employee is someone who makes mistakes, is careless, and dresses badly.

FACT: While a person whose work product is inconsistent and whose appearance is sloppy is frequently a disgruntled employee, those workers who try to hide their dissatisfaction and gossip or make cruel remarks behind others' backs are frequently the worst kind of employee because they poison the workplace atmosphere.

FICTION: Workaholics make the best employees.

FACT: Workaholics frequently become burned-out or are so focused on one aspect of their job that they can no longer perform at their best.

FICTION: Disgruntled employees bring only trouble to their organizations and are not worth keeping.

FACT: Many employees perform brilliantly on some parts of the job while exhibiting symptoms of discontent. Sometimes an employee who is unhappy with certain aspects of his or her position can be "rehabilitated" by changes in responsibility or acknowledgement of a job well done.

3 handling disgruntlement

General
Principles Learn to distinguish between truly disgruntled employees and those who are just temporarily out of sorts. When a troubled employee has been identified, it's important to address the problem directly and without hesitation. Every day you delay, your problem child gets worse, and it becomes more difficult to rectify the wrongs he causes himself and the workplace. Usually your best first step is to spend one-on-one time with Mr. Disgruntled. In the best-case scenario, he will be comfortable and honest enough to share his concerns and complaints, and you will reach a quick solution.

Glenn Shepard, author of the books *How to Manage Problem Employees* and *How to Make Performance Evaluations Really Work*, was a guest on my radio show and he adamantly agreed, "Too many managers today are scared to confront problem employees. A big problem today, with such low unemployment, is that managers are scared to death that they are going to lose an employee if they actually hold him or her accountable. They make the situation even worse when they do that." I agree with Glenn; you need to confront the disgruntled employee, because no matter what business you're in, your people are your greatest assets. That may sound trite but it's true. A good manager needs to have close working relationships with all of the people who report to her. Just because someone is disgruntled doesn't mean you're going to lose him or that he can't change. We wouldn't trade in a car because it had a flat tire or a knocking noise in the engine. We would take it to the shop to fix the problem.

Immediate Feedback

It is important to meet face-to-face with a dissatisfied employee as soon as possible without adding stress by making it seem as if the meeting itself is a crisis. Then clearly communicate your concerns and work to determine the source of the problem. It may be something that's easily dealt with, and if this is a valued employee, you should be able to remedy the situation to everyone's satisfaction. Employees expect honesty, respect, cooperation, acceptance, and trust. Even in the midst of addressing a performance or personal issue, focus on the individual's strengths, suggest an area in which she might grow or even excel, and always end the meeting with a reinforcement of those positive critiques.

Attack Problems While They're Still Small

"Attack a situation with a disgruntled employee when it's a molehill instead of a mountain," Glenn Shepard said on my show. "For example, if an employee comes to work five minutes late, that's not the problem; it's a symptom of a problem employee who doesn't respect boundaries."

Whether the issue is gossip, personal hygiene, tardiness, cynicism, or any other warning sign, deal with it as soon as you become aware if it. Don't let it fester until it becomes a much larger issue.

Have Job Descriptions and Responsibilities (and the Mission) in Writing

This is Human Resources 101. Company HR managers and others involved with hiring and firing use descriptions of job duties not only to define the function and responsibilities of the job, but also to train and develop the employee. It's quite common for a job description to change as an employee's skills grow and develop. The job description can also be used as a benchmark to measure the organization's positions against others in its field, especially with regard to salaries.

In addition to sitting down with a new hire and explaining the details and duties of the job, always put the complete job description in writing. Make sure her roles and responsibilities are clearly defined in a mission statement that can be referenced if workplace issues arise. For example, consider you're hiring someone to manage your small office. The duties, in your mind, are fairly clear. The office manager will supervise the receptionist, order office supplies, get materials printed, handle shipping, and make copies—normal administrative stuff. But you also expect this person to run some personal errands, such as going out to get your lunch when you get busy, picking up your dry cleaning, and maybe even your kids from school if your spouse can't make it in time to get them. This sounds simple, but you neglect to put all of it into the job description. You figure you can just tell the person when he or she starts work. But you're wrong, my friend. Because if you don't have those duties written into the job description, the first time you ask your new office manager to grab you a tuna on rye and a diet soda, and he stares and then glares at you, what will you do? To you, it's an expectation; to him, it's an insulting exception to the job he signed up to do and an imposition on his professionalism. No one ever told him he would have to get your lunch, and he considers it demeaning. You're going to engage in a bit of backpedaling when you have to explain that you thought he knew that getting your lunch (not to mention your kids!) was part of the job.

What if you hire a manager whom you expect to work with outside vendors, but it's not in the job description, and it turns out that the person you hired is painfully shy and doesn't feel comfortable dealing with anyone outside the company? If she had known the full extent of the job and its responsibilities, perhaps she wouldn't have accepted it. Or if you had been aware of the shyness, you may have screened her out during an interview.

Make it easier on yourself and your workers. Think about as many of the duties a job could entail as possible and put them in writing as part of the job description. Because really, how many of us like surprises at work?

Clarify Duties One of the most common types of disgruntled employees is the person who insists that certain duties are "not my job!" If the written job description clearly states what the employee is responsible for, down to the smallest details, then it will be evident when an employee is, in fact, shirking responsibility. In the case of shared duties, be clear what each employee must contribute to the team effort. Distinguish between supervisors' and other employees' tasks. Be careful, especially if yours is a start-up or a small organization, not to practice what I call "seat-of-the-pants" management. I think it's a good exercise every once in a while to have people put in writing what they think their job description is and what their mis-

66 99 **Advice for employees:** Understand the ebb and flow.

Too many of us dream of the perfect everything: a trophy wife (or husband), kids who bring home straight As, not just a house with a white picket fence, but a country place and vacations in Paris, white, straight teeth, and lots and lots of money. Of course, advertising and celebrity watching feed these unrealistic expectations. Life ebbs and flows. The ups and downs are part of the natural cycles we experience. Job satisfaction is no different. Very few of us love everything about our jobs. That's why it's called work. Once you recognize that some days will be better than others, it is much easier to work through those times when you think you hate your job. One device to try is to consider what you enjoy at the office while you're doing some mundane task that you'd rather not do. Realizing that there are aspects of your work that you really like can help prevent you from becoming a discontented clock watcher.

sion is. You'd be surprised to find out that people don't necessarily think about their mission in the same way that their manager or supervisor does. As Terry Bacon, who specializes in helping companies develop and manage employees, puts it, "When somebody says, 'Well, you know, somebody else was supposed to do that,' it is usually a sign for me that you need to redefine the purpose of the organization and the roles of the people within it. There's no substitute for clarity in a case like that; you just have to sit down and get people to rethink what they're doing and clarify their roles and responsibilities."

If your company doesn't yet have a mission statement, this is the time to get one. A mission statement can play an important role in unifying employees and management behind a single, coherent long-term goal. A mission statement can also inspire. Consider Google's mission statement: "Don't be evil." That sums up what a lot of company employees felt—and still feel—about why they joined the company in the first place. Or Nike's slogan: "Just Do It." It is succinct.

Develop Clear Policies about Appropriate Behavior

Whether it's as formal as an employee handbook or as informal as making sure your employees understand guidelines for behavior, be sure to develop clear policies when it comes to on-the-job performance. Let it be known that sloppy work, consistent tardiness, poor work product, and other such bad behaviors are not acceptable. Don't be afraid to be tough when performance expectations fail or behavior is inappropriate. Written policies concerning behavior will carry more weight. Include examples of appropriate conduct in written job descriptions and discuss them during performance evaluations.

Establish Clear Consequences for Violations

My radio guest Glenn Shepard sounds like a drill sergeant regarding workplace troops. "When an employee doesn't heed a manager's warnings, you get tougher; you hold them accountable. Allowing bad employees to get away with bloody murder," he warns, "will cause you to lose other good employees who'll go looking for a better-run organization for which to work." In other words, set clear guidelines that outline the consequences for violations of company policies and then act accordingly. Be consistent; the consequences should be the same for top executives as for clerks.

Sometimes employees are completely unaware that they have done or are doing something that goes against company policy. They may even be surprised when you confront them. Not only should you have documentation that describes the problem, you should also clearly and succinctly articulate the problem. Make sure that disciplinary measures match the severity of the behavior. Customize the discipline to fit the crime. For example, if someone is consistently tardy, your first step might simply be to meet with the person and point out that work starts at 8:30 A.M., that the start time was discussed when he was hired, and that it is written in the job description. Then discuss ways to solve the problem; maybe he needs to take an earlier bus or join a carpool. Agree to revisit the issue in a month's time, and be sure to follow up. After such meetings, it's a good idea to write a memo to the employee, summarizing what was discussed, so you have a clear paper trail in the event of a dispute.

Use the dress code and other company policies to set boundaries and workplace standards. But if you find someone dipping into the petty cash or making personal overseas phone calls on the company's dime (boy, that dates me, doesn't it? Who remembers the ten-cent telephone call?), not only should you confront the employee in a private meeting, you should write up a warning and put the worker on probation for a specified time. This kind of violation might warrant termination. As a manager, you need to let employees know what misdeeds require dismissal. The employee handbook should also spell this out.

Have a Policy on Using Company Resources for Private Business

We've all brought home a pen or a pencil from work, but what about the employee who raids the storeroom for his personal stash of office supplies? Most organizations have written policies about appropriate use of company resources, often in the employee handbook. But if yours is a less formal workplace, it is a good idea to stress at the beginning of employment that company resources are only for company use, period. If you learn that someone is using those resources for personal business, he must be confronted at once.

Establish Policies on Attire and Attendance

In the same vein, make certain all employees understand your organization's dress code. Again, it's best to put it in writing. For example, if you run a restaurant and you expect employees with long hair to wear it up or in a hairnet, tell the employees when you hire them, but also post this guideline, along with other rules, in a highly visible spot. The same goes for attendance. Even if an employee isn't punching a time clock, expected hours or shift times should be put in writing at the start of employment, along with the consequences for noncompliance.

Have a Conversation

I find the best solutions for dealing with disgruntled employees always develop where and when I'm free to hear and listen, not just to talk. As a manager, you need to sit down face-to-face with someone who's having a hard time or showing symptoms of dissatisfaction. This conversation may feel tense or even uncomfortable at first, but it is absolutely necessary to determine whether you're facing a chronic or a temporary problem and to learn just how deep dissatisfaction lies. You want to remediate the situation, and you want to set an example of being an aggressive, hands-on, early-stage diagnostician and problem solver for the rest of the company. This is because the crew wants to see that their coworkers get a fair shake.

Spare-Time Stealing

Suppose a caller named Sarah phones in to tell me about a difficult situation she is dealing with as the principal of a private girls' high school.

SARAH: I pride myself on hiring the best teachers for the job. I've been doing it for more than fifteen years now, and that's why I can't believe this is happening!

ME: Fifteen years is a lot of experience. Tell me what's going on? What's the problem?

SARAH: Mary is one of our senior science teachers. She's taught at two other schools, came in with great recommendations, and graduated from one of the best colleges in the country. The girls love her; she conducts the most interesting labs. But apparently she's been, well . . . basically, she's been stealing from the school!

ME: You mean she's been caught taking things?

SARAH: No, thank goodness. But it appears that she's been using the school's computers and printers to work on a book she's writing in her spare time. She's been making long-distance phone calls from work. I think her publisher is in another state. And I know her parents don't live in the area.

ME: Just how many of the school's resources is Mary using? Can you quantify them?

SARAH: Yes, that's what's so upsetting. This is rather a long book, more than two hundred pages. And I caught her printing it out after school one afternoon. She said it was the only time, but it made me wonder. I went over the long-distance phone bill, and there were a whole bunch of calls from the extension in her classroom. They really added up.

ME: So you confronted Mary when she was copying the book. And then again after you'd looked at the phone bills?

SARAH: Exactly. And she said she didn't realize she had made so many calls. She told me again that she had only printed out the book once at school. I asked her if she was writing the book on the school's computers, and she admitted that sometimes during lunch she wrote on our computers but then copied everything onto a memory stick and took it home.

ME: How do you feel about that?

SARAH: Honestly? I don't think she should work on the book at all at school.

ME: Does your employee handbook say anything about the use of school resources being off-limits to staff?

SARAH: That's just it. We're a pretty small school, and I handle all the personnel decisions myself. We don't really have an employee handbook. I just figured most people know not to use the school's resources for personal projects.

ME: Now that you've confronted Mary about this, what do you want to do next?

SARAH: I definitely don't want to lose her. But I also want her to stop using the school's resources.

ME: I recommend that you call her in for another discussion. You need to let Mary know that what she's doing is taking time and resources away from the school. Even though there is no formal policy that states what she is doing is wrong, she should understand that this is a possible conflict of interests, and that she cannot continue working on the book at school. Let her know you value her as a teacher, but that she's bending what you considered were obvious, if unspoken, commonsense rules. Now that the limits have been strictly defined, tell her you expect her to adhere to them.

SARAH: You're right, that's just what she's doing.

• • •

Sarah's school would do well to put all policies having to do with employee behavior and expectations, from appropriate attire to use of the organization's resources, in writing. A human resources or employee handbook solves the problem, even if it is just a few pages long. Under those circumstances, management is covered if an employee such as Mary is caught red-handed. Since there is no written policy, Sarah should meet with Mary and, without focusing on wrongs already committed, clearly define the school's policies on the personal use

of its resources. It is important to keep track of all employee evaluations. If you ever need to fire a worker, she may have grounds to sue you and the company if she can produce a track record of all-positive evaluations previous to the termination. A judge and jury could interpret the lack of criticism as a failure on your part to give the employee a chance to meet your standards. Keep a paper trail to protect yourself, and make sure you evaluate your employees accurately. With skill and compassion you can criticize and chastise without offending or alienating your workers. The resulting employee files will then protect you when you need to discipline or discharge workers.

FOLLOW-UP

Under the best circumstances, I would get a call like this back from Sarah, seeming both relieved and elated.

SARAH: I had a really good meeting with Mary. And I'm so glad that I didn't have to let her go and that she wants to stay.

ME: That's great. What happened in the meeting?

SARAH: I explained that the school had a strict policy on using its resources—including supplies, equipment, and phones—for personal use. I told Mary that I was sorry if that hadn't been clear, but that I was working on a pamphlet explaining all the school's rules to the staff. I think she was

The BUSINESS
Shrink

(continued)

kind of ashamed at first, but then I started talking about what a great teacher she is and how the girls adore her. I even said I admired her for writing a book—on her own time.

ME: Sounds like you handled it just right. My only suggestion now would be that you check in with Mary in a month or so to see how she's doing. And you can reiterate the school's policies at that point if you feel it's needed.

SARAH: I probably should do that. But I think she got the message.

• • •

When he talked about dealing with problem employees on my show, Terry Bacon said, "Go right back to the basics, and establish a charter for each person that explains that person's roles and responsibilities, and establish some basic measurements for how the organization is supposed to work." Sarah needs to make sure Mary, and the rest of her staff, are clear about not only their duties but overall school policies. ■

Ask How the Disgruntled Employee Sees the Situation

Erika Andersen, founder of Proteus International, a consulting firm, and the author of the book *Growing Great Employees: Turning Ordinary People into Extraordinary Performers*, was a fascinating guest on my radio show. She made intriguing analogies between gardening and the grooming of good employees. "Anyone who gardens knows that one absolutely essential component of a good garden is preparing the soil properly. Even if you get great plants and you're willing to care for them, unless you create soil that is good and rich and loose, the plants aren't going to grow. I think the analogy for managers is listening," she suggested. "Listening creates an environment that's open, that's rich, and feels trusting and respectful to employees." When you're meeting with a troubled employee, take the time to ask how she sees the situation, and then really listen to the answer. You might be surprised. Frequently workers see things quite differently from their bosses.

Name Specific Behaviors

Let's say you're meeting with someone who's chronically late. Maybe she also comes in hung-over every Monday, and her coworkers have noticed the tardiness and mentioned it to you. In your meeting, discuss both the late arrival on the job and the hangovers. Don't gloss over the details; tell the employee exactly which behaviors you and others see as negative or problematic and suggest ways to improve. It's okay to say, "Brenda, your office mates smell the whiskey fumes on your breath during meetings, and they're starting to worry about you. Also, I've noticed you've been coming in late, and that goes against company policy." Offer help, from the informal to the professional.

Assure Confidentiality

If you have an employee in your office and you're planning on talking with her about a personal hygiene issue—maybe she wears too much perfume, and it's nauseating—assure her that what is discussed will stay with you alone. Can you imagine how embarrassed your employee would be if she thought you were going to tell everyone else in the office she was stinking up the joint? Even if they already know, and that's why she's in your office, always keep these kinds of discussions confidential. Make it part of your organization's policy, and stick to the rules. Don't let the gossiping start with you. The principle of confidentiality extends to any of your private discussions with your employees. What happens in your office should stay in your office.

Discuss Future Opportunities

When I chatted on my radio show with Susan Gebelein, executive vice president of client relationship management at Personnel Decisions International, we honed in on the importance of making good employees feel valued. If you're having a conversation with a disgruntled employee who has stalled out or begun slacking on his responsibilities, maybe it's time for a change. Gebelein pointed out, "One reason people leave organizations is because they don't see an opportunity there. You want to make sure that you are listening and hearing what it is that employees want to do besides what they are doing right now. Maybe you have an employee who is in a

66 99   **Advice for employees:** Compartmentalize problems.

All of us, both bosses and employees (and in some sense, we're all both bosses and employees), suffer from personal and professional problems. Minimize your frustrations and conflicts on the job by learning to leave the irritating minutiae of your home life back on the ranch. There are enough irritating minutiae at work to fill your 9 to 5. Once you're back home with your dog barking, your spouse yelling, and your kids crying, practice dealing with those domestic problems free of the hassles you face at work. Bifurcating your life—leaving work at work and home at home—will reduce stress and make you a happy camper in both venues.

customer service position but is interested in supervising in a customer service role. And you may think to yourself, 'Gee, I don't see this person as a customer service supervisor.' Rather than dismissing the idea and saying, 'Look, you're great in the job you're doing now,' spend some time talking with the person about what gives them the idea that a supervisory role is a goal for them. You might discover that you've got someone who has been very active in leadership roles in the community or in a church organization and so has a whole lot more leadership experience than you may have thought." If you want to hang on to someone, discuss other opportunities that might exist within your organization.

Getting Tough (When You Must)

There are always going be some employees who just aren't going to work out. Or maybe they will if they're capable of making a whole slew of changes, but you doubt they can manage such radical transitions. If you have a disciplinary discussion with someone who gets defensive, who doesn't seem as though she wants to improve, or is carrying so much emotional baggage that it is seriously interfering with her work, you must be candid and explain that she is not meeting your expectations and that her job is in jeopardy.

Don't Be Afraid to Be Firm

My guest Glenn Shepard gives the example of a nurse who was a manager saddled with some problem employees. "She had to get rid of some people," Shepard told me and my radio audience, "so she laid down the law and fired them. When I spoke to her, she said, 'It's like a whole new organization. People want to work for us now because I finally stepped up to the plate and became the manager I needed to be.' And that's the most common story I hear all over America."

If you're a supervisor, at times you will need to stand firm, no matter how difficult or how much of a "bad guy" you might feel. As Shepard pointed out, "Sometimes you might have to say, 'You can't come to work late. You can't just call in sick. You're going to have to play by the rules.' People either shape up or ship out; it's their call."

Give Accurate Performance Appraisals   During performance appraisals, focus on the goals set at the beginning of employment or at the employee's last review as well as the overall goals of the organization. Start with the positives; put the interviewee at ease, especially if you can see he's sweating bullets. Performance reviews can be extraordinarily stressful for some types of personalities, especially if their work product is being challenged and criticized. Talk in terms of preventing problems in the future, and make it clear that your comments pertain to specific performance and not to the employee as an individual. Ask him or her for feedback and suggestions. Always keep written records of employees' performance evaluations, listing any action items or behavioral issues that were discussed. It is important to keep track of all employee evaluations. If you ever need to fire a worker, he may have grounds to sue you and the company if he can produce a track record of all-positive evaluations previous to the termination. A judge and jury could interpret the lack of criticism as a failure on your part to give the employee a chance to meet your standards. Keep a paper trail to protect yourself, and make sure you evaluate your employees accurately. With skill and compassion, you can criticize and chastise without offending or alienating your workers. The resulting employee files will then protect you when you need to discipline or discharge workers.

Give Fair Warning   If an employee is exhibiting negative behavior or is clearly disgruntled, review your expectations and corporate policies with her. Engage in a conversation about what she sees as concerns or issues. Then agree together on specific changes that need to be made and a time frame for completing them. Go on the record in your conversation about what you determine is not working and then develop a program response. Put it in writing. Maybe your strategy is to move her to a new department or to assign her different peers or supervisors. Maybe you're going to watch her work product more carefully in your role as boss. Make it crystal clear that if she does not meet the goals and criteria you have discussed within an agreed-upon time frame, the lack of progress may be grounds for disciplinary action up to and including termination.

Set Up a "Program for Improvement"

When the soles of your favorite shoes are so thin you can feel the sidewalk, you take them to the cobbler and get them resoled. If you're anxious to hold on to a disgruntled but basically productive employee, set up an improvement program. Sit down with the employee and make sure you ask him for input throughout the entire process. Revisit the situation within a specified period to see if he's making the improvements you requested. Just as you would write up a job description, create specific goals and benchmarks detailing how the employee can improve his behavior or performance, all in writing.

Write a Disciplinary Letter

The purpose of a disciplinary letter is never to punish or chastise but to let the employee know that there is a serious behavior or performance problem. It offers an opportunity for her to change, but it obviously is also ammunition for you if you decide you must fire her. The tone of the letter should be matter-of-fact, describing the problem(s), yet also supportive, offering to help or guide her back to a secure berth in the company ship. To protect the company, the letter is an on-the-record report of her transgression. This is a self-protective measure for you as an employer. It serves as a formal warning that her negative attitude or inappropriate behavior is unacceptable. By documenting everything, if you have to let her go, you'll have a paper trail to use as proof that you didn't fire her capriciously. The reality is that many disgruntled employees try to sue their former employers. If that happens to you, you want to be protected with proof that your decision to fire the problem worker was not arbitrary and was well grounded in documented facts that were made clear to the employee in a timely fashion.

Don't Be Scared to Lose Employees

When an employee is physically harmful to others, steals or lies, is emotionally unstable, or simply unable to perform his job, you will have to fire him. Unfortunately, we live in such a litigious environment that sometimes managers are intimidated when they must discipline an unruly or underperforming employee, because they fear legal reprisals.

Don't be afraid. If you document your case against a disgruntled employee, you need not worry about court actions other than nuisance suits. But be prepared to be sued.

"That's a very real thing to keep in mind," Glenn Shepard said during our conversation on my show. "And the answer to that is to always make sure that you document everything you do and be able to prove that you were fair and consistent in how you treated people. The flip side of not disciplining or holding problem employees responsible for their actions is that you could wind up with legal problems with others who *have* been held accountable. So it's got to be across the board."

You must be consistent in your treatment of your employees, at least from a legal standpoint. And you must remember that you have a responsibility to yourself if you own the business, or to the board or proprietors of your company, to rid the organization of employees who do not serve its current needs. Always consult with your human resources and your legal department, if you have them, for advice on disciplining or terminating your employees.

Education in Response to Violations

Not only can you provide written warning to a problem employee, but you can also work to educate her regarding what's expected in your workplace. Discipline should never come as a surprise to any employee. You don't want to blindside your workers with a sudden assault. Sit down with your employees—disgruntled or not—on a regular basis to talk over the issues. (This makes me wonder about the opposite of a disgruntled employee. Funny, isn't it, that we don't call them "gruntled"!) Some organizations develop communication and conflict-resolution training for all employees. Strive to inform, not just criticize; give employees a chance to shape up if they're making errors.

Tips for Dealing with Specific Types

There is no one across-the-board solution for dealing with unhappy employees. You must tap your creative managerial talents and adjust your reactions to individuals. Just as unhappy workers come in a smorgasbord of flavors, there are different ways to handle specific types. Some employees may just need someone to listen to them; some must be instructed specifically how to change. Others might need outside professional help, while still other workers could benefit from a new supervisor or an increase or reduction in responsibilities. Just as I've covered many of the types of disgruntled employees, I've compiled tricks and techniques for coping with the array of characters that exist in the workplace (and in life, of course). I've encountered most of them over my many years in business, and eventually so will you. Having a game plan prior to meeting with them will help save you some of the on-the-job training I was forced to undergo.

Cynics and Naysayers

Naysayers and cynics are perpetually pessimistic and love to disagree with everything and everyone. The best way to deal with them is to ask them why they are disagreeing. Make them explain their negative point of view. Try to get them to develop a more positive attitude toward work and to focus on their strengths. Demonstrate how their negativity affects their coworkers. Start allowing them to take charge of individual projects whenever possible.

*Establish
Appropriate
Avenues/
Times for "Venting"*
We all need to let off steam. Sometimes you can diffuse a negative employee by allowing him to vent about his issues and concerns. But it's not appropriate for people to talk behind each other's backs, or worse, to infect coworkers with their pessimism. Develop a strategy for appropriate venting. It might be a peer meeting, where everyone is encouraged to gripe about his or her problems and then brainstorm about solutions. Or you may choose to take your employees out for a drink once a month and let them blow off steam in a casual setting. As long as you keep negativity out of the workplace, venting can be a beneficial exercise.

Do-Littles

If an employee is not performing up to par, missing deadlines, or turning in shoddy work, maybe it's time for a change. Don't start with criticism; simply observe the behavior. Then ask her if she has changed her attitude toward her work. Ask if she is interested in new responsibilities or some other change that will inspire her to be more productive. Sometimes a "do little" is bored or insufficiently challenged and just needs a change. In other cases, employees are doing little work because they are actively seeking new jobs. Still others may be slowing down in productivity as a way of protesting something they don't like about their job or about the organization.

If a worker is underperforming where she once was a superstar, take the employee aside and frankly ask what has happened to affect her level of performance. Without being accusatory or hostile, let her know that you know she can do better work, and try to find out what has caused the change in attitude and behavior. Ask pointed questions,

"Are you looking for work elsewhere and just marking time here?" "Has someone or something offended you?" Make it clear that the current pattern cannot continue, but that if she wishes to remain with the firm, you're ready to work with her. And if she says she is seeking employment elsewhere, make it clear that her work product cannot suffer while she finds another job or she'll lose the one she has and jeopardize a positive referral.

Perhaps the slacker correctly figured out that she was marked for a layoff or termination. If that's the case, you will be hard-pressed to change her attitude and the best move is to simply accelerate her firing. Better to call in a temp to fill in for her than to keep her around doing a poor job and grumbling.

Disaffected Workers If an individual feels he is a "bad fit" within the organization, he may become sullen and uncooperative. It is almost impossible to work with a person like this. A disaffected worker can infect coworkers with feelings of disappointment and frustration. Listen carefully to the employee's complaints and try to understand his basic concerns and needs.

66 99 | **Advice for employees:** Recognize your frustrations.

A first step toward minimizing what makes you disgruntled on the job is to pinpoint exactly why you're unhappy at work. Once you learn what is causing you distress, you're in a much better position to address your frustrations and reduce your sense of displeasure. With a specific complaint, you may be able to talk with your boss and achieve immediate relief. Even if you cannot convince your supervisor to make the changes you desire, simply recognizing what is making you unhappy is a productive leap. With the knowledge of what's bothering you, you may be able to develop work-arounds—both psychological and actual—that remove, or at least relieve, your problem.

Is the employee really a bad fit, or does he simply have unrealistic expectations of the position? Explain your own expectations and see if you can reach some kind of agreement, an agreement that may well be a divorce. Negotiation and compromise are key components to the solution for disenchanted employees and their employers, even if that solution is a resignation or a termination agreement.

Indifferent and Bored Workers

You may not know you have a bored employee. Someone who is bored may just start slacking off, taking long lunches, or coming in late and leaving early. Her symptoms of dissatisfaction mimic other types of disgruntled workers. You need to meet with someone who appears unhappy or unproductive and start by complimenting the things she is doing right. Then ask outright if she is feeling challenged. If boredom turns out to be the problem, ask her what she thinks would make her job more fulfilling. Be willing to experiment within the basic job description, to offer more interesting or challenging work. Perhaps she needs to be transferred to another department, position, or manager.

Dealing with Victims and Whiners

Employees who whine and complain feel victimized all the time, but really they are crying out for attention. They need a supportive environment and lots of encouragement and positive feedback. Deadlines and worries about job performance stress these people out and fill them with anxiety. While you can't get rid of deadlines, and you expect quality work, assure the employee that he is doing a good job and that you have faith the work will come in on time. Remind him of past successes. It sounds as if I am saying to treat this person like a child, and so I am, a little. But it works, just as reinforcement of positive behavior can stop children from whining, too.

Agitators/
Obstructionists
People who are actively slowing things down or stirring up trouble in the workplace need to be stopped cold. Meet with an agitator, point out the problem, and discuss how to preventing it from recurring. Ask her if she realizes the effect the behavior is having on coworkers. You can remind her that she is part of a team, no matter how small, with a common objective. Work to get to the root of the problem, and ask her to suggest how she might change her behavior. Decide on specific actions, and follow up to make sure she is working toward change. But be firm and watch her carefully. And, if necessary, get rid of the troublemaker. Don't tolerate poison in the office.

Workaholics
Sometime a workaholic might just seem like a dedicated, hard worker. It's part of the American work ethic to praise and even reward those who put in long hours, take work home, and show up at the office on weekends. Yet the long hours and lack of a life outside work will take their toll as the workaholic becomes less productive and burned-out. If you're worried an employee may be heading in this direction, ask him if the workload is too heavy. Even if he denies it, suggest that he may have taken on too much work and responsibility. Propose ways to ease back and reduce stress while still emphasizing his value to the organization. In extreme cases, you may need to ask him to take enforced time off in the form of paid or unpaid leave. Assure him that you will welcome him back once the leave is over and he's less tense.

Snipers
Snipers feel bad about themselves, so they spend their time slinging arrows at others as a way of deflecting their own negative feelings. When you meet with someone who has been verbally attacking her colleagues or organization, tell her that her negative behavior is hurting people. Do not be confrontational but be specific, such

Sam the Workaholic

Sam had a successful gardening business; he'd been the sole propri-
etor since he opened the business more than ten years ago. Because
his business had grown so much in the past several years due to happy
clients' word-of-mouth recommendations, Sam had recently taken on Eric, an
assistant. Eric enjoyed working for Sam who was a nice guy, a fair boss, and
had a good sense of humor to boot. But lately, with orders for new lawns
and landscaping coming in every day, Sam's good moods seemed a thing
of the past. Eric noticed that no matter how early he got to work Sam was
already there, tending to seedlings, watering plants, or going over new orders.
And whenever Eric left work, no matter if he stayed late, Sam stayed later.
Eric had overheard some angry-sounding phone conversations between Sam
and his wife, always ending with Sam saying, "You know this business is my
life!"

Early one morning, when Eric came in and found Sam collapsed in his
office chair, sleeping in yesterday's clothes, he decided to confront his boss.
Eric cleared his throat. Sam shook his head wearily and gave Eric a small
smile.

"Sam, what's going on?" Eric asks. "Did you spend the night here?"

"Oh, hey, Eric. Yeah, I guess I did. I've been really worried about those
roses we promised Mrs. Fells. You know, with the early frost, I'm not sure
we can deliver. I've been trying to convince her to buy something hardier
instead."

"I know she loves those roses," Eric says. "But couldn't it have waited
until this morning? I mean you can't have spent the night here worrying
about roses."

"No," Sam responds. "I was doing some invoices, just trying to catch up
on paperwork. It can get really overwhelming this time of year with the holidays coming."

"But, Sam, isn't that what you hired me for?" Eric asks. "All you had to do
was ask, and I would have taken the invoices home or stayed late. You know
I'm single and you've got a family. You should be getting home to your wife
and kids."

"Yeah, that's what my wife says," laughs Sam. "But I just feel better when
I know everything is taken care of. Not that you're not a big help, Eric. You
are. I guess it's just that I've been running things on my own so long I'm not
used to having anyone else take over."

"I know, Sam. But honestly, you look like hell," Eric says. "You ought to go home early today and get a good night's sleep. I'll take care of the roses and whatever else comes along. I promise, if I don't know what to do, I'll give you a call."

• • •

In this scenario, Sam is a workaholic in disguise. Because he owns his own business in a non-technology or financial industry, many would say he's a typical entrepreneur, working long hours and rarely getting home to see his family. Yet, because he had the good sense to hire a capable assistant when his business expanded, Sam didn't have to be at the shop every minute. Unfortunately, old habits die hard. Sam was so used to being solely responsible for the business that even though he'd enlisted Eric's help, he couldn't relinquish control. He had become obsessed, spending all of his time at work, and neglecting his wife and family. With no boss to recognize what was happening, Sam just kept going.

If I had been his boss and noticed he was there every morning when I came in and still there when I left on a daily basis, I would have had a frank talk with Sam. I would have said while I admired his work ethic, he seemed run-down. I would have pointed out that Eric was perfectly able to take on some of the responsibility for the shop and that was what Sam had hired him to do. I would have asked after Sam's health and possibly learned that the long hours were affecting him. I would have insisted that Sam cut back on his hours and learn to delegate. Since I can't "boss" Sam around, I would hope that he might listen to Eric and give his assistant more responsibility. ■

as "Karen, you know those things you were saying about Tony in the staff meeting were mean, and they made him feel horrible." Acknowledge her emotions, and try to focus on the positive contributions she makes to the business. Ask her what she likes about her work. Offer to make any changes that make sense, and monitor her actions carefully, checking in often.

Gossipers and Rumormongers

Rumormongers may feel a lack of control over their environments. They often feel uninformed and spread rumors as a way of regaining control. Try to head off more gossip: Give your employees as many facts and as much information as you can so they feel more powerful. Point out specific instances of rumors that aren't true without placing blame on those generating the gossip. Suggest that it is better to wait until information is confirmed before spreading it about the workplace. Make cutting down on rumors an organization-wide goal.

Understand the limits of what you can do to stop rumors. It's human nature to gossip. Keep focused on the rumors and gossip you believe is damaging and destructive; don't waste your time with the casual chatter.

When a company's stock is performing poorly, when there has just been a round of layoffs, or if the money just isn't flowing in at the pace expected, rumormongers love to take the slightest bit of negative news and run with it to the water cooler and the e-mail lists. As a supervisor, it is your job to tackle rumor control by being very open with all of your employees about exactly what is happening within the organization, even if the news is bad.

Thieves and Exploiters

There is no pleasant way to deal with the issue of a thief in the workplace. Before you confront the employee, carefully document all records of theft, no matter how petty, and be prepared to give specific examples in the meeting.

Make sure the employee knows that the behavior is inappropriate and will not be tolerated. You can give a written or verbal warning to be followed up with another meeting within a short time frame. If the theft is egregious, you may feel compelled to fire the employee and call the police and attempt to prosecute the ex-employee. Such as action certainly will make it clear to others that illegal activity is not tolerated in your workplace. Check in with your human resources or legal department (or adviser if your firm is too small for a legal and HR department) to make sure you handle this matter with the sensitivity it demands.

Manipulators   Sometimes a worker will come to you if he feels manipulated by another employee. Document the complaint and schedule a meeting with the manipulative employee. As with many other disgruntled employees, a manipulator may feel a lack of control over his circumstances. Ask him how he feels about his job. Review other employees' complaints with the manipulator. If the manipulative employee feels stalled out or as though he doesn't have enough leeway within his position, and you want to save him, try to find opportunities that will give him more control over his work.

Harassment is a variant of manipulation. We'll talk specifically about harassment later.

Passive-Aggressive Employees   Deep down, a passive-aggressive person is full of anger. While you need to be extremely direct in dealing with her, you can't be accusatory; that feeds the anger. This kind of employee believes, or says she believes, that she is complying with your wishes and meeting job obligations.

People suffering from this disorder may appear to comply with your wishes and may even act enthusiastic about a project, but when you request action—finishing a report or meeting with a client—a passive-aggressive personality either performs late or somehow sabotages the job so that it doesn't meet your expectations. A passive-aggressive employee may say, "I thought the deadline was next Monday, not this Monday!" Avoid this situation by being direct and clear in your communication, and by ordering in writing specific tasks and deadlines whenever possible. Establish firm, reasonable consequences for behavior and goals, and make sure the employee knows what to expect from you. Always make it clear that these same consequences will apply to you as well.

Ranting Egos   Underneath the bravado and arrogance of a worker with an overdeveloped ego lies an insecure person. But the egomaniac's ranting, raging, and always being "right" is disturbing to everyone in the workplace. You need to document instances of rude conduct and inappropriate outbursts and print a list. When you meet with the employee, calmly discuss each item, and explain that the behavior is unacceptable. Consider suggesting that the employee go outside the office if she needs to blow off steam or rant. Try to get her to see things from a coworker's point of view. Continue to document egotistical behavior, and make a plan of action if the worker's ego continues to get the better of her, a plan that includes termination if the foul behavior does not cease.

Appearance and   If the organization has a clearly stated policy against body
Hygiene Issues   piercings other than the ears, and an employee comes to work with a nose ring or pierced tongue, the solution is simple. Meet with the person, refer to the policy, and ask for compliance. In other cases, where personal hygiene or appearance is offensive or unprofessional, the employee may be disgruntled or he may be unaware there's a problem. Meet with him. Find something positive to say

about his performance. Then, without making it sound like a personal attack, address the appearance or hygiene issue, and explain that he might enjoy a better chance for advancement once he makes the appropriate changes. If he doesn't clean up, follow up with a written warning. And refrain from calling him Stinky or Tattoo Boy during the meeting!

Clinical Psychological Issues

It's no secret that mental illness has invaded the U.S. work force. According to the organization Mental Health America, depression alone ranks as one of the top-three workplace problems for employee-assistance professionals, following family crises and stress. Despite its traditional stigma, employers and workers are much more open about mental illness in today's environment. When dealing with an employee who has emotional or psychological problems, first assess whether the symptoms—such as mood swings or unpredictable behavior—are temporary or signs of a more lasting psychological problem. Workers may try to camouflage their illness due to shame or fear of losing their jobs. Meet with the employee in question and offer your support while working to discover the depth of the problem. The Americans with Disabilities Act strictly limits the circumstances under which you may ask questions about an employee's disability or require a medical examination. Understand your legal responsibilities, obligations, and restrictions. But if you have a strong feeling that the employee is suffering from overwhelming emotional or psychological problems and can no longer perform the job, you may step in and suggest outside help or offer some time off. Again, record every conversation and symptom of distress in writing to stay in compliance with all laws surrounding this complex issue. For specifics on how employers can learn the details of the Americans with Disabilities Act and its impact on workers, go to the ADA's Web site at *www.ada.gov.*

Garlic Breath

I had an interesting situation in my own business not so long ago. I had a guy, let's call him Ed, and he liked to go down to the local Italian restaurant for lunch almost every day. And Ed loved garlic. Not only did he love garlic, somehow his skin and his body oozed garlic, so much that after lunch he'd come in my office smelling like a garlic clove with a fan around it.

Now, the truth be told, I didn't mind the guy sitting across from me. But I felt the problem was with the other people in the office. Maybe they didn't like the smell of garlic or they didn't enjoy having such a strong food odor at work; either way, it wasn't fair to the rest of the staff.

So one day when I'd had enough, I called Ed into the office, closed the door, and put my proverbial arm around him (I didn't do it literally because I didn't want to smell like garlic!), and our conversation went like this:

"Hey, Ed," I said. "You know it's very obvious when you go out to lunch and when you come back. I think you need to save your garlic eating until after-hours, at dinner, because everyone else is noticing it, and some people like garlic and others don't. I think they should have a choice, and the garlic odor shouldn't be in the office."

I could tell that Ed was a bit nonplussed because he started to blush. I'm sure he felt both embarrassed and a bit humiliated.

"Um, yeah, I get it," said Ed. "Okay, I'll stop eating so much garlic at lunch."

"Thanks, Ed. I really appreciate your cooperation on this."

"Okay, thanks. I didn't mean to offend anyone."

"Sure, no problem."

Now, I was lucky. Because the conversation was held in private, and I went out of the way to be polite and not to use ridicule, I got the response I wanted. If I had talked to Ed in a group setting, it would have been awful—or if I'd called him "Stinky." You would think most people would be too professional to stoop to name-calling, but some are not.

Several years ago a *Wall Street Journal* article profiled an employee who had a sweating disorder and was fired because of it. That employee ended up collecting a lot of damages because she told the company, Look, it's not my fault, it's a glandular problem, and I'm not trying to harm anyone. She felt she shouldn't have been fired.

Now if Ed had said to me, "Listen, boss, I do a good job, my numbers are in order, my desk is neat, I like my spaghetti and meatballs with extra garlic at lunchtime, and I'm not going to change," things would have been different. Depending on how valuable he was, I would have continued working with him, or I would have checked my legal situation to see what my options were. This kind of situation is not black-and-white; it's a gray area that needs to be handled with delicacy. Most likely, Ed and I would have reached a compromise involving breath mints or eating garlic only once a week. But as a supervisor, always make sure you're not challenging your employee's legal rights. ■

Mixed Bags   You may have a good employee who performs well on most projects, has lots of experience, but everyone on the team dislikes her because, well, she's kind of a prima donna. She can be rude and demanding, but she doesn't actually abuse her coworkers; she's just no fun to be around. In fact, even after you meet with her and explain the problem, she just doesn't change. Being self-centered and rude is just hard-wired into her personality. On an interim basis, say in the middle of a project in which this employee has a key role, you might just have to put up with her. It would be disruptive and potentially destructive to make a dramatic change or to fire or replace her. But once the urgent circumstances have passed, you need to do real work to reposition this disgruntled employee by addressing the problems she is causing in the workplace.

At one point in my career, my staff came into my office and threatened to quit because of one fellow who worked in the finance department of my real-estate company. He was a whirling dervish of deal activity. He was able to get all kinds of creative financing and do amazing things. The problem was that although he would stretch the envelope and do far better than everyone else, he did it very manipulatively, with lots of miscommunication to each party involved in the deal. Once everyone got together and realized that this very creative, sales-oriented guy hadn't told them 100 percent of the facts, there were always all kinds of pieces to pick up and crises to deal with. To save the deals, many of my people were left with the unenviable task of having to clean up the mess that this guy made. They came into my office en mass and told me that this guy was very productive but geared to showboat. I was left with the choice of getting rid of this fellow who was very productive but created a lot of problems and mess in his wake, was not particularly honorable in his communications and his business style, and miserable to work with, or lose a big chunk of the department I had put together. I tried various techniques—from group meetings and discussions to corrective action—but this guy could never quite comprehend his mistakes and change, so I fired him.

Sometimes the solution to a disgruntled employee is the ultimate punishment: "You're fired!"

Giving the Benefit of the Doubt

I like to say on my radio show that my favorite color is gray. I also say to expect the worst and hope for the best. You can have a manager who's great at his job, is terrific with customers, gets along with the employees, but then it turns out he has a blind side when it comes to numbers. He can't say no to people. Yet his competence is so high in other areas that you don't get rid of him. Instead you work with him to overcome his weaknesses, celebrate his strengths, and bring in other employees to help support him. Enroll him in a basic accounting class so he can learn the additional skills he needs to do all the parts of his job. Part of being a boss is looking for the best in people and helping them develop those qualities so they can grow.

Dealing with Physically Dangerous Employees

When someone is so disgruntled or disturbed that she is making threats to hurt herself or others, you must confront this employee immediately; never ignore somebody who is exhibiting unusual behavior. Physical threats mandate firing the employee who made the threat, and perhaps calling the police. Take no chances with threats of physical harm.

If no threat has been made but you perceive potential danger, immediately meet with the employee you're worried about. In your conversation, talk about specific, work-related behavior. Rather than framing the discussion in vague terms such as a "negative attitude," focus on specific behaviors. Give examples. For instance, you might say, "During the staff meeting you spoke out of turn several times and seemed angry with Danny." Or, "Sarah says you have been lurking outside her office. It is frightening her. This is not part of our organization's policy regarding teamwork." Do not attempt to analyze the employee or argue with her at this stage; simply listen to what she has to say. If she is willing to talk, you may gain insight into how she perceives the workplace. Sometimes, being heard is enough to defuse an angry employee. Explain specific things you'd like to see her do differently, especially with regard to behavior. Ask if she has any thoughts on how she can be part of the team, and strategize devices and techniques to solve problems. You must always document in writing the worker's behavior and any complaints from others, your comments, and the employee's reactions.

If your organization has an Employee Assistance Program (EAP), discuss its benefits with the employee. These programs offer employees some form of counseling or medical assistance. The EAP provides confidential and professional help for workers facing personal problems that may have an impact on their job performance, their overall health and well-being, and safety of the entire work force. The program can help employees cope with family problems, marital difficulties, substance abuse, and other mental or emotional issues that may not be job related but can have a severe effect on their work.

Use compassion and diplomacy when you explain how the program can reduce workplace stress. But if you feel the employee is physically dangerous, your safety and that of your staff should always be your first priority. Don't be afraid to call for help if you think it is warranted, whether it's company security personnel or the police. Remember to notify the individual's spouse, parent, or close friend if possible—check their personnel file for this information. If someone is threatening suicide, attempt to get her to professional help immediately.

Getting Outside Help When an employee is having long-term difficulties, whether emotional or psychological, or is simply unable to perform his duties, it might be a problem too big for one supervisor to handle. National Institute of Mental Health studies show that untreated mental illness is costing the United States an estimated $50 billion a year in absenteeism, lost productivity, and direct treatment costs. Companies are starting to expand their mental health insurance coverage and treatment programs. The EAPs often provide on-call counselors and referrals to other professionals. They may also offer programs designed to provide confidential, professional help to employees facing personal problems that have an impact on their performance, their health and well-being, and the safety of others.

If your firm doesn't have an EAP, suggest that the employee seek outside counseling.

Counseling and Mediation From psychologists to social workers to crisis coaches, there are a variety of professionals equipped with the skills necessary to help a troubled employee through a difficult time. These people can help you figure out whether the problem employee is clinically depressed or if there's a temporary crisis. Have a list of local experts on hand. If you are faced with an employee in the midst of a personal crisis, refer him to an expert. Career counselors can help employees tackle tough problems at work and get back to being productive parts of the team, whether the problems stem from the job itself or from trying to find a work/life balance. Workers may not want to admit to mental health issues; if you notice the warning signs, step in and offer to help. In many cases, help will come in the form of a referral to an experienced professional, but sometimes just a collegial chat and a pat on the back may be the best treatment of all.

Psychological Training for Staff

I've described the many different kinds of troubled employees who have called in to my radio show and the warning signs to look for. If you're completely at the end of your rope regarding the inappropriate behavior of one of your workers, and you don't feel your managerial skills are up to the task of dealing with a severely problematic individual, seek professional training in how to manage these types of employees.

Given the rise in mental illness in the workplace, it makes sense to enroll senior managers and human resources staff in a psychological training program. Such a program will help you identify and interpret unusual behaviors and symptoms of emotionally disturbed employees. I think every organization's human resources manual should contain a section on common issues that arise in the workplace involving unhappy employees. These can range from complaints of harassment to lack of discipline, from workplace violence to substance abuse. The HR manual should also include a section that deals with the different personality traits of people who are in a major crisis or who are acting out their disenchantment and disengagement, and what a manager can do about it. There is no dearth of professionals who are trained to deal with inappropriate behavior in the workplace. A seminar focusing on disgruntled employees and their issues might well be valuable to your management or HR team.

Psychological/ Placement-Oriented Tests for Employees

Psychological profiling helps managers select and retain candidates who have both the skills and the temperament to succeed in their business. Psychological assessment is often used in hiring to test for various traits and behaviors including honesty and likeability.

Many organizations today rely on personality tests such as the Myers–Briggs Type Indicator to help them in their hiring process. Myers–Briggs was designed to use the theories of Carl Jung to identify certain psychological differences in people. Now, that sounds pretty heavy, but basically Myers-Briggs divides individuals into types or "combinations" and may help predict how they will perform in different settings. For example, one combination is "ISTJ," or "Introverted, Sensing, Thinking, Judging." You can find a complete description of Myers-Briggs combinations at *http://en.wikipedia.org/wiki/Myers-Briggs*.

Another kind of personality test popular with hiring managers is the enneagram, which identifies people as one of nine personality types (such as a peacemaker or an enthusiast). More information on that test can be found at *www.enneagraminstitute.com* for a nominal fee.

I invited Ben Dattner to be on my radio show, the head of Dattner Consulting. Ben works as an executive coach with a variety of corporate and nonprofit organizations, helping them become more successful by developing a better understanding of the impact of individual psychology and group dynamics on their performance. He's also a professor at New York University. When I asked him about psychological profiling and testing in the workplace, Ben said, "Companies are realizing that people are their only enduring source of competitive advantage. Particularly as organizations all now have the same technologies and the same information, they've realized in order to compete, they really have to pick trained staff and get the right people on board. Psychological tests can be used both to select new employees and to assess and develop employees. The tests not only assess intellectual ability, but they also assess personality fit. For example, somebody who's very effective at founding an organization from an entrepreneurial perspective might not be nearly as effective when more bureaucratic systems and structures need to be put in place."

Before you hire a new employee, or if you want to check the fit of your existing employees, you can test them to make sure you've got the best person for the job. Whatever assessment tool or personality test you use, make sure you understand the legal limits of what you can test for and how you should administer tests. You must be able to show that the traits being tested for are necessary for the worker to be able to do the job. There are many Web sites that do a pretty good job of personality testing. One of the leading quiz sites is *www.personalitypathways.com/type_inventory.html* and for a more Myers-Briggs approach try *www.knowyourtype.com.*

Avoid Creating Disgruntled Employees!

One of the most important things a manager can do is to avoid having unhappy employees in the first place. You need to be aware of what's going on in the workplace and have fluent and close working relationships with the people who report to you. Then, issues are easily observable and can be nipped in the bud. As my radio show guest Erika Andersen says, you have to listen to your employees, and you have to respect them. Erika told us, "The most difficult thing about listening is that to really listen, to really take in what the other person is saying, or how they feel about it, what it means to them, you have to put your own thoughts on hold. You have to stop thinking about what you're thinking about and really just focus your attention on them." This is probably the best piece of advice I can give to anyone who's managing employees at any level: just listen. It's pretty good advice for your life outside the office, too.

Acknowledge a Conflict or Problem

One of the benefits of listening to your employees is that you will know when something is wrong. A supervisor might come in and report a difficulty with a subordinate, or a worker might come in with a complaint of her own. Don't shy away from dealing with the issue, whatever it is. Take the bull by the horns and tackle the problem (how's that for a mixed sports metaphor!) by having a one-on-one conversation with the disgruntled employee or employees, and let your colleagues know what you're up to. If you catch a problem when it's small, it's less likely to spread like a virus and contaminate the rest of your work force.

Affirm Your Investment in the Relationship

Erika Andersen told my radio show audience that a good business manager ought to have the mindset of a coach. "What I discovered over and over again is that people who are good managers, who are good leadership people, tend to hold a particular set of beliefs about the people who work for them. They believe in their employees' potential to succeed, and they want to help them succeed." I like to refer to this as "enlightened self-interest," meaning that you invest in open, direct, and fair relationships with the people reporting to you, and you hope that they in turn will be happy in the workplace, adjusted to the task at hand, and proud of their work and of the company.

Avoid a Lack of Direction/ Misdirection

Employees often run into trouble when they aren't clear about their job responsibilities. Sometimes those duties change, and management neglects to make them aware of the changes. It sounds simple, but so much of creating a contented and productive work force is good communication. Be direct about what you expect from people, down to the smallest detail. My radio show guest, Susan Gebelein, knows that such managerial detail work is key to keeping good workers, "If you want an employee to stay around, their expectations for their job keep increasing, so we always need to be developing our employees because the jobs and what we want them to do gets greater and greater. A very smart supervisor is one who's very, very in tune, in lockstep with the employee and able to assess their potential as their expectations keep changing." Be very clear with employees about how and when you expect them to complete projects, and always leave time and encourage them to ask questions. Leave nothing in doubt.

Micromanaging/ Looking Over Their Shoulders

How do you feel when your spouse or friend tells you how to drive? When they remind you to put on your blinker, adjust your mirror, speed up, slow down, and turn left here? One of most frequent complaints I hear from disgruntled employees is that their boss is looking over their shoulders, micromanaging every aspect of a project. I mean there are literally bosses out there perusing people's penmanship and counting paper clips! If you've hired talented people, and you've established an atmosphere of trust among your team, challenge them and then let them do their jobs. Back off. Establish benchmarks or check-in points, and wait for them to come to you. If there's a problem, you're sure to find out about it without hovering like an anxious parent.

Conformity That Stifles Creativity

An article by Carol Hymowitz in the *Wall Street Journal* on October 1, 2007, caught my eye because she writes that one thing that troubles executives the most is employee turnover. Not only is an employee revolving door hard on the managers but the employees who stay often feel threatened because they perceive there's some reason people are leaving. They became disenchanted. Those workers who quit may have gone on to new jobs that were more challenging. While it is important that employees meet their supervisor's expectations and conform to the organization's rules and corporate culture, they also need some freedom. Many need to feel challenged. "Analyze why talent is going out the door," advises Hymowitz. That assignment is critical. Let employees' creativity and individuality shine on the job through new assignments. Listen to what they have to say, and find ways to help them grow within the framework of their job description.

Neither people nor jobs are black and white, just many shades of gray.

Missed Bonuses

Imagine telling your child, "After you finish your homework, you may have some cookies and milk." After the homework is completed, you say, "Oh, great job, but sorry, we ran out of cookies, so you'll have to do without." You'd expect the child to be disappointed and angry, wouldn't you? That's how employees react when they're promised an end-of-year or any other kind of bonus and the company fails to come through with the cash. Plan ahead. Never promise a bonus unless you are certain you'll have the money to assure it is paid on time. Short of bankruptcy, there is no excuse for failing to pay out a promised bonus if the employee has met his or her end of the bargain.

Unnecessary and Humiliating Scolding

Discipline is important in any workplace. But there is a time and place to discuss an employee's behavior, and that is never in public. Remember Ed, the lunchtime garlic lover? If I had brought up the garlic stink during a staff meeting, not only would Ed have been humiliated in front of his peers, but he would have gotten pretty angry with me, too. Monitor an employee's inappropriate or noncompliant behavior, and call a face-to-face meeting behind closed doors or away from the work site. Calmly go over each item and distinguish between the person and the actions of the person. Never berate an employee—it makes them feel awful. You will look bad, and it will probably not result in the person changing his or her behavior.

Denying Employees a Voice

Susan Gebelein uses a tool she calls "360 feedback." Not only does she provide feedback and coaching to employees, but she elicits feedback from them as well. She told us on my radio show, "The employee wants to know, does the boss care about me? And that means hearing the little hints the person is dropping about him or herself and just interacting a little bit around those things that people care about. And then you start talking with people about what they're interested in doing within an organization."

Many organizations build 360 feedback tools into the formal performance appraisals all employees undergo on an annual or semi-annual basis.

The key to the approach is listening and allowing your employees the freedom to express themselves and to do their work in a way that not only meets the needs of the organization, but allows them to have a say in how they're doing their job.

Lavishing All the Attention on the Troubled One

As children, most of us have experienced jealousy when our sibling was sick or in trouble, and our parents lavished extra attention on her. If little Susie got appendicitis or Billy kept coming home with notes from the principal, our troubles or pains seemed inconsequential to Mom and Dad. It was all we could do to get our parents to even hear us, much less help with the math homework! So we wound up feeling jealous and alienated and throwing a tantrum. And finally, this negative behavior got us some parental attention, even if it meant being sent to our room.

In the workplace, a troubled employee tends to get a lot of attention, too. If this person is constantly at fault or has ongoing problems, you may be neglecting the very competent workers going about their jobs nearby. Because you deal with the problems first and put out the fires, the people who are doing a great job feel neglected. When you have to deal with a disgruntled employee, you can't neglect his or her coworkers. They still need praise, advice, and the same kind of attention you usually devote to them. The more feedback an employee gets, even the occasional negative feedback, the more responsive, productive, and content she will be.

"Punishing" Good People

Perhaps even worse than ignoring good employees when a coworker is disrupting the workplace, is saddling them with extra work to make up for what the problem employee isn't doing. Or, because you're caught up in the drama of handling a difficult situation, you may deny capable workers who are interested in advancement the opportunities they need to move forward—such as attending conferences, going to training classes, or managing a new project. By focusing all of your attention on the difficult employee, you may be turning the rest of your staff against you, forgetting that they are your greatest resource, and, as Erika Andersen would say, need nourishment just as a plant does to grow.

There are various techniques to avoid such a trap. Despite the fact that one of your workers may be giving you grief, continue meeting with *all* of your employees as usual, without singling out the problem employee. Offer praise and encouragement when it is due, and when possible avoid discussing the troubled worker's issues with his coworkers. While you may have to spend extra time meeting with the problem employee, focus as much as possible on the day-to-day business at hand.

Achieving Balance: Coddling Versus Too Critical; Understanding Versus Leniency

My radio show guest Terry Bacon said, "It's up to the manager to set a positive tone in the workplace and manage relationships with employees so that they are positive. I also advise managers to set boundaries. For example, if someone is sick, you should give him or her the day off. And if they have a sick child it's important to be humane and to allow them to take care of that. But if somebody starts taking advantage of your compassion, you have to draw the line." It's fine to let your employees take sick or personal days when they really need them, but you have to be careful not to be too lenient. If you constantly grant days off or let employees leave early, you're sending the message that workers can walk all over you.

Summary: Handling Disgruntled Employees

FICTION: You should wait until a problem is really big and everyone knows about it before you take action.
FACT: You should handle any kind of employee issue immediately, no matter how small.

FICTION: Employees should be taught to stay quiet about their concerns.
FACT: Sometimes venting about a problem, in an appropriate setting, can solve an employee's problem and clear the air.

FICTION: The best way to handle whiners and complainers is to complain to them about their behavior and tell them to change their attitude.
FACT: Employees who whine, complain, gossip, and exhibit other forms of anger or unhappiness often feel bad about themselves and need a chance to be heard. They might also benefit from a new job challenge, a different supervisor, or some time off.

FICTION: Employees just need to hear there's a problem, and they'll know how to fix it.
FACT: Take the time to talk to an employee about specific concerns. Tell the worker exactly what behavior or action needs to change.

FICTION: Employees are either good or bad.
FACT: Sometimes an employee has one bad habit or quality that makes working with her difficult but is so good at her job that you might have to temporarily overlook the problem.

FICTION: If one of your employees has a nervous breakdown or depression, it's none of your business, and you should expect her to solve it on her own.

FACT: If an employee has a mental or emotional health issue that is affecting his ability to perform, consider referring the individual to an outside professional such as a psychologist, social worker, or career coach.

FICTION: Employees must follow the rules and accept the facts even if it means not getting a promised raise or bonus or picking up the slack when someone else is having a problem.

FACT: Listening, being fair, allowing employees to be heard, rewarding them appropriately, and giving them a voice in how they do their jobs goes a long way in preventing disgruntled workers.

4 legitimate disgruntlement

Is that paycheck in the envelope the best motivator for a happy and efficient workplace? Of course, most workers show up at the office or factory to trade labor—physical or mental—for money. But that's not the whole story. As counterintuitive as it may seem, time and time again, when asked what they want from their jobs—in addition to enough cash for food, clothing, and shelter—employees scream out for recognition. That's right; they want to be recognized for a job well done by their bosses and colleagues. Employees complain all the time about the lack of recognition. Some managers remain unaware of this simple truth and still ask, "Why should I pay special attention to him or thank him? He's just doing his job." But managers who make employee recognition a priority understand just how powerful a tool it is. Workers in any industry will tell you that what makes them feel warm and fuzzy and happy to go to work is praise and attention from their supervisors, and acceptance from those laboring alongside them.

When less than half of all Americans say they are satisfied with their job, we know we have a problem and we're fools not to take action to fix it. Hefty bonuses and promotions may not be as satisfactory and motivating to employees as their bosses think. Employees are unhappy with long hours, long commutes, and little family time. As a boss, there may be little you can do about those issues. But when asked what would make them feel as if their organization cared about them, employees again and again respond that praise and attention from their supervisor would make them feel as though the company cared about them and their health and happiness—so they want such praise. A large part of satisfying these types of noncash needs is to know your employees, their goals, what causes them stress, and what excites them about their jobs. This will help you provide them with challenging, stimulating work, the chance to succeed, and the chance to be rewarded for that success.

The flip side of a corporate culture where employees are praised and recognized for their contributions is one where managers offer no positive feedback at all. This results in the employee who feels undervalued and unappreciated. Not only does he feel bad about himself, but he also feels bad about his boss, bad about his company, and just bad enough to become the kind of disgruntled employee you don't want in your workplace.

This is a problem that is so easy to fix, it's absurd for it to plague your shop. If someone does a good job, tell her how much you appreciate her hard work. Give her a (figurative) pat on the back. Sing her praises in front of coworkers. Reinforcement is often more important than a raise, especially a token raise. When you can offer more money, make sure you combine that cash with a public display of appreciation.

Jobs That Create Discontent

Journalist Barbara Ehrenreich joined me on my radio show to talk about her firsthand research on what types of jobs and mismanagement create disgruntled employees. The author of *Nickel and Dimed* and *Bait and Switch: The (Futile) Pursuit of the American Dream* embedded herself in the world of American wage slaves. She learned that even the highly skilled and well-educated suffer in today's labor markets.

"People who get laid off or fired or outsourced out of their jobs, often face disaster," she told me. "First, they just try to cut back on expenses and job search as diligently as they can. They may have to sell their house. They may have to auction their goods off on eBay. They keep on trying like that but eventually they probably say, 'Well, I'm going to have to take any job,' a so-called survival job, the white-collar people call them. You're talking at seven, eight, nine dollars an hour at a place like Wal-Mart or another big-box store. That can often be a complete dead-end because then you don't even have time for job searching or for interviews, and a lot of people just get stuck at that level."

A skilled and educated professional working a "survival job" is likely a disgruntled employee as soon as she puts on the big-box uniform. I suggested to Ehrenreich that perhaps the bait and switch that she sees society foisting on so many workers started a generation ago when students found themselves buying a high-priced education with expectations that the education would all but guarantee a satisfying, secure, and well-paid job.

"I think you're right, Peter," she agreed. "Business is the most popular major on American college campuses. People study management or marketing as undergraduates not because they love those subjects compared with poetry or philosophy, but because the promise is there of a secure income and possibly even wealth."

I agree with Barbara Ehrenreich's criticism of business education and believe students should consider spending their time studying history, languages, literature, and poetry. They should have a good time and broaden their perspective, then go out to work and understand that being street-smart is probably more important than a business education per se. I know that certainly was the case with my education. I was encouraged to go to law school, and I went to Harvard Law School. I never

Find the Hat

Let's take the case of Bill, a composite I've constructed from stories I've heard over the years. He's a finance professional whose life revolves around business travel. Bill likes the company he works for, and he's gotten used to life on the road. He's adept at packing in a hurry, racing through the airport, and working on his laptop when his flight is delayed. He's a master of expense reports and managing difficult clients with very little sleep. But after returning from four days on the road, Bill shows up in his boss's office. Paul, his boss, is surprised to see Bill in the doorway because Bill hardly ever wants a one-on-one meeting, and he almost never complains. But today is different.

"Bill, good to see you," greets Paul. "I hear things in Philly are going well!"

Bill walks into Paul's office and sits down across from him. "Yeah, the meetings went well. But I kind of have a personal problem."

"Really? Are you sick? Do you need a day off?" Paul asks. "I know all that travel can get to you."

"No, it's not that. I'm fine," says Bill, looking down at his lap. "It's just that I lost something on this trip. I think I must have left it in the hotel, but when I called, they said they couldn't find it."

"Well, what was it?"

"When I fly somewhere, I always wear a baseball cap," answers Bill. "It keeps my head warm, and it's kind of a personal trademark. Actually, I think it's a good luck charm. It's a Mets cap, and I've had it forever."

Paul is completely surprised because Bill has never worn the baseball cap to the office. Of course he wouldn't; hats aren't allowed in the office. But he's never seen the guy so worked up.

"I'm really sorry about that," Paul says. "Maybe you should check back with the hotel. Or did you try the airline?"

"Yeah, I've talked to the hotel people twice, and they have no idea where it is. It could have gone out with the laundry or the maid could have thrown it away. And the airline was useless."

"Sorry, Bill. I guess you'll have to get a new hat."

"I know. I will. It won't be the same, but I've got have my hat to fly. Here's the thing, though. I'd like to put the cost of the new hat on my expense report."

"Seriously? I mean what could it cost, like twenty, thirty bucks?"

"Yeah, but since I lost it on a business trip, and I always take it with me, I figure the company can cover the cost of a new hat. As you say, it's not a lot of money."

"No, but it wasn't the company's fault you lost the cap."

"But if I had lost, say, my cell phone, wouldn't you pay to replace that? And that would be a lot more expensive. What's the big deal?"

Bill's face is getting red, and he is clearly getting angry. So is Paul.

"Look, Bill. Expenses cover things like dinners and rental cars. We can't go around paying for people to replace personal items they lose on trips."

"Why not? This hat really matters to me. And it's cheap. And if you won't pay for a new one, then I think you're being cheap."

• • •

It's easy to see both sides of the situation here. Bill is making a somewhat unusual request. And Paul doesn't want to give in to what he views as an unreasonable expense. But if Bill is a great employee, and this is the first time he's ever really asked for anything, how hard would it be for Paul to reimburse Bill for a new "lucky "cap? If he doesn't, he's going to wind up with a disgruntled employee. Bill may buy himself a new hat, but he'll hold a grudge against Paul, and over time this little incident may result in Bill not feeling respected and valued. He might walk out the door. Despite the fact that Paul clearly feels Bill is making an unreasonable request, if he wants to keep him on board, clearly he should swallow his pride and buy the guy a new hat—but make it clear that company policy does not *require* the business to replace personal property lost on the job. ∎

wanted to practice law, and I'm glad I didn't. I found the knowledge very useful, but not because I was going to be hired by a big Wall Street law firm and feel like I was on easy street; that would have been a miserable existence for me. I wanted the knowledge of the law to practice business. Being successful in business—whether it's as an employee, or an entrepreneur—requires emotional intelligence. I'm not convinced studying for an MBA is the best method for obtaining emotional intelligence.

Ehrenreich suggested that the insecurity in the corporate world adds to employee frustration. "Corporate jobs offer very little stability anymore. There's been a real seismic change, disrupting the old notion of loyalty between the company and the employee. In the eighties, if you got to a certain level as a white-collar person, you were likely seen as a treasured asset by your company. No more. This whole thing that started in the nineties of getting leaner and meaner, downsizing, smart-sizing, right-sizing, reorganizing, offshoring—there's just no stability anymore. We haven't talked enough in this country about the psychological consequences of that. You do everything right; you play by the rules, you conform and go get the right degrees, and you do a good job, and that's no guarantee of anything."

The instability Barbara Ehrenreich documents in her books fuels the potential for disgruntled employees. In addition to individual fixes on a job-by-job and worker-by-worker basis, we need to seek long-term solutions and realize that some costs to keep employees content will generate returns on investments that will provide valuable dividends of consequence to society.

Employees with Serious Personal Problems

There are all sorts of reasons people start having trouble focusing on their jobs. Emotional problems such as depression and anxiety, family issues including a sick child or spouse, or a divorce—these types of life-shocking events can cause even the most stalwart employee's work to suffer. When someone is going through a personal crisis, it is common sense to give him or her some time off. It's hard to concentrate on work when a loved one is in the hospital or you are haggling over selling a house, child support, and other personal concerns. These kinds of unhappy employees aren't taking out their problems on the organization; they simply need time to recover and regroup. If your organization has an EAP, suggest the employee meet with an EAP expert to see whether short-term counseling might be in order. A constructive alternative would be to offer the worker a short paid leave of absence for a mutually agreed-upon length of time.

Depression   A great number of American adults suffer from depression, especially those in their prime working years. Depression can hit anyone, from an assembly worker to a CEO. It's not uncommon for a formerly outstanding employee to become depressed; the disease knows no boundaries. Depression is one of the three most-common workplace problems dealt with by employee assistance professionals, according to studies conducted by the National Institutes of Mental Health. Yet depression is also very treatable; the nonprofit organization Mental Health America estimates that more than 80 percent of people with clinical depression can successfully overcome the sickness.

A depressed worker may experience a variety of symptoms ranging from a persistent sad mood, sleeping too much or too little, weight gain or loss, difficulty concentrating, along with physical symptoms such as headaches or stomachaches, and plaguing thoughts of suicide or death. Yet a depressed employee is not always aware that he suffers depression. Frequently, depressed workers won't seek help because they're worried about drawing attention to their problems and the effect this will have on their job status. Others don't seek help because they're not aware they need it or they're afraid their insurance won't cover treatment. Depression can also affect a worker whose spouse or child is depressed. If family members are down in the dumps, it can disrupt working hours and affect the employee's mood just as severely as his own personal blues—their depression naturally becomes his. This is another situation in which an Employee Assistance Program can be of value. If you don't have one, but you have a good rapport with the employee, suggest that he seek the help of a professional. Be ready to provide some names or organizations that you know might help. Start by looking on the Internet for local resources that provide counseling for various kinds of emotional illnesses.

Family Problems Family and problems seem to go together like cheese and crackers. Who hasn't suffered through a difficult time with family, whether it's a rebellious teen or a rough patch in a marriage? Family woes such as sickness, divorce, and death can have a serious effect on a worker's job performance. Missed work is common during a family crisis. It's not unusual for a daughter to fly miles away to cope with an ailing parent, leaving her husband to deal with the demands of the home and the children. Family problems are among the most stressful occurrences in people's day-to-day lives. If you know one of your employees is struggling with family issues, offer as much help as you can, either through an EAP or other counseling resource. At the very least, work with the person to see if a condensed work week, telecommuting, or another solution might give the employee a little more time to take care of his family but still have the ability to do the job.

Helping the Employee Through a Crisis I refer to myself as the Business Shrink because everybody must be a bit of a psychologist to be good in business. Although you may not consider yourself a therapist, all good bosses must play shrink at one time or another, even if you hate the idea of an intimate chat with a worker you wish would smile while she punches in and punches out. Most employees, at some point in their careers, develop a personal problem or emergency that can be helped by counseling or medical assistance, but the first conversation about it may well be with you. A temporary crisis such as a sick child, a car breaking down, or a parent who falls and breaks a bone is usually resolved within a day or two without any intervention from you. But suppose your top salesperson finds out his wife is cheating on him. And she wants a divorce and custody of the two kids.

This is a man who is shattered. He can barely eat, sleep, and breathe, much less have a productive day at the office. He does come to work, yet you know something's up when he sits in an important sales meeting with a vacant stare on his face, doodling on his notepad. Perhaps you feel uncomfortable discussing any of the very personal details of his problem. So you try to ignore his behavior and hope he gets his act together on his own. Instead you could lend a sympathetic ear. I'm not suggesting that you offer to let him sleep on your couch or promise him a trip to Tahiti. But you can listen and suggest the name of a good therapist, counselor, or mediator. You can be reassuring. When an employee is undergoing a personal crisis that is so powerful it's interfering with his ability to work or endangering him, you, as a manager, must help. The sooner that you recognize the problem and offer help to a worker undergoing a personal crisis, the sooner he can get back to being a productive part of the workplace.

Meet with him and hear him out. Encourage him to talk about the problem, but don't probe too deeply if you sense he wants to keep the issue private. You can find out how serious the problem is and what you can do to support the person; you do not have to know every detail of the issue. Often when someone is in a failed relationship or finds out a family member is very ill, he wants to keep the facts to himself. If an employee is reluctant to talk, assure him that the conversation will be confidential. Offer to refer him to your human resources department, outside counseling, or your organization's Employee Assistance Program. EAPs are there to help workers deal with family, marital, and relationship problems, substance abuse issues, stress, financial difficulties, depression, anxiety and eating disorders, and other mental or emotional problems. EAPs can help even if the problem is not work related. Many programs provide short-term counseling as well as referrals to other services or outside professionals. Even if you don't have a company EAP, you have empathy. Show the employee that you care by providing whatever support you can, including a leave of absence.

It's also important to realize that while the employee is in crisis mode, she might display signs of sadness, anger, or anxiety. She may withdraw temporarily from social interactions and need more time off. As long as you believe she will return to full productivity once the crisis has passed—and you've had a discussion about this and agreed that this needs to happen—cut her some slack as she works things through for herself.

Here are some typical kinds of "crisis" employees.

The "Stuck"
Employee

Have you ever been stuck in your job? You know—you come in every day and you do the work and you do a darn good job, but somehow it never gets noticed. You don't get promoted, you don't get a raise, and you don't get to go to a seminar to learn a new skill. You're trapped doing the same thing, day in day out, like a hamster on a wheel. Most of us have felt that way at least once during our careers.

Lots of top-notch employees feel stuck in their positions. For whatever reason, management is ignoring them, letting them do their jobs without recognition, without the perks or any of the positive feedback that is needed to enjoy their jobs. Stuck employees become bored due to lack of a challenge, and they also get mad. They want to grow professionally, to make more money, and to be rewarded for their hard work. Without the opportunity to accomplish those goals, they start to hate their jobs, their bosses, and their organizations.

The Misplaced Employee Sometimes we managers forget to check in with employees who may feel stuck or unchallenged, and sometimes we are bad matchmakers. When a person is assigned a job for which he doesn't have the right skills, he can't help but feel inadequate. The employee who lacks the ability or even the personality necessary to complete a work assignment is set up for failure, and failure breeds frustration. You wouldn't hire a house painter to fix your computer or a diesel mechanic to bake a cake, would you? Yet that is exactly how an employee who is equipped with the wrong skill set for an assignment feels.

The Chronically Disappointed Employee Another way a manager can set employees up for failure and disappointment is to have unrealistic expectations. Sometimes you can get so caught up in the overall organizational goals, you expect an employee to tackle an assignment he just doesn't have the skills for. Or you may assume that someone has a faster learning curve than she does, or that she's interested in advancement or more responsibility when in reality she's happy doing what she's been doing. Consistently expecting or demanding more of people adds stress and provokes anxiety in many otherwise skilled workers. (Other employees, of course, may thrive on consistent challenges.) Plenty of bosses make the mistake of assuming an employee has the same goals and ambitions as the boss or the company's star performers. When the targeted worker doesn't want more challenge, the boss is disappointed.

Maybe you're grooming your assistant to take over the job of a manager. You offer outside training, you talk with her about the job, and you do everything in your power to bolster her confidence and prepare her for this new challenge. Yet when the time comes to offer her the job, she politely declines. She tells you she is perfectly happy in her existing position and has no interest in managing. You can't believe it! How could she turn down such a great opportunity? Well, some people just aren't cut out to be managers, and it was very mature of your employee to realize this. If you had been paying attention and listening to her when you discussed the promotion, if you had read the verbal and nonverbal cues she gave you, you would have realized she wasn't the right person for the job. Just because you imagine that this is the right move for an employee doesn't mean it's what the employee wants or needs.

Hanging on to unrealistic expectations for your employees reminds me of those "helicopter" parents who hover over their children, constantly pushing them to make choices based on the parents' interests and goals, not on the kids' desires. These parents nag and cajole; even worse, they try to bully their children into after-school activities, sports, and even high school and college choices. And you know what? Those kids are the most likely to rebel when they're older by making a decision that goes completely against the parents' wishes, such as not going to college at all, and there's absolutely nothing their parents can do about it.

The Mismatched Employee

The flip side is not recognizing a successful worker's potential to move to a new assignment. It's the old cliché: It's not broken so why fix it. An employee who has been in the same position for a long time may have learned new skills on the job that makes him the perfect candidate for a different role or department. When Susan Gebelein was a guest on my show, she touched on the importance of understanding the overall performance and abilities of each employee. "You really need to develop all employees, because expectations keep changing," she told us.

"A boss needs to keep his or her eye out for folks who really do have the potential for higher-level roles. What is the person's career goal? Are they interested in advancement or not? You want to look at the psychological characteristics that an employee has that might lead him or her to a different role, as well as the cognitive skills that they have that might lead them toward higher-level roles in an organization." If you keep a talented worker stuck in an unfulfilling job, she will most likely go somewhere else where there are more exciting possibilities for growth.

The Disenfranchised Employee

Some employees become disgruntled because they just don't fit into the workplace. Say you have a chronically shy person who has to deal face-to-face with customers. Or you've got a vegetarian promoting your special on steaks. What about the nerdy guy who doesn't like to go to lunch with the gang or chat after meetings, who just sticks to his cubicle?

An employee may also disengage from his job due to boredom, or the opposite may happen—he may feel overwhelmed by too much work. Either way, the disenfranchised employee will do little work because there is little appealing about the job as far as he is concerned. Maybe Sue in bookkeeping just doesn't understand the new computer system, or Jimmy in client services would rather be handling payroll. In both instances the employees have given up and become disenchanted with their responsibilities and their positions.

These people are probably fine, even talented workers, but they are disenfranchised or disengaged from what they're doing because they don't have much in common with their colleagues, and maybe their boss. The workplace isn't always the place for blooming friendships, but on the other hand, someone who's stuck in what my guest Martin Yate, author of the book *Knock 'Em Dead: The Ultimate Job Search Guide,* calls the "outer circle" is going to have a hard time.

Training for Promotion

Now imagine that Kerri calls my show, full of pent-up anger. She works for a fitness center as a receptionist, and she also handles enrolling new members. Her boss is the gym's owner.

KERRI: I feel like calling you is the last straw. I'm so fed up with my job that I just want to scream!

ME: What's wrong with your job? Don't you enjoy what you do?

KERRI: No, I really don't. I spend my days checking the gym's members in, answering the phone, handing out towels and locker keys, and sometimes giving new members tours of the facility. I mean, I do it just fine. But it is sooo boring!

ME: Sounds like it. Is that what you were hired to do?

KERRI: Yes, but when I took the job, I told my boss I wanted to do other things as well. And he told me being a receptionist would just be temporary.

ME: What would you rather be doing?

KERRI: I want to work as a personal trainer and an aerobics teacher.

ME: Have you told your boss? And are you trained as an instructor?

KERRI: I have told my boss, Phil, so many times. I've been taking a class at night, and I'm almost certified as a personal trainer, and I've also taken a ton of aerobics classes at the gym. I've even had clients come up

to me and tell me I should teach. I would just need to take one more instructor's class and maybe learn CPR. I'm totally up for it, but Phil keeps shutting me down.

ME: What does Phil tell you?

KERRI: Oh, he talks about what a great receptionist I am and how I've gotten to know all the members. That they look forward to seeing me when they come in. And that he has enough instructors right now. But you know what? He just hired a personal trainer from the YMCA last month. And I would have been perfect for that job!

ME: Are you sure Phil knows you're ready to be an instructor? Does he know about the certification class and all? It could be that he thinks you don't have the right qualifications. I'm just giving him the benefit of the doubt here.

KERRI: Phil totally knows. I brought in a brochure from the class. And once, when one of our aerobics teachers was running late, I started the class. I put on the mike, found a CD for the stereo, and warmed everybody up. And when she got there, she told me I had done a great job. I mentioned it to Phil, and all he said was "Thanks." Seriously, I just can't stand sitting at this stupid desk for one more day.

• • •

Kerri is mismatched for her job, and it's making her crazy. Clearly she's an active person who wants to help others get fit. But Phil hired her for a desk job, and although Kerri's tried to show him that she's ready for a new challenge at the gym, he's not listening, even though it sounds as though he promised her he would consider making her an instructor at some point. Can you predict what might happen?

FOLLOW-UP

Let's consider a best-case scenario conversation if Kerri calls me back.

KERRI: Guess what? I quit the gym!

ME: You did? And what did Phil say?

KERRI: He acted all surprised, like he hadn't heard me tell him a million times that I wanted to teach. And then he practically begged me to stay and told me I could start teaching next month. But I already got a job with the gym that certified me as a personal trainer. All I had to do was take that CPR class, and now I've got three clients already. I love it!

• • •

That's what I thought would happen. Phil had blocked out Kerri's requests for a change in responsibilities; he wasn't listening. It wasn't that she was doing a bad job; quite the opposite, he liked her a lot. Managers often fall into the trap of wanting to keep a good employee in the same role forever because, frankly, it's a hassle to replace the person. But if you don't let people develop and use new skills, you'll likely lose them anyway. ■

"As a career coach, I have people coming to me all the time," Yate explained on the air with me. "They want to change jobs, and they want a promotion because no one appreciates them, and they're not growing. Now sometimes that is true, and in the real world we do move if we're in a job for a number of years, and we haven't had significant pay raises, significant promotions. The chances are we've been stereotyped, categorized, and pigeonholed. Fact of the matter: sometimes change helps. But sometimes we don't have to make the move. I think everyone listening to your radio show recognizes that in their department, their company, there's always an inner circle and an outer circle. And we all know which part of that circle we belong to." Of course, employees in the outer circle feel isolated and misunderstood.

Employees in the inner circle think they have a window into what the boss is thinking and feeling, and they are secure in the knowledge that their needs will be met. Therefore, they are not afraid to tell their supervisor what they want and expect from their job. Outer-circle employees, on the other hand, feel less connection to their bosses. As a result, they are unlikely to speak up when they become disgruntled, thus feeling isolated and misunderstood.

Yate told us, "There are so many ways we can get disgruntled. I think very often employees can feel left out of things. There are some people who get the plum assignments, the special projects, the biggest raises, and the promotions. And yeah, those are the guys who are in the inner circle. So if you're not one of the ones who is making a difference with your presence, it's probably by making the wrong alliances, and you become part of the outer circle." Yate suggests that rather than changing jobs, disenfranchised workers should try to change some things about themselves to gain access to the inner circle and start growing within the company.

Being a "Matchmaker" Managers have to be good matchmakers. We have to recognize when someone just isn't a good fit, either with her job or with her boss or coworkers, and we have to make a change. Like putting together a jigsaw puzzle, you have to look at all sides of a person, figure out what she wants and how she works, and then find a corresponding niche within the organization. Maybe it's as easy as having the employee report to a new supervisor. Perhaps you can shift her to a different department. Recognize what drives a worker. Understand her skills and ambitions. Then figure out how to best take advantage of those traits.

During the hiring process, it may make sense to administer a personality test or quiz to help determine where the new employee will best fit in. If she is shy, for example, you don't want her at the front desk dealing with new clients every day, at least not until she gets used to the organization. Someone who works best alone would not do well in a group setting all of the time and perhaps should have his own office or cubicle. Some of these solutions are simple intuition, and the rest require taking the time to learn the strengths and weaknesses of each new hire so you can fit the person into your organization in the most productive manner. Usually it will take some time to get to know a new employee well enough to take full advantage of his assets and to minimize his weaknesses, so don't be surprised if you have to adjust things after a few months.

Some workers are troubled—disgruntled—because there are severe problems in the workplace that need management attention. These workers are the canaries in your mine. They don't need to be fixed. On the contrary, they are assets. They may save your company from disaster. Pay close attention to them.

Whistleblowers Did you know that the term *whistleblower* comes from the practice of British bobbies? The London police would blow their whistles when they noticed someone committing a crime. A more formal definition of a whistleblower is an employee, ex-employee, or member of an organization or business who reports misconduct to people or entities that have the power to take corrective action. Whistleblowers are the folks within your company who see someone doing something wrong, and their moral code compels them not to ignore it. They have to tell someone.

Danielle Brian, the executive director at Project on Government Oversight (POGO), defines a whistleblower as "a person who is aware of misconduct and wants to do something to stop it." The most common type of whistleblower is the internal whistleblower who reports misconduct within his own organization. External whistleblowers report the problem to outside people or entities. When I talked with Brian on my radio show, she told us, "At POGO we advise most people not to go public because there's almost never a happy ending. A person who goes public almost every time will lose his or her job, or if they keep their job they are shoved into a corner. So often we find whistleblowers with their desks moved to the basement of their building, or they're not given any resources or jobs to do, they don't get invited to the office party; these kinds of things happen constantly." It is absolutely illegal to fire someone for whistle-blowing. However, it's extremely difficult to prove you were dismissed because you blew the whistle.

Most whistleblowers are angry about things their coworkers or supervisors are doing. These often are relatively small ethical violations such as calling in sick and going to the ballgame rather than more significant violations such as a boss having an affair with his secretary and returning her favors with inappropriate raises and bonuses. But there are plenty of whistleblowers who've reported on high-level corporate wrongdoing, from Enron to the FBI. Whatever the motives, if there is a whistleblower in your ranks, pay attention to his or her complaints.

Train department managers and supervisors about the rights of employees to blow the whistle without fear of retaliation from the employer. Take the time to provide several options for workers to raise legitimate concerns, including the ability to voice a concern anonymously.

Although Danielle Brian says whistleblowers sometimes wind up quitting because they feel marginalized, perhaps you can learn from a whistleblower and save yourself serious problems down the road. Perhaps you can be the type of boss who helps a constructive whistleblower remain in the fold.

Always conduct prompt, thorough investigations of any employee concerns if the issue involves fraud or securities law violations. It is critical that whistleblowers be provided with the chance to come forward and voice their concerns without fear of adverse consequences. Take immediate disciplinary action against workers who violate the company's policy prohibiting retaliation against whistleblowers (if one exists). Remember that if an employee comes to you with a clear case of corporate malfeasance and you do nothing, you can be held personally liable.

Employees' Rights

Human resources departments are rife with stories of employees and employers both unhappy, yet unable to amicably or gracefully settle their differences. The fact of the matter is when troubled employees are in a company, it's probably plagued with troubled managers as well. Personnel problems are often a two-way street, and compromise is not always easy. Human resources laws now require recordkeeping and dialogue and opportunity for a resolution of differences short of termination. Managers cannot just come in one day and decide that they don't like the cut of someone's hair or the way she's chewing gum and say, "Hey you're fired." That's illegal in today's environment; it invites a lawsuit.

Pat's Last Call

Whistle-blowing can be a factor in any type of organization. A whistle-blower played a role in the demise of Enron. An FBI whistleblower tried to point out the failure of the U.S. national security apparatus prior to September 11, 2001. And whistle-blowing can disrupt the corner bar. Consider if a bartender we'll call Pat showed up on my *Business Shrink* radio couch.

PAT: Peter, I've got a moral question for you, which may seem odd coming from a guy who tends bar—who pours drinks all day.

ME: I'm not judgmental, Pat. At what kind of place do you tend bar?

PAT: I guess you'd consider it a dive. It's just a neighborhood bar here in Cleveland. It's been here forever and so has my boss, the owner.

ME: So tell me, what happened to you?

PAT: I was fired for not watering down the booze. Well, I wasn't exactly supposed to water down the booze. The boss wanted me to pour cheap whiskey and tequila into the Jack Daniels and José Cuervo bottles. You know, take the generic stuff he was buying at the supermarket and fill up the call bottles with it. He told me that no one really can tell the difference, so why shouldn't he make a few extra bucks.

ME: So what did you do, Pat?

PAT: Well, for a couple of weeks I did what he asked. And you know, Peter, he's right. No one said a word. I even poured extra into their drinks. I guess I felt guilty about

charging premium prices for the stuff. And maybe that's one reason why there weren't any complaints; I was fixing some stiff drinks. But, you know, it just didn't seem right, cheating. Especially cheating working stiffs.

ME: So after a few weeks your conscience started bothering you.

PAT: Yeah, my conscience. And I guess my sense of self-preservation. One of the old-timers questioned his drink. He asked me if I made a mistake when I mixed his tequila and tonic. "Not strong enough?" I asked him. And I gave him an extra splash. But something about his tone made me wonder if he suspected what was up. And that made me nervous. I work the night shift. I don't need drunks turning on me at closing time.

ME: No kidding. Then what happened?

PAT: The next day I told the boss I didn't want to keep cheating the guys, that it was the wrong thing to do. My way or the high-way, he told me. So what I want to know is this: Should I go to the alcoholic beverage control boys, the licensing authorities, and report him? And if I do, what happens to my job? Can I report him anonymously?

ME: Seems like you're in a no-win situation, Pat. You go to the authorities and they'll probably close down the bar—suspend the license. Or at least fine your boss. And you'll be out of work. Even if he's only fined, just who do you think he'll blame for the bust? You, right? And then he'll likely fire you. Now maybe that's too severe for me to say you're in a no-win situation. If you report him, at least you'll feel good about putting an end to his cheating. And you probably can find another bartending job.

PAT: So I can't save my job since he's the one watering down the drinks? I thought there were laws protecting whistleblowers.

ME: You're right, Pat. There are such laws. But look at this with a dose of reality. Your boss can just say he doesn't like your attitude. How can you prove that he fired you for reporting him? It's sad but true, whistleblowers often end up doing what's right and suffering for it. Even in circumstances where their jobs are protected, the companies they work for marginalize them. They often become stigmatized within their industries, looked at as troublemakers. Sorry not to offer better news, but I do hope you get back in touch after you decide what to do.

PAT: Bummer. But okay, Peter. I get it. And thanks for the straight scoop. I will call you back when I figure this out.

• • •

Here's a transcript of a call back from Pat that I'd like to get.

PAT: Hey, Peter. Pat the bartender here. Remember me? Cleveland. Phoney Jack and José Cuervo?

ME: Of course I remember you, Pat. What did you decide to do? Stay on the job pouring cheap liquor or report your boss for the old bait and switch?

PAT: I turned him in, Peter. It was just wrong what he was doing. He was fined and closed down for a few days. But he's back in business, and without me. You were right. I was fired, and I couldn't figure out anything to do about it. He said I was fired because I wasn't cheerful enough. Ha.

ME: You did the right thing, Pat.

PAT: You bet I did, Peter. I felt better immediately. And a week after, guess what? I got another job. I make more money. The tips are great. And we pour the real stuff!

ME: Good to hear, Pat. Congratulations.

• • •

A lot of business is about interpersonal relationships, which is what makes it so hard. Employment can begin with a handshake. But what's really needed is a mutually agreed-upon, negotiated, written agreement. And it's wise to include in that agreement an exit procedure, explaining what happens when an employee is terminated.

- What behaviors are grounds for termination?
- What are the employee's rights?
- What procedures must be followed when an employee is terminated?
- What will be the terms of severance?

I never did hear back from Pat but I hope he worked something out. I hope, too, when he gets offered his next job that he gets the terms of employment in writing, from the outset. ■

Even small-business owners can't arbitrarily decide for themselves who's going to be terminated. Employees expect certain rights on the job, including the right to be treated decently. When people have a job and they work for a company for an extended period, they build non-monetary equity. They build a track record and a reputation. They build accomplishments. A boss who just says, "You're fired," would be abridging the worker's rights and the privileges that come with them. A manager who thinks he's clever and annoys the worker enough to make her blow up (because he knows the employee is a hothead) is involved in behavior fraught with risk. That's just a capricious termination if no good reasons are documented. If the fired employee fights the termination, the government usually assesses some form of compensatory package to the employee. In addition to the cash settlement the discharged employee may receive, a judgment is also a slap on the wrist to the employer for firing a worker without just cause.

Valuable Web sites provide a wide range of information on employment rights. For example, AHI's Employment Law Resource Center, *www.ahipubs.com/FAQ/index.html*, is aimed at managers and human resource personnel and offers answers to frequently asked questions about many aspects of employment. The Employment Law Resource Center, *www.coloradolawyer.com/discrim.html*, summarizes the major federal laws that prohibit employment discrimination. This is a good place to begin your search if you're looking for an overview. Employment Law Memo, *www.lawmemo.com*, is a great site offering both free and paid services for those researching labor law, arbitration decisions, civil rights law, and more. FindLaw, *http://employment.findlaw.com*, is a comprehensive site that covers a wide variety of employment laws and provides numerous fact sheets and links, including information on state employment laws. LaborNet, part of the Institute for Global Communications, is a group of labor unions, activists, and organizations using computer networks to share information about pending and recent legislation, labor movements and disputes, and international labor issues.

Summary: Legitimately Disgruntled Employees

FICTION: Employees care only about monetary compensation.
FACT: Employees often care more about feeling appreciated and respected by their supervisors than they do about money. Reward workers for a job well done; give positive feedback, and make sure you make your recognition of their efforts public.

FICTION: Employees should keep their personal affairs out of the office; it's no concern of the manager if a worker has a serious personal problem.
FACT: When a worker is suffering from a serious personal or health problem, including family crises or mental illness such as depression, show your concern and offer to help. Most employees can be rehabilitated with counseling, treatment, or some time off.

FICTION: It's up to employees to let you know if they're not challenged.
FACT: Employees who feel stuck in their jobs, or not sufficiently challenged, are prone to becoming disgruntled. Review your employees' skills and responsibilities on a regular basis and discuss their interest in advancement. Follow through on requests for new responsibilities or projects whenever possible.

FICTION: If an employee can't do his job, he should be terminated without further discussion or investigation.
FACT: Sometimes an employee is mismatched for his job. Encourage the person to tell you what he envisions as the right job, and work to match his talents and interests to a different role. If someone is a "bad fit" within a department or work group, see whether it's possible to match

the employee with a new supervisor or another department where he will feel more comfortable.

FICTION: Whistleblowers are just troublemakers whose employment needs to be terminated immediately.
FACT: If someone comes to you with a complaint about someone else in the workplace acting inappropriately, follow up immediately. You don't want a whistleblower to go public, and you don't want to lose a good employee.

5 handling the vindictive employee

If you've got a dissatisfied employee on your hands, she might turn against you and cause serious damage. Whether you let her go, or you just had an ugly encounter at a meeting and you had to follow up with a disciplinary letter, the person on the receiving end of these types of actions is probably going to be mad. Often, when an employee gets riled and feels she has been misrepresented or treated unfairly, she will react, and you must be prepared. In today's litigious and occasionally violent environment, you need to protect yourself against vindictive employees.

My radio guest, Sanford Sherizen, president of Data Security Systems, calls such people "insider threats." While speaking on my show, he cautioned, "There are a huge number of people who work within organizations who have a tremendous amount of information about how transactions occur, how finances function, about strategic plans, access to computer systems—all kinds of things that are potentially very serious problems. What we're finding out is that people have all kinds of capabilities." He means capabilities to seek revenge using access they gained to your business while they were working for you and cashing the paycheck you signed. The first step toward protecting yourself against a hostile worker or former worker is to be simple, direct, and honest in all your dealings with all employees.

Document All You Do

It is critical to document every consequential managerial interaction you have with your employees. Whether it's a performance evaluation, a raise or promotion, a disciplinary conversation or letter, everything—I repeat, *everything*—needs to be in writing. Follow up all of your substantive communications—letters, memos, notes, e-mails—with employees by documenting them with a file memo just in case you have to prove these exchanges actually occurred.

Have a Witness to Conversations

If you need to have a conversation with an employee about a subject that may concern sensitive issues such as work performance or mental health, do not talk to the employee alone, especially if you are a male supervisor with a female employee, or vice versa. For example, let's say that some of your staff members have complained that a coworker has been making sexually suggestive remarks that are making them uncomfortable. Since this goes against your organization's no-tolerance policy for sexual harassment, you want to deal with the situation immediately. Even if there is no specific company policy, you must act, both because the law may have been violated and because you want no disruptive behavior in your workplace. You schedule a meeting with the problem employee. Do you need a witness? You bet your bottom dollar you do.

What if when you schedule the meeting, the accused worker says he won't come without a coworker present? Most companies do not have to agree to this request unless a collective bargaining agreement mandates it. While nonunion employees have the right to ask for the presence of a witness at any disciplinary meeting or interview, the company isn't required to honor the employee's request. This issue arose from a 1975 case in which the U.S. Supreme Court ruled that union-represented employees had the right to bring a union representative to any investigatory meeting that might result in disciplinary action. Following that ruling, nonunion workers began to request the right to bring a coworker or even an attorney into meetings with their supervisors if they felt the interview could lead to discipline.

There is no legal requirement that you honor such a request. But no matter the law or the sensitivity of the agenda, it may make both you and the problem worker more comfortable to have a witness there.

Consider meeting with the troubled employee along with a human resources manager. If your organization doesn't have an HR department, ask another supervisor or manager to sit in on the meeting. Let the employee know why you are doing this, and get the other manager's promise to keep the issue private. If privacy is a special concern, make each party sign a confidentiality agreement. If there is no appropriate supervisor available, have another member of your staff—say, your assistant—act as a witness to any sensitive confrontations. The accused worker cannot legally demand a witness (unless he's

66 99   **Advice for employees: Don't expect fairness.**

Your mother may have been fair to you when you and your sister got in a fight. Your teachers, if you went to some dreamy school, may even have been fair to you. But, despite the best efforts of government and business, the workplace is often unfair. I'm not saying, "Expect the worst." But I am suggesting that if you appreciate that one of the pitfalls of the workplace is that you will feel mistreated periodically, you'll be prepared for those times when work life is just unfair. Someone else will get credit for an idea you generated. You'll work hard, and a slacker will get an extra day off (making it necessary for you to work even harder!). Try not to resent these incidents. Read some books by Charles Dickens to remind yourself how awful work used to be, and get on with the task at hand. Unless there is systematic abuse in your workplace, these anomalies will pass and if you do not fixate on them, you'll be the winner.

represented by a union), so he certainly cannot dictate who the witness is going to be. If your assistant or some other management staffer is in the meeting with you, it is much less likely that any future disputes will degenerate into a he said/she said scenario.

Have an Established Grievance Policy in Place

Even if yours is a very small workplace, it still pays to have certain policies and rules in place and in writing.

Employees with serious issues should have a formal way to register complaints. Have a grievance policy available that is written in clear, plain English and let all your employees know it exists. Make sure your staff knows that if they file a grievance the complaint is not grounds for termination, simply the proper way to lodge a complaint. The grievance policy should be general enough for the employee to fill in the blanks with the specific issues at stake.

Having a written set of procedures in place will minimize the risk of an angry employee taking you to court—always provided, of course, that *you* follow the procedures outlined in your employee handbook. Remember, the handbook is essentially an agreement between you and the employee, one you both must abide by.

Types of Post-Termination Sabotage

During the past twenty years, society has grown more sensitive about what is said in and out of the workplace.

Slander/Libel

Workplace defamation can happen any time a person comments about a current or former employee. Defamation encompasses any slanderous spoken remarks and libelous written statements. Slander is a form of spoken defamation, or harm, to a person's character directly caused by a false statement or act by another person, and libel is a written form of defamation. Slander and libel related to the workplace usually happen when an employee who's been terminated tries to ruin the reputation of his former employer by making false accusations—lying—either verbally or on paper. This is more serious than name-calling or spreading rumors. Defamation can cause serious harm to a person's character, reputation, or career. Watch out: employees sometimes sue their employers, charging that their reputations have been ruined. In one intriguing Minnesota case, a jury awarded $60,000 to a fired salesman. The fellow's former manager claimed publicly—in a letter to his new boss—that the employee left his old job with a briefcase full of confidential business records. These materials were later found safe and sound in the employee's former office.

While laws vary from state to state, most often judges are authorized to dismiss lawsuits filed against employers who have legitimate reasons for disclosing information that could embarrass current or former employees. If a terminated employee tries to ruin or harm the reputation of her former employer by outwardly lying about the organization, the employer can make this information public.

The flip side is that an employer who is trying to protect his company's image from bad publicity by calling attention to the slander or defamation can be accused of slandering or defaming the employee. This is a very slippery slope and potentially harmful to both employer and employee.

Computer Hacking   Our total reliance on the Internet and e-mail as preferred forms of communication makes everyone vulnerable to computer hackers. But bosses especially need to worry about ex-employees who know too many passwords and other information. These kinds of hackers can break into an organization's technology base, crashing computer systems and wreaking total chaos. On my show Sanford Sherizen shared his own experience with computer crime as president of Data Security Systems.

When It's Okay to Speak Up

The BUSINESS Shrink

Suppose you have an employee who witnesses an inappropriate conversation between another employee and the boss. Even though the worker who is being harassed does not report the incident, the employee who witnessed it decides to report it. It might go something like this:

Angie and Lisa are both young women in their twenties and administrative assistants for a large manufacturing company. They've been good friends for a while. Over lunch they've discussed the various people who work at their company, and one thing they agree on is that Jack, the head of their department, is a slime ball. Jack is married and has two kids, but that doesn't stop him from hitting on most of the woman in the office. So far, he's never bothered Angie or Lisa, at least that's what Lisa thought until she happens to be walking by the copy room and sees both Jack and Angie inside. Angie is making copies, and Jack is standing in the doorway, basically blocking Angie from leaving. Lisa walks past but stops just past the room when she overhears part of their conversation.

"So, I was going to head out for a cocktail after work, and I'd love it if you'd join me," Jack says.

"No, that's okay," Angie responds. "I may have to stay late to finish up some things."

"Well, that's even better," Jack says. "What if I run out and get us some booze and we can enjoy it here after everyone's gone home? You know, I'd really like the chance to get to know you better. You're probably the prettiest girl in this office."

Angie moves toward the door, but Jack stays put so she can't get past. "Thanks for the compliment. Um, I'd better get back to work."

"Oh, come on. It'll be fun. I bet you look really sexy without your glasses."

"Jack, you're making me kind of uncomfortable right now. Can you please get out of the way so I can go back to work?"

Jack moves just enough that Angie still has to brush against him on the way out. At this point, Lisa has walked a little farther down the hall so that neither Jack nor Angie can see her, but she has seen and heard the whole thing. At lunch she brings up what she's seen.

"Listen, I was walking by the copy room yesterday, and I heard what that scumbag Jack was saying to you," Lisa says. "Are you okay?"

"Yeah, I'm okay. But he made me feel super uncomfortable. I didn't really know what to say, and he wouldn't get out of the way, so I actually had to touch him. Gross!"

"I know. I saw," says Lisa.

"I've been trying to avoid him all day, but he keeps giving me this creepy smile. I hope he doesn't try it again. I am never, ever going for a drink with him or anywhere else!"

"No kidding. But you know what I think you should do? Report it to HR. I mean, I heard it, too, and I'm happy to go in there with you. Jack's been hitting on half the women in the office, and no one ever says anything."

"That's because we don't want to lose our jobs!" Angie exclaims.

"I know, but now you've got a witness. Will you at least think about it?"

"Okay. The whole thing is just nasty."

A couple of days later, Lisa makes an appointment for her and Angie with Joyce, the head of human resources.

"Let me get this straight," says Joyce. "Lisa, you heard Jack ask Angie to go out for a drink. Angie, when you said no, he proposed drinking in the office after-hours?"

"Yes," answers Angie.

"And he wouldn't move to let you pass by when you tried to leave?"

"Uh-huh."

"Lisa, you witnessed this entire event?"

"Yes, I was standing just down the hall."

"Well, it sounds like a clear case of harassment. Lisa, if you're willing to be a witness, and if Angie files a grievance form, we'll be able to take care of this unpleasantness once and for all. I've heard things about old Jack, but this is the first time someone has actually come to me. Thanks."

• • •

If this had been a real-life situation, Angie would have been lucky to have Lisa as a witness. But even if she hadn't, if Jack was acting in a way that disturbed her and made her uncomfortable, Angie had every right to go to the human resources department or to another manager within the company and lodge a complaint. And HR can now go ahead and deal directly with Jack, likely resulting in some disciplinary action. ■

Sherizen specializes in protecting business data from disgruntled employees who are not just irritated and want to cause some trouble but who also have the technical knowledge to do just that.

"I have found employees who have been able to delete very critical types of records," he pointed out. "For example, there was a person who worked for a major stock company, a multinational, who was able to bring down all of the system so that the employees from around the world were unable to work for a limited period of time. Here's somebody who had the knowledge of how the computers operated and had a scheme that worked. He had what criminologists and investigators often talk about: MOM—motivation, opportunity, and means."

Leaking Sensitive Information

Just as a terminated employee may leave with a head full of handy computer passwords, he or she may also be privy to confidential company information. Disgruntled employees sometimes release information about upcoming plans or gain access to records for use in identity theft. Some vindictive employees will even break the non-competition or confidentiality agreements they have signed and spread the word about a new product or client to the public or the competition.

Tampering with Data

Remember those cocky kids in high school who snuck into the principal's office and changed everyone's algebra grade to an A? They weren't disgruntled, just crazy teenagers. However, an angry former employee may have the same urge to tamper with data or other information in the workplace. All it takes is a copy of a key or knowing a combination or password, and the vindictive worker has access to sensitive confidential employee records and other information and can easily destroy or change sensitive company data. Always have an exit interview for each employee and state firmly that all keys and other company property must be returned at that time. During the interview, have the employee sign a nondisclosure and a noncompete agreement stating that they will not, by law, share any confidential company information with anyone. If you do not trust the ex-employee, change the locks and passwords.

66 99 | Advice for employees: Say goodbye to an unfair boss.

Maybe your boss is a real jerk. And you slipped up once, just once, and he or she came down on you hard, and now you're out of a job. How do you feel about that person? Odds are, you're mad as hell, and maybe you want revenge.

Having irreconcilable differences with your supervisor is a worst-case work scenario. As my guest Tom Markert, author of the book *You Can't Win a Fight with Your Boss*, put it on my radio show, "I think over time you learn in business that the most important person in your business career is your boss. He or she really makes the decisions about how far you're going to go in a company and how fast you're going to go in that company. The boss really holds the keys to the kingdom in terms of your ability to get ahead. Even if you have a boss who is difficult to get along with or is difficult in other ways, you have to work really hard at finding ways to win them over and to understand their objectives. Because like it or not, they are your boss, and they do hold the keys to your future."

If you can't get along with your boss, you've got trouble, my friend.

Markert offers a step-by-step approach to solving conflicts with a boss. "The first step is always to approach your direct boss and see if you can resolve the conflict in an honest and open way."

If that doesn't work, it is probably time to consider looking for a new job. When you like the job, but not the boss, and if the company is big enough, Markert suggests you seek a transfer to a department where you would report to a different supervisor. "But I will say that if you are not achieving your objectives year in and year out, you're simply not going to get ahead. Employers are looking for people who are working really hard and are really, really smart. You've got to be able to adjust your style and your tactics. It's really important that you spend a little bit of time studying your boss so you're doing the kinds of things he or she wants you to do."

**Preventing/
Limiting Damage**

Clearly, your first concern must be to prevent the employee from doing any permanent damage to the company.

Limit Access

There is a reason we don't let our three-year-olds use the stove. They might hurt themselves, or they might even burn down the house. In any organization, it is critical to limit access to certain equipment, passwords, and confidential data. Only a few trusted employees should have access to information and equipment that is easy to sabotage. Make sure these authorized individuals sign confidentiality or other agreements that state clearly that they are dealing with secure data that must not, under any circumstances, be shared with other employees or organizations. An open-door policy at work is fine; an open file cabinet or accessible e-mail box is not. Keep all passwords, combinations, and keys in a safe, secure place that only a select few know about.

"There are three approaches that I take in helping companies protect themselves against security breaches," Sanford Sherizen told my audience. "The first is to look at the policies and procedures that are in place. It may be than an employee does something, and when they are detected, they may point out that they were never told it was wrong. Sharing passwords is a simple example. That may not be a violation of a company's policy. There may not even be a policy." His second concern is technical. "Use tools and techniques to make it more difficult for people to commit crimes." Employers may want to take advantage of protection offered by several different "e-risk" and other computer and network security systems to ward off electronic sabotage problems. Firms such as Computer Forensics, *www.forensics.com*, and ERisk, *www.erisk.com*, can offer suggestions about different types of electronic and Internet security tools. For a list of network security tools, go to *http://sectools.org*.

His third approach fits right in the intersection of psychology, business, and strategy that is the key to my own business theories. Sherizen says organizational behavior must send positive signals. That means not allowing what he calls the "criminogenic environment" to develop—that is, a workplace that gives informal messages to employees that says no one takes security seriously here. In such workplaces, employees learn quickly that it's very easy to steal, and no one will care. "That's really a motivation for certain people, and they may very well take advantage of it," Sherizen says.

Nondisparagement Agreements

Nondisclosure and noncompete agreements have been around the work force for some time. They restrict employees from divulging company secrets and forbid workers from going to rival companies for a specified time. But today more and more companies are also asking employees to sign nondisparagement agreements. This type of agreement is usually tied to a financial incentive and forbids the employee to say anything negative about the organization. Companies put these agreements in place to head off bad publicity that can cause a stock to drop or can scare away potential investors. But nondisparagement agreements can be difficult to enforce when they clash with workers' rights. It may also be tough to prove violations. And just as you would ask an employee not to make derogatory remarks about you or your business, you may be asked to sign an agreement not to do the same about the employee.

There are several types of agreements that you, as an employer, can use when hiring employees to assure their loyalty not only while employed by you but after they leave or are terminated. Confidentiality agreements cover public domain information, confidential information—for example, the identity of a former employer's customers to a new employer—and trade secrets. Noncompete agreements usually focus on geography, customers, or knowledge and generally forbid employees from working for rival companies for a specified time.

Nondisparagement agreements restrict employees from making derogatory remarks against a former employer that might damage the employer's reputation and cause financial damage.

Have a Security/ Surveillance System Installed

Many of us have security systems in our homes to prevent break-ins and theft. What you're protecting in the workplace is different than what you're protecting at home, but the principle is the same. I always recommend installing a security or surveillance system in any business, large or small. It gives you peace of mind and can keep former employees with a grievance against you and the company from coming back and ransacking your business. It also lets you monitor your work force and catches any unwelcome intruders, not only ex-employees.

Station Guards and Install Pass Codes

In the period following September 11, 2001, many high-traffic organizations stationed guards at all entrances and asked employees to wear badges. They installed pass codes for employees to use when entering different parts of the facility. Maybe you think this sounds a little too paranoid. But trust me, when you've got a building with several entrances, multiple floors with elevators and stairwells, and people—from bike messengers to clients to employees and other visitors—coming and going, having guards, sign-in sheets, and pass codes helps keep track of who enters and leaves; that is a valuable asset.

Bar Past Employees from Your Facility

Once you've let someone go and he's packed up his belongings, he does not belong in your workplace. Maybe he's had a few weeks to use his old office while he looks for another job, but the day he turns in his keys and security badge should be the last time you see him onsite. Clearly and firmly state that past employees may not enter the facility, and have the employee sign an agreement that he will not enter it again uninvited or he will face serious

charges. When we spoke on my show, security special-
ist Sanford Sherizen said, "There are many ex-employees who are very, very knowledgeable. Sometimes they're
leaving with nondisclosure agreements, but the reality is
they carry in their brain a whole lot of information." You
want them off-campus.

They may know how transactions are conducted in
your organization. They may have intimate knowledge of
your IT systems—how they work and their contents. If
they decide to become vindictive and seek revenge on the
company, the potential for damage is much greater if they
are on the premises. Keeping them away from the workplace reduces the likelihood that they can damage it.

More worrisome even than an ex-employee stealing
data or other information is the chance that she might
"go postal." That nasty term originated in August 1986,
at a post office in Edmund, Oklahoma, when postal clerk
Patrick Henry Sherrill (known around Edmund as "Crazy
Pat") shot and killed fourteen coworkers—including
two supervisors—and injured seven before killing himself. The trend toward workplace violence is showing
up in every industry from factories to law firms. Workplace violence has been rising in the past several decades.
According to the U.S. Department of Justice, up to three
supervisors are killed every month in the United States.
The seemingly common thread among those employees
who turn violent is a change in status in their employment, such as quitting or being fired. Changes in shifts,
a bad performance review, a decrease in hours, and canceled contracts can also trigger an unstable employee to
"go postal." These attacks, however, rarely come out of
the blue. In most cases, the employee has exhibited some
unusual actions such as threatening or aggressive behavior toward coworkers and supervisors, talking about plans
to kill his boss, family violence, and other warning signs.
Crazy Pat didn't get his nickname for nothing.

There are two worrisome characteristics that you should watch out for:

A person who's not just irrational and irascible but also prone to outbursts of anger—This lack of anger control is especially problematic when its triggering event is relatively mild and could be handled gracefully by a healthy person.

A person who is completely withdrawn and sulks—These characters act sullen, tend to be loners, and are uncommunicative to everyone in the organization.

Human resources training and psychological training for senior staff will help your crew recognize the early warning signs of serious personnel problems in your shop. When we hear stories about students or workers "going postal," coworkers or neighbors often say, "Herbie was a great guy, he did a good job, he was a great father." Well, I think that's hogwash. If people are trained to be observant, they'll see warning signs. Of course, at times, behaviors and warnings are not noticed or are ignored out of fear or discomfort over how to deal with this kind of employee.

If you have an unstable employee, and you fear for the safety of yourself or your staff, you need to get rid of the individual. By barring entrance to the workplace to any ex-worker whom you feel bears a grudge or might literally go crazy, you can prevent any violence from taking place at your business.

Pay Severance in Staggered Installments

Some employers like to pay out severance in a lump sum at termination. But offering an employee severance pay or benefits in staggered installments can ease the pain of unemployment. The fired worker may then feel as if he is still "making money" and may be less likely to be vindictive.

Smoothing the Separation/ Termination Process

I've described the type of vindictive or troubled employee who can cause a real problem when he or she becomes an ex-employee. Yet sometimes terminating a worker is inevitable. It may be a case of poor matchmaking or a bad fit, or you may have to fire someone who is stealing from your organization or slandering you. There are ways to terminate employees that leave both sides, if not exactly happy, at least somewhat satisfied with the outcome.

Very few people (with the possible exception of Donald Trump) actually enjoy firing workers. Even if you have good reasons, delivering bad news can make the most polished manager squirm. But sugarcoating or obscuring the message with a lot of legalese will just make matters worse. Meet with the employee in your office, an empty conference room, or in the HR department if you'd feel more comfortable with a witness, but not in the employee's space, and certainly not in a visible public place within the organization. Make sure this is a private, closed-door conversation. Review with the worker all warnings and performance evaluations leading up to your decision. Clearly share your feelings on the degree of unacceptable behavior that led to your decision. Use simple, short sentences that explain your point of view without sounding cold. Ask the employee if she has any questions or comments. Explain the organization's policies on severance, benefits, and vacation pay. Let the employee know if the termination will take effect immediately, and if not, state a specific date for her last day. Usually a worker has a hint that she is in danger of being fired, but sometimes she is caught by surprise. Be sympathetic but firm. Above all, don't get drawn into an argument. The time for arguing is past. Now is the time for action.

Give Plenty of Advance Warning with Documentation

If you've done your homework, you'll have plenty of documentation ready when you're going to terminate someone. You will have copies of written warnings, disciplinary letters, e-mails, and unacceptable performance

Debra's Story

A caller to my show named Debra inherited a business along with her brother when her father became ill. Debra called in because of problems stemming from a disgruntled ex-employee.

DEBRA: I inherited a material-handling business—forklifts, pallet jacks—anything to move material we work with, and we've been in business for twenty-eight years. In 2003 this disgruntled employee quit my firm. He's married to my sister, so he's also my brother-in-law. He proceeded to tell us he was going to put us out of business and has been working very hard to do that.

ME: Whoa. Now is your sister in the business with you, or no?

DEBRA: No, she's never been involved with the business at all.

ME: And is your brother-in-law a competitor or just a detractor?

DEBRA: He went to work for one of my competitors.

ME: Has he made a dent in your business with the competition?

DEBRA: He's made a little dent, but the story goes he also has a side business that is in direct competition with me. He runs the same type of business out of his home.

ME: Let me ask you a question. When he worked for you and your family, did he ever sign an agreement not to compete?

DEBRA: No, because he was a member of our family.

ME: He was trusted.

DEBRA: Right. I never thought he would do something like this to the family business.

ME: So what's your strategy, and what are you trying to do now to mitigate this problem?

DEBRA: Our strategy is we take the high road. We do a lot of advertising, letting people know that we're still here; we're not going anywhere. The first thing he did was tell everybody we were going bankrupt.

ME: Well that doesn't last too long once people find out you're still in business.

DEBRA: No. And it hasn't helped him at all because we're still here. But he's a thorn in our side.

ME: Is he still married to your sister?

DEBRA: Yes.

ME: This hasn't caused him any marital problems, huh?

DEBRA: No, not really.

ME: Well, something's wrong with your sister then, huh?

DEBRA: She doesn't associate with the family very much.

ME: So the whole family's split apart over this?

DEBRA: Yeah.

ME: Now, what are your ideas on how to mitigate this problem? What would you like to do to make things better?

DEBRA: Well, I would like to get hold of the company that he's working for and let them know what he's doing. But that's not really ethical for my business, because it's going to look like sour grapes.

ME: No, wait a minute. Hold on. Is he doing things that are negative toward your business that you can prove, either bad-mouthing or disinformation?

DEBRA: See, that's where it gets sticky because we have heard from our customers what he has told other people, but my customers do not want to get involved with my legal issue. I have contacted a lawyer about this.

ME: And the lawyer has said?

DEBRA: The lawyer has said he can write a letter telling him to cease and desist, and it's going to cost me five hundred bucks to get this letter written. Right now my company doesn't have an extra five hundred dollars to have this lawyer write this letter.

ME: I bet you right now that you can get a friend who's a lawyer to write the letter who won't charge you five hundred dollars. You can write the letter and ask him to cease and desist. Or why don't you just set him up? Have someone you know who is aware of what he's up to make this nega-tive comment to them. Then you'll have a case against him, and you'll have a case against the company that employs him and is probably aware of what he's doing and benefiting from it.

DEBRA: I hadn't thought about that, but that's a good idea.

ME: You know, you need to be street-smart, and you're making yourself too helpless for your own good. I think you should be more direct in dealing with your brother-in-law and his company. They're both benefiting from this type of attitude and these actions. The way he's doing it so carelessly and openly, it would be very easy for him to talk to a few people whom you had set up who would be willing to sign an affidavit or be a witness—and then boom, you've got him where you need him.

DEBRA: Right. Yes.

ME: There's a saying in Chinese philosophy called thick face, black heart. It means there are times you have to be a bit ruthless. The art of thick face, black heart is that you don't do it to hurt harmless people. But if you have a virtuous cause and you're defending your business, you have to be tough sometimes.

• • •

Debra's problem was complicated because her ex-employee went to work for her competitor and because he was her brother-in-law. I would never tell anyone not to go

(continued)

into business with his or her family; this country was built on mom-and-pop stores. Many of them are successful. What I would say is that you have to be extra cautious when working with family members—siblings, parents, in-laws—and it is critical that you follow company policies and procedures, document everything, and have the appropriate noncompete, nondisclosure forms in place if a falling out does occur. Business and money issues can cause friction among even the closest families. The other lesson to take away from this story is that as a boss you can't be too lenient; to be successful you have to be tough and develop a thick skin.

FOLLOW-UP

Debra never did call me back. But I'd like to assume that she did stand up for herself. Maybe she got in touch with a lawyer, who, as a friend, could write that letter to tell the brother-in-law to cease and desist, and stop bad-mouthing Debra's company. But even better, I hope she set the guy up, and if she did I would bet that stopped him cold. I hope it was a happy ending. ∎

reviews, plus any negative comments or complaints from coworkers, supervisors, or clients. If you've given the employee multiple warnings and she has failed to follow through on a promise to change or improve, you will have that in writing as well. Then, during that uncomfortable meeting, you will be able to show her the chain of events on paper that led to your decision.

Sometimes those firings may not be as unpleasant on the boss's side of the table, and they sure can inspire fellow workers to toe the line. My colleague Peter Laufer tells a story from a radio station where he was program director. Prior to the launch of the new program schedule, he spent some time with the staff in a classroom environment, instructing them in the techniques and style he sought for the new operation. For the first couple of sessions, one fellow who had been hired as an announcer was perpetually late. Not too late, just by a few minutes. But it was disruptive to the class, and he arrived with a chip on his shoulder: he was arrogant and acted as if it was just fine that he rolled in when he felt like it. Twice Peter made it clear that his behavior was unacceptable, stressing that in addition to violating policy, being late is an egregious dysfunction in live radio. The result is dead air. The third time this problem child showed up late, Peter said to him, "You're late again." And the guy just shrugged. With no change in his tone of voice and in front of the entire staff, Peter calmly told him, "You're fired. Go to the business office and pick up your check." The guy looked shell-shocked. He sat in his chair and thought Peter was joking. Peter repeated his announcement and motioned the loser out of the classroom. The result: one bad apple out of the barrel and you can be sure none of the other employees were late for the remaining training sessions.

Give a Generous-as-Possible Severance

What's the point in shortchanging an employee you're firing just to save a few bucks? To make the termination process as smooth as possible, be generous with the severance package you offer the employee. Remember, you still have a job and a paycheck, and she doesn't.

Not only can you offer a nice severance package, you can extend the employee's other benefits, such as the ability to cash in unused vacation or sick time. You can offer the worker job search resources and career counseling, to ease the transition from employed to unemployed.

Help the Ex-Employee Find Employment Elsewhere

If you had to let someone go because she was a bad fit or simply outgrew the position, she's probably well qualified for another, similar job at a different organization. Use your connections and see if you can't help her find a new position. Even if you don't know someone who's looking for this sort of worker, let the employee work with your human resources department or hiring manager to get a sense of what's available out there.

Use of Office Equipment

If an employee is fired due to theft, harassment, or violence, you'll want him out of your facility pronto. But if the termination came about because of some smaller issue, and you're giving the employee one or two weeks' notice before his last day, let him use an empty office and office equipment to prepare a resume, write letters, research job boards, and so on. As long as you explain that he can only use your resources for a defined period, let him take advantage of copy machines, computers, and fax machines. In the best-case scenario, the employee might find a new job, or at least set up interviews, during this phasing-out period.

Restrict Internet Access

Once you have made the termination official, it is critical to restrict the employee's use of confidential company resources and equipment immediately—especially the corporate computer files. Coordinate the firing with your IT manager so that the former employee cannot access confidential company documents. Lock out the employee's access to the corporate intranet and e-mail systems.

Explain to Remaining Staff   After someone is let go, the remaining employees tend to get a little nervous. Address this immediately by calling a meeting or sending out a memo explaining exactly why you had to terminate their coworker. Don't beat around the bush, but don't be unnecessarily harsh either. The other employees were most likely aware of the problems and will tend to respect your decision. Be as specific as you can when talking about your rationale, but there is no need to go into much detail. After the termination, be especially aware of your staff's accomplishments and compliment them whenever you can. This will help to keep a positive atmosphere in the workplace. While you should keep focused on business as usual, look for opportunities to recognize people for their good work performance.

Chatting about hiring and firing on my radio show, my guest Erika Andersen, author of *Growing Great Employees: Turning Ordinary People into Extraordinary Performers*, suggested, "Be really clear with people, make sure you're taking care of the team after the person is fired because—even if no one liked the person and everybody's glad he's gone—it's still traumatic to have somebody suddenly gone. And you know, firing people when they deserve to be let go and doing it well and cleanly, really impeccably, is a critical management skill."

Exit Interviews   I recommend you conduct an exit interview with any employee who quits. Now you may be thinking, "Hey, they're out of here. Why should I waste time talking with that person? It'll likely be all sour grapes!" In fact, exit interviews are a great way for the employee who's leaving to vent her feelings and for you and your staff to find out what's working at work and what isn't. Analyze what happened: Was it a personality conflict with a boss or a lack of challenging assignments? Was the employee disgruntled due to personal problems?

By talking frankly with the employee, you can gather information about her colleagues and supervisors, along with other aspects of her job. This gives you a chance to make improvements and changes before you hire or promote a replacement, and you can discuss this information with existing employees and enlist their feedback as you restructure or re-evaluate the position.

"Front-End" Protective Measures

To avoid firing or creating vindictive employees intent on sabotage, build the best workplace you can create. Hire a strong, capable team of workers you trust and respect, workers who have the right skills for the job. You're a matchmaker connecting talent with positions and duties. Keep the employees satisfied in their current roles, and offer them new and more interesting work whenever possible. Listen to your employees, reward their achievements, and show empathy when necessary. Be the type of person whom workers seek for a boss: demanding but fair.

Check References Before Hiring

Before you hire someone, check his references. That's just logical, right? But you'd be surprised how many employers just accept what's on a resume. Hiring decisions are often made on gut feelings. That's fine, but it's mindless not to check references, too. Would you buy a car based on your gut feeling without even a test drive? Trusting your instincts is an important business tool, but you should always ask potential hires for at least two or three references. Past employers can verify that the job-seeker did in fact hold the jobs he's claiming even if they are hesitant—fearing a lawsuit—to provide the reasons he no longer works for them. Some smaller, less formal business owners or managers may be happy to give you the straight scoop, and even the most paranoid former employer may let slip the real story with a tone of voice or clever choice of words. Remember, if a prospective employee is giving you a list of references, that list is sanitized. These are people he expects will say only good things. It's a good idea to check with past employers who are not listed as references.

"Prenuptial" Hiring Agreements   When celebrities—top-ranking business moguls, politicians, or elite athletes—decide to marry, any details of their prenuptial agreement makes the news. While there is no such thing as a "prenup" in the business world, you can make sure that the work an employee does for you remains your property and not theirs when you part ways. Too many times I see employment begin with a handshake or a brief memo, not a negotiated agreement. A work-for-hire agreement states that the employer, not the employee, is considered the legal author or owner of work created by the employee. Imagine, if you will, a large software company or an advertising agency. In both cases, employees are creating something—software, operating systems, ad copy, illustrations—yet the end products or creations are released under the name of the company, not the employee. To protect yourself from a former employee taking credit and ownership of a product developed in your workplace, especially if you run a creative business, ask new hires to sign work-for-hire agreements. You can give them plenty of credit and compensation for the finished work while you keep the rights to the intellectual property as well as to specific products.

Invest in an Employee Assistance Program Counselor   Employee Assistance Programs (EAPs) exist to help workers deal with every kind of personal problem, from family issues to mental and emotional health to work-related issues. An EAP counselor is a trained professional who can provide confidential help to employees in trouble. If your organization does not have an EAP in place, you can still refer employees, or soon-to-be former employees, to an outside EAP counselor with whom you have established a relationship.

Summary:
Limiting
Damages Caused
by Vindictive
Employees

DO:

- Document everything you do from e-mails and memos to disciplinary letters and warnings.
- Keep a confidential file for every employee.
- Establish a grievance policy for your workers so they have a safe, legitimate way to make complaints.
- Have all employees sign noncompete and nondisparagement agreements upon hiring.
- Limit access to all sensitive materials, computer passwords, building pass codes, and office equipment. Install a security and surveillance system as well as stationing guards at entrances if your business is large.
- Give plenty of advance notice in writing when an employee has been warned and is failing to live up to acceptable expectations.
- Be as generous as possible with severance and the use of office equipment during the transition from employee to former employee.
- Explain a termination to remaining staff and look for ways to compliment them on their work.
- Conduct exit interviews to find out what went wrong from both sides of the issue and consider making changes before hiring a new employee.
- Always check references before hiring a worker.
- Invest in an Employee Assistance Program or an Employee Assistance Counselor.

DO NOT:

- Assume that former employees can be trusted to the same degree as current employees.
- Ignore warning signs of a worker's tendency toward violence and aggression.
- Save money by cutting back on severance packages.
- Use informal or verbal agreements in which there can later be disputes about who said what.

6 cultivating a nondisgruntled workplace

Manage Your Attitude

If you're a grumpy, disgruntled boss you're going to have a bunch of disillusioned, disgruntled employees. It's hard for anyone to look forward to the workday when the boss is a grouch. While it's just as difficult for you to check your emotions at the door as it is for your workers, as a supervisor you need to do all you can to compartmentalize your off-site problems and frustrations. A big part of your job is maintaining calm and exhibiting a positive attitude despite the inevitable miscommunications, missed deadlines, and plain old mishaps that occur in every business from time to time. Treat yourself well, exercise to reduce stress, eat right and get enough rest, and make an effort to enjoy your life outside work. You'll bring a fresh, positive outlook to work, and your coworkers and staff will appreciate that. Just as a disgruntled employee can contaminate a workplace, so, too, can a bummed-out boss.

Listen

The results of good listening are profound. Listening enhances the value of any conversation. Too many people don't listen; they only appear to listen. Since we talk and listen at about 90 words a minute while we talk to ourselves internally at as many as 800 words a minute, we tend to distract ourselves very easily from listening. Make a supreme effort to focus on what the other party is saying. Whether it's a grievance or simply a data-dump, truly listen when your employees talk to you. Block out distractions and focus on what's being said. Let your staff know they've been heard. It'll go a long way in maintaining a conflict-free workplace.

Believe in People   If you make a point of hiring smart, capable people who have the right skill sets to fit the job description—if you're being a good matchmaker—then you should believe in your work force. Your employees don't want to feel that you are second-guessing them every step of the way. Trust your instincts and have faith in your ability to build a strong team; your employees will know you have confidence in them, and they'll be motivated to do a good job. If there is a problem, address it right away, and work with your employees to stay challenged and engaged in what they do.

Set a Positive Tone   There are too many whiners and complainers out there in the world of employment, and many of them are bosses. Do you find fault with everyone and everything? Do you chastise people for their weaknesses rather than patting them on the back for the things they do well? Do you come to work with a cloud of negativity hanging over you?

66 99   **Advice for employees:** See the good in a bad day.

It is important to realize that a problem you face at work may well be an opportunity. Just as physical pain is a tool to inform you that something is wrong with your body, a difficulty at the office can be a blessing. If something or somebody is causing you stress, that may mean there is a glitch in the system. If you can isolate the problem and fix it, you may not only relieve your own anxiety but also increase the efficiency of the business. You will be a hero to yourself and your boss. It is a tired cliché, of course, but when you're faced with a pile of lemons, look for the opportunity to make a cool, refreshing drink.

Strive to create a positive atmosphere in the workplace. The author of *What People Want: A Manager's Guide to Building Relationships That Work*, Terry Bacon, said on my show, "Everybody gets up on the wrong side of the bed, and sometimes you have to come in, and you feel negative; you don't feel good. What I tell managers is that you've got to park that when you get to the office. You've got to try to set your moods aside and manage your relationships with employees so that they are positive. It's up to the manager to set a positive tone in the workplace, and I think if you do that people will reciprocate."

When you're setting companywide goals and objectives, inform and involve your workers. Empowering employees to meet the company's goals means giving them the power to help the company meet its objectives. Workers who understand the organization's goals also understand their role in achieving success, and they can act to help both the company and their individual jobs.

Be Optimistic   Setting a positive tone in the workplace means more than simply recognizing and capitalizing on people's strengths. Your optimism and confidence rubs off on those around you. Don't forget to enjoy yourself. Studies prove that laughter burns calories, makes blood pressure drop, and relaxes muscles. Inject a little humor and lightness into your business. Joke. Don't be afraid to laugh at yourself (but don't make fun of others). Be the person who always believes the glass is half full, not half empty. Seek to reduce stress in the workplace. I call this sense of optimism the Fun Factor. The Fun Factor can become a catch phrase in your office. When fleeting depression or a note of negativity creeps into an employee or a meeting, you can add this easy line to your speeches and orders, "Remember the Fun Factor."

Kanter's Law   Rosabeth Moss Kanter touts confidence in her book, *Confidence: How Winning Streaks and Losing Streaks Begin and End.* When I welcomed Kanter to my radio show, we talked about the importance of confidence in the workplace. Kanter was quick to point out that leaders and companies build confidence when they don't treat their people as disposable. She made an intriguing team sports analogy.

"There was something I saw on the winning streak side that is not only part of business but a part of all the great sports teams in countries all over the world and anyplace where there is the ability to keep succeeding time and time again, over long periods of time," Kanter reported to me and my audience. "There were not only the investments on the people side, but also leaders themselves believed that people had the potential to achieve. One of the great arts of leadership is to build confidence in advance of victory. Those leaders who were able to turn around losing situations really impressed me, like Jim Kilts at Gillette, who turned Gillette around and then sold it to Procter & Gamble for a lot of money, or Gordon Bethune who turned around Continental Airlines, or Nelson Mandela who turned around South Africa. They all believed in human talent, and that's why they made those investments."

I love it that Kanter was able to stir Kilts, Bethune, and Mandela in the same pot. Too often, we isolate business from the rest of our lives. Techniques that work in sports and marriage and politics often are exactly what work in business. Nelson Mandela was critical, of course, to South Africa's evolution. That's where his talents were needed. But he probably would have made a killer CEO.

In her book, Kanter writes that great leaders view success not as a one-shot deal but as a marathon. They are able to embrace the ambivalence of what she calls the middle. Talking with me, she said, "Something I observed in leaders I call Kanter's Law, which is that everything can look like a failure in the middle. Anything that we undertake, whether it's a new venture, a new product, construction on our home—there are always more obstacles ahead of us, potential trouble, and knowing we can get through it, that's what confidence really brings. It's the ability to believe that success is possible; that's all confidence is. Those companies that have built a great deal of confidence in their people, those people believe they can do anything, they can perform miracles. They can get through any crisis. Those companies are more likely to bounce back from troubles, and troubles affect all of us."

The Continental Airlines turnaround is one of Rosabeth Kanter's favorite case studies, especially since the company was facing the same troubles all the major airlines suffered at the time of the Continental crisis. The company's response to the New York City blackout in summer 2003 was textbook correct according to Kantner.

"Every other airline closed when the power went out for two days, and hundreds of flights were canceled. The Continental people had a culture of confidence; they believed that they could keep those planes flying. The most important performance measure was on-time performance, so they had to keep those planes in the air. No one called in sick. Everybody came to work. They found very innovative solutions. It turned out to be a beautiful day. There was no danger flying that first day just because there was no electricity at the airports. Air traffic control was not affected by the outage, and the Continental team devised creative workarounds to compensate for the lack of electricity on the ground.

"While the blackout in the Northeast impacted Continental's operational performance in the quarter, the airline was the first to restore its flight schedule, canceling only 45 flights on Aug. 14 and 15, for a completion factor of 98.3 percent.

"Change to Continental not only kept their airline flying, but they made money during the worst disaster the airline industry had had since September 11.

"It's all about this idea of persisting in the middle, that's what confidence gives you. It's easy to be successful when every condition is in your favor, but what we all need is the ability to bounce back, to keep going. When you do it, you get that confidence because the team around you believes in you, and you don't want to let them down."

Yup, it's easy to succeed when it's all working perfectly for you. It's selling ice to the Eskimos and coal to Newcastle—or flying in and out of New York with no juice—that takes talent.

Insist on Respectful, Sensitive Treatment

Employees everywhere, at all levels, complain about one thing: lack of recognition. People want to be recognized and rewarded for their good work. They want—no, they *need*—to know when they've done a good job. Praise and attention from supervisors motivates workers. How do you do this without fawning all over someone? Write a note and put a copy in the employee's file. If it's a big accomplishment, a plaque or a gift certificate might be in order. If an employee is going through a rough time, let her know that you still value her contributions. Ask if she needs a day off or to see a professional. Treat your employees the way you want to be treated, with respect, honor, and recognition.

Call People by Name

One of the most valuable techniques you can use around your office or factory is name calling. No, I don't mean, "Hey, quit that slacking, you jerk!" I mean, make it a priority to learn the names of those who report to you. Knowing a spouse's name and a little something about the kids is also of great value.

Maybe you're terrible with names. You hire someone, and even though you've been staring at his resume for two weeks, two days after he starts, you run into him in the hallway, and he says "Good morning, Peter," and you say, "Good morning, uh, how's it going, big guy?" because you've totally forgotten his name. Go to your office and look it up. Make a point of going by his workstation later that same day and addressing him by name. Do whatever it takes to fix the names of your employees into your brain. The staff may just call you, "Boss." That is the corporate culture in some companies, but most supervisors would rather be on a first-name basis with employees.

Show Trust   Just as you should get to know the people you employ, you should trust them. Some employers like to make a big deal about perks—cushy chairs, fancy new computers, or corner offices—but more important are the human conditions in the workplace. I'm talking about values like trust, communication, equity, respect, challenge, appreciation, and feeling like part of a team while still feeling like a successful individual. These are more important than fixtures in an office, and sometimes they're more important than a raise—especially a token raise. Trust is at the top of the list because if you think someone mistrusts you, it's really hard to enjoy doing your job.

66 99   **Advice for employees:** Embrace positive peer pressure.

Peer pressure is a term that's been saddled with a bad reputation. We tend to think of peer pressure in the context of negative influences. But peer pressure can be a tremendous asset. Just as when you were a kid in the schoolyard, those you hang out with influence you and the perception others have of you. Analyze your coworkers. Don't hang out at the water cooler with the complainers and the kvetchers, the rumormongers and the gossipers. That crowd is bad for your reputation and bad for your attitude. I'm not suggesting you seek out the ever-cheery Pollyannas of the office. But find those who tend to be the glass-half-full types. These are the people who try to make the best of a situation, and they usually end up the happiest and the most successful. Learn from them and team up with them whenever possible.

Don't Treat People as Disposable

How many times do you hear, "Our people are our most valuable asset?" Many organizations make this claim, but how many actually mean it? If you've assembled a great team of talented workers, make sure they know that you value and care about them as people, not just people you pay. Don't be stingy with insurance, raises and bonuses, and other benefits. Share your corporate mission or vision with your employees. Get to know your employees. It's the people, not technology, office equipment, or a new software program, that will make or break a business.

Manage Your Moods

Maybe you just can't check your emotions at the door when you come to work, but you can manage your moods. Is it your employee's fault that your dog threw up on your best carpet, that your kid forgot his homework (again), that your mother's in the hospital, or that your mother-in-law wants to visit? Of course not, and even if it is an employee's fault that the conference room is double-booked, you still shouldn't lose your temper at work. If you're having a bad day, or you just feel rotten, don't take it out on your staff. Close the door to your office and take some deep breaths. Go outside and take in some fresh air or go for a short walk. Remember that your bad mood will affect others in the workplace. Try not to spread it around like a virus. Put your mood aside and focus on whatever positives you can find, or just let the negativity dissipate before you engage your staff.

Manage Your Mindset and Beliefs about Employees

All of us have developed certain mindsets by the time we are adults. We have set expectations of people, of how they behave, think, and act. But just because someone has a different mindset from yours, it doesn't mean he or she won't be a good employee. For example, Gen X and Gen Y employees may value their personal time more than workers from previous generations. A worker may leave at 5 P.M. every day, only working late when it's absolutely necessary, while other employees stay late all the time. Ask yourself if the 9-to-5er is producing good work, meeting deadlines, engaged in the job? If the answer is yes, then don't judge her for having a different mindset. A strong working team is made up of a diverse group of people with their own mindsets and beliefs, and that promotes growth and creativity.

Watch Your *Projections*   You know how you instinctively stay away from that bleached blonde at the gym with the black roots showing who reminds you of your cousin Rhonda who was always gossiping and complaining? We all tend to avoid people who have the same mannerisms, looks, or even names as someone from our past who hurt us, didn't like us, or with whom we didn't get along. But that's crazy. That woman at the gym may be a lovely, accepting person who is completely different from your cousin Rhonda. You shouldn't judge that new employee with the tan and big biceps because he makes you think of the guy who stole your girlfriend in high school. Scratch below the surface when you hire or meet new workers. Cast aside your preconceptions and get to know the person for who she is.

Temper Your *Preferences*   Maybe there's an employee who has a look or a habit you really can't stand. It could be the guy in the warehouse who has tattoos up and down his arms—and who knows where else—or the woman in accounting with the long dreadlocks. These choices in personal style may be completely opposite from yours. You may even disapprove. But ask yourself if the tattoos or the dreadlocks or anything else that doesn't mesh with your personal preferences is affecting the employee's abilities to perform her or his job. No, you probably wouldn't assign the tattooed guy to close a deal with your best client. But what harm is he doing in the warehouse? As a manager, be tolerant of others' differences unless they are affecting the work product.

Annoyingly Cheerful

Now, let's say Robert, the owner of an auto body shop, calls in to my show.

ME: Hi, Robert, how are you today?

ROBERT: Just fine, thanks.

ME: Great. What made you call in?

ROBERT: Well, it's a tricky subject. I almost feel bad about calling you . . .

ME: Well, that's not good. What's going on?

ROBERT: So I hired this new receptionist, Kathy, for my shop about a month ago. She seemed perfect for the job. And actually, she's not doing anything wrong. It's just, uh, well, she just has some mannerisms or whatever that really bug me.

ME: Such as?

ROBERT: I know this is going to sound nuts, but she's just so cheerful. Like all the time, she's smiling and happy. First thing in the morning, she's all, "Hi, Robbie, isn't it a great day? Did you have a nice night?" And I'm not a morning person. I don't feel like making chitchat. It's all I can do not to tell her to shut up. Not to mention that nobody's called me Robbie since sixth grade!

ME: Ah, those early birds can be pretty annoying, can't they? Let me ask you, do you think Kathy's behavior, or her perkiness, is bothering anyone else?

ROBERT: Um, well a couple of the mechanics were sort of making fun of her in the shop the other day. But it was good-natured.

I don't think she's getting on their nerves as much as mine.

ME: And you say she's doing a good job otherwise?

ROBERT: Yeah, she's real organized, and she's never late. And I think the customers like her.

ME: Do you think the customers like Kathy because she's so cheerful?

ROBERT: That's the thing. I'm sure they do, but they don't have to listen to her every day. But yeah, I know people like the way she smiles when they come in. And she's helpful and all.

ME: So, Kathy is doing exactly what you hired her to do. She just rubs you the wrong way.

ROBERT: Right.

ME: Well, Robert you have a dilemma on your hands. You certainly can't fire Kathy or even give her a disciplinary warning, because she's doing nothing wrong. And you need to be very careful what you say to her. You can't tell her she's too cheerful for the job! But I do think you can call her into your office and have a confidential meeting. You can say, "Kathy, I'm just not a morning person, so don't take it personally if I don't make a lot of conversation first thing when I walk in the door." And you can also say, "You know, Robbie was my childhood nickname, but I really prefer Robert these days." More important, though, is that during that meeting, you need to tell Kathy what a great job she's doing. Your goal isn't to make her feel bad, just to get her to understand you better. And

Robert, you know what? I think you need to learn to be more tolerant. So your receptionist comes on a little strong. At least she's got a positive attitude. Wouldn't you rather have a smiling, happy person running your front desk than a crabby grouch?

ROBERT: Yeah, you're right about that last thing. And I guess I could try talking to her.

ME: Okay. Why don't you try, and then give me a call back and let me know how it goes.

• • •

If you allow your mindset and your personal likes and dislikes to interfere, you could wind up like Robert, who has a perfectly fine employee he's having trouble with because she rubs him the wrong way. If Kathy was Robert's business partner, or they worked together on a team every day, I would say they were mismatched. But the fact that her chipper comments rankle him in the morning when everyone else, especially the customers, seems to like Kathy means this is Robert's problem. As a boss, you need to cast aside your preferences and ask yourself if you value this employee, and if she is making a contribution. If the answer is yes, then it's time to take a look at how your personal feelings might be getting in the way of your professionalism.

FOLLOW-UP

A couple of days later Robert calls me back with good news about his conversation with Kathy.

ROBERT: So I talked to Kathy.

ME: How did that conversation go?

ROBERT: I started out by telling her how much the customers liked her cheerful smile.

ME: Perfect. Great icebreaker, Robert. And then what?

ROBERT: I told her I hated mornings and could barely manage to say good-morning until after ten, so she shouldn't feel bad if I didn't talk much to her when I came in.

ME: How did Kathy take it?

ROBERT: She was fine. She laughed and said her boyfriend was the same way. She promised not to try to have a conversation with me until I'd had my coffee. I was pretty relieved!

ME: I'll bet. What about the "Robbie" thing?

ROBERT: I lost my nerve on that one. I'll just save it for another time. Actually, now that I talked to Kathy, she doesn't bombard me with questions in the morning anymore, so it's not such a big deal.

ME: Well, done, Robert. You handled the situation beautifully. I hope things work out for both you and Kathy at work. ∎

Establish Proper Boundaries

When we think of boundaries, we think of lines that can't be crossed. In the workplace, boundaries exist whenever a person or a team interacts with others. Personal space and setting limits are part of establishing boundaries. These boundaries can be emotional, physical, and personal. You don't want another person to invade your physical space by standing too close to you at the office; you don't want another employee to pry too deeply into your personal life; and you don't want to share every emotional crisis with your coworkers. The best way to establish proper workplace boundaries is to have a frank discussion when hiring a new employee or when starting a new project. Talk about responsibilities, goals, and priorities, and the organization's mission statement. Discuss how you'd like people to work together and the division of responsibilities.

Don't Be a Control Freak

It's one thing to be involved with your employees and the jobs that they do; it's another to go try to control every little detail of each project. By the same token, it's great to get to know your workers and their interests, but it's different when you expect to know exactly what's happening in their personal lives on a daily basis. Your role as boss does not give you the right to be Big Brother. One of the biggest lessons managers have to learn is when to let go and hand over the reins to somebody competent. Delegate. You can't do it all.

I'll tell you, that's a failing of mine. I'm a bit of a control freak myself, but I'm also an odd duck as a manager and not nearly as talented as I am as a creator. So I can become a bottleneck in my own company and my own worst enemy. On one hand, I want to control everything, and on the other hand, somebody else needs to control a big chunk of it and report to me. I need to find people I can trust to do that, and this is one issue I grapple with all the time. A boss is not a parent, but a mentor and a teacher, one who leads by example. If you don't want your boss breathing down your neck, challenging and interfering with your every move, then don't be that kind of supervisor to your own employees.

Establish a Balance: Micromanaging vs. Being Out of Touch

People who are control freaks are usually guilty of micromanaging. Worse yet, they usually have no idea they're even doing it. Micromanagers are addicted to control. They're often perfectionists who are extremely detailed oriented, or they are so self-centered that they believe that only they can do the job right. Other micromanagers are so worried about the end results, as well as their own jobs, that they seek ultimate control over every aspect of their work. If you are a micromanager, your employees are probably calling you ugly names behind your back like ruler, tormenter, and tyrant.

As Professor Derrick Neufeld, who teaches at the Business School of the University of Western Ontario, told my radio audience, "We all know that the enlightened manager is not the one who watches the clock and watches the employee minute by minute, but rather sets some objectives together with the individual. The idea is to look at the quality and productivity at the end of the week or the month, or the project itself, rather than simply monitoring time. That seems like a very old-fashioned notion yet there are still many middle-level and supervisory level managers who seem to operate that way."

Ask yourself the following questions: Is there a way I can be in touch with what my employees are doing without micromanaging? Can I let go of some of the little stuff? Can I take a day off without calling in to ask how things are going? Would it kill me to stop reacting to every grammatical mistake I find in interoffice e-mails?

If you have a strong, skilled team in place, you must give them control over their work. Strive to be less critical, and wait for the project to be completed before you jump in and pick it apart. Exude a positive expectation and get out of the way. Your workers will thank you.

Model a Strong Work Ethic   You need to model all of the qualities you want to see in your workers. If you leave early, dress sloppily, and show little respect and trust in your team, then how can you expect them to be respectful of you and your demands? Your behavior and your attitude reflect how your employees will think about you and act. Be honest and fair and face up to your mistakes and weaknesses. Remember the importance of your own role models and their value as you moved forward in your career. Stay up-to-date with the latest information and technology in your field, and your employees will want to stay current.

Show You Care   Team-building activities, retreats away from the workplace, and special employee recognition lunches or dinners will demonstrate to your staff the investment you have made in them and that you care about their job satisfaction. Remember not only workers' names and those of their partners and children but also a bit about their interests and hobbies and whatever else they've shared with you about their personal lives. These gestures help people feel secure in the workplace. One of the biggest problems for employed Americans today is balancing work/life responsibilities. Many employees feel overwhelmed and exhausted from trying to cope with both family and work demands. When you take the time to ask someone how he's doing, where his teenager is applying to college, or how his golf game went over the weekend, you are making him feel like not just an employee but an individual whom you care about and understand.

Take an Interest in Their Careers   My guest Susan Gebelein, the executive vice president of client relationship management at Personnel Decisions International, talked on the air with me about how to gauge if an employee is worth developing. "Not only do you need to develop all employees because expectations keep changing," she told us, "but a boss needs to keep his or her eyes out for folks who really do have potential for higher-level roles. You have to look at a number of different factors, only one of which is current performance. What's the person's career goal? Are they interested in advancement or not? What are the psychological characteristics that they have that might lead them into more advanced roles? And what are the cognitive skills that they have that might lead them toward higher roles in an organization?"

Investigate What Makes People Flourish

You may think you've won half the battle once you've hired a great team of workers, but actually that's only step one. You don't want your employees to get disgruntled or bored; what's more, you want them to grow and succeed in their jobs. But you're not a mind reader, and not every employee will be bold enough to ask for new challenges, so you need to play private investigator. Watch, listen, and learn what makes your employees tick.

Business consultant and executive coach, Ben Dattner, when he appeared as a guest on my radio show, pointed out that employers often call him for consultation because they feel an employee doesn't work well on a team or is not assertive enough. Dattner told me and the audience, "What I'll do is say, 'Before we even start the coaching process, why don't I do some interviews with you and the person in question and with any colleagues or subordinates, just to try to get a read on what's going on.' Often what you can find out is that the lower-level employee is being accused of not being assertive enough, but maybe it's because the boss is domineering or bulldozes the employee and doesn't give the person the chance to be assertive. The problem may be that this worker isn't assertive enough. Maybe it's the team dynamic where people are punished for speaking up. Maybe it's the organizational culture where you're not supposed to say anything that can be perceived as disloyal. So before you start solving the problem, before you take the approach of being a hammer when the whole world's a nail, it's important to figure out what's really going on." Dattner is adamant that managers should do this background work.

Learn your employees' preferences and interests. No, you don't need to know it all, just enough to help figure out what motivates or inspires your workers.

The "Gruntled" Worker! This book deals with the problems facing and caused by the disgruntled worker and, of course, strategies to deal with him or her. But there are some nice, even inspiring, stories in the debris of corporate unhappiness. I've decided to coin a term. Let's call the opposite of the disgruntled worker the "gruntled" worker! Okay, I agree. That doesn't sound so nifty. But it does describe the status of some lucky employees who find themselves working for an organization that does double backflips to make the staff not just content but blissful.

Consider the outdoor activity supplier Patagonia. I enjoyed the distinct pleasure of talking to Patagonia owner and founder Yvon Chouinard on my radio show when he published his inspiring book *Let My People Go Surfing: The Education of a Reluctant Businessman*. What a great title, and what a great story! Chouinard told me he never wanted to be a businessman. He liked to climb mountains and make tools. He made his own mountain-climbing equipment, and when his pals saw the stuff, they wanted him to make more for them.

"Since I never wanted to be in business," he said, "I had to make business a pleasurable thing." He devised what he considers "an experience that kind of blurs the distinction between family and work, and work and play"—and that explains the title of the book. "We have a company policy that when the surf comes up you drop your work and you go surfing." Company headquarters are next to the blue Pacific in Ventura, California.

The Patagonia philosophy extends from play to productive corporate citizenship. "Our mission statement,"

explained Chouinard, "is to make the best quality clothing and cause the least amount of harm. The least amount
of harm is something that not many clothing manufac-
turers care about. We do an environmental assessment of
every process and of every material that we use." Cotton is an example. The company determined that a 100
percent cotton garment is damaging to the environment
because of the pesticides used growing industrial cotton.

"In 1996 we decided that we would never again use
industrially grown cotton. We use organically grown cotton everywhere we use cotton. Organically grown doesn't
use any pesticides or toxic chemicals. And it doesn't use
defoliants to take the leaves off the plant so the mechanical
pickers can pick. Those defoliants are like Agent Orange."

The result is a garment that may cost the consumer a
few dollars more than the competition, but Patagonia has
carved out a niche of customers who are willing to pay
the premium. It's an example of how it costs relatively
little to do the right thing, all the way down to the avoidance of sweatshops in Second- and Third-World countries, where the difference in a product's cost could be just
pennies and yet the lifestyle of the workers is miserable
if it's a sweatshop. A cost-benefit analysis can prove that
there's often very little cost difference to a business's bottom line when a company decides to practice global corporate responsibility. There may even be a nice upside.

"Our customers," Chouinard is proud to report, "tend
to be very loyal, and they're responsible people. For them
the fact that it's organically grown cotton adds value to
the product, and there's less guilt in buying it." And here's
the critical news: "I found out that every time we make
a decision because it's the right thing to do we end up
making more profit." Of course, that translates directly
to the factory floor and the office cubicle, resulting in a
team of gruntled workers.

One device that helps Yvon Chouinard keep his workplace free of unhappy employees is to monitor the hiring

process carefully and closely. "I try to hire people who are very passionate about something—it doesn't matter whether it's music or food or surfing or whatever, they have to be passionate about something. I think it's easier to teach a passionate person about business than to try to teach a businessman to be passionate. We all think that we're kind of on a mission. We're sort of pessimistic about the fate of the natural world and we want to do something about it. At the end of the year we take one percent of our total sale, which last year was $2.3 million, and we give it away to environmental causes. I think when you're really into doing some good with your work, you don't call in sick unless you're really sick. We have child-care centers right there so your kids are there with you." He designed the Patagonia offices to be "not different than your home life; it's all just part of your living."

Growing Great Employees   The founder of the consulting company Proteus International and the author of *Growing Great Employees: Turning Ordinary People into Extraordinary Performers*, Erika Andersen, kept returning to her gardening metaphor during our interview on my radio show, "You can't actually make plants grow. What you can do is buy the right plants for your garden and give them the optimum conditions they need to thrive, which is precisely what you can do with employees as a good manager. You can make sure that you get the right people for the workplace that you're trying to create and then give them the optimum conditions to thrive. And you don't just pick them, you nurture them." Andersen talked about what she calls the mindset of the coach, "What I discovered is that people who are good managers, good leadership people, tend to hold a particular mindset or set of beliefs about the people who work for them. They believe in those people's potential to succeed, and they want to help them succeed."

Andersen and I agreed that sometimes managers in positions vital to nurturing great employees don't know how to stimulate growth. "Think about it," she mused. "If someone's going to be a lawyer they go to law school and they pass the bar; they put a lot into it. If they're going to be a doctor, they go to medical school, and then they do an internship and a residency first. If someone's going to be a manager, generally what happens is they wake up one morning and they go to work and their boss says, 'Congratulations, you're a manager.' And they're supposed to automatically know how to manage people. We don't give managing the respect it deserves as an art and a craft, and there are a lot of people who do it very badly. Many managers look at the leading of people as something that they do in the cracks around their real job, because the real job, whether you're head of finance or something else, it's more nuts and bolts, and to manage people you have to think and feel. It's a very complex process."

More business gardening advice from Andersen: Don't be afraid to prune. "One of the things most gardeners I know find difficult, and this is certainly true of me as well, is pruning, because it is counterintuitive to take a sharp implement to a living plant. The analogy to managing people is giving them corrective feedback. Most of the managers I've spoken with over the years say this is the single hardest thing to do, to tell somebody that they need to do something differently or that you don't like what they're doing."

Give employees very specific advice and action points. As well, mix in some compliments to soften your managerial pruning shears.

Keep Your Eyes and Ears Open

Stop, look, and listen. Listen when you see a group of workers gathered for a meeting or a lunch and pick up on clues about what different people like or dislike. Susan Gebelein said on my show that a great way for bosses to show they care about their workers is to take the time to hear the hints people drop about themselves. "They may make a comment about having gone horseback riding," she says, "or they may make a remark about the NAS-CAR race they went to. You don't need to get into long, enormous personal conversations, but interacting a little bit around those things that people care about is another indicator that you care."

Let Them Know Their Needs Are a Priority

It is not enough simply to listen to employees and get to know their preferences. You also need to let them know that their needs are a priority. If someone comes to you and asks for a raise or a new project, don't string them along with false promises. If a disgruntled employee comes in to your office and says, "You know, I haven't had a raise in a year and a half. Sally was just hired, she makes the same as I make, and I'm doing more work than she is. What about me?" As a manager, I would stop and take note of that complaint. I'd say, "Guilty as charged; let's make that raise now."

Of course, as a boss, you need to investigate the situation to make sure that there aren't other factors involved. The lesson is to make sure you aren't overlooking people but instead are nurturing and encouraging them.

Create an Environment of Fairness

Loosen your control of employees and make them feel more empowered at work by cultivating an atmosphere of fairness. Make sure employees receive information on a timely basis and explain how supervisors make decisions. Provide opportunities for workers to give advice to decision-makers. It's a good exercise to have people periodically put in writing what they think their job description is and the company mission. You may be surprised to find that people don't necessarily think about their role in the same way their managers do. Terry Bacon, author of the book *What People Want: A Manager's Guide to Building Relationships That Work*, said on my show, "One of the things that people expect in the workplace, and it's a fairly high expectation, is fairness. If you've got a situation where some workers see that other people are being paid the same or in some cases paid even more and doing less, there's no faster way to mess up a workplace."

Guest Ben Dattner pointed out that in business we are constantly negotiating transactions, and each party wants an equal piece of what he calls the "mythical fixed pie." He said, "We often approach situations in business and everywhere else believing that they are win-lose when in fact they're really win-win. So our natural bias is to compete rather than to collaborate. If we don't trust, we're not as likely to communicate our real priorities and concerns and therefore less likely to find what's known as integrative solutions."

To create fairness in the workplace, we need to remember that we're all on the same team, and we're all going to get some of that pie if we work as collaborators not as competitors.

Set Out Clear Expectations and Give Equal Treatment

Human beings are creatures of habit. In general, we don't really like surprises. In the workplace, it's important to set out clear expectations in terms of behavior, responsibilities, and corporate culture. It is critical to treat all of your employees with the same level of respect and consideration. Remember that lonely boy in grammar school who always was chastised by the teacher no matter what he did? And then all the other kids picked on him and teased him at recess? Employees want to feel a part of the "inner circle." Make workplace policies and procedures public, and apply them consistently, from top to bottom. If you offer a top manager time off beyond family leave when his wife goes through a difficult childbirth or a death in the family, you should do the same for the assembly-line worker. Make sure everybody within the organization receives public company news and information at the same time. The trickle-down theory doesn't apply in the workplace. By the time the news trickles down several levels, it is likely distorted and far from the truth. Make everyone aware of companywide news such as layoffs or a takeover; otherwise, you run the risk of alienating a large portion of your work force.

Build Mutual Loyalty If you encourage and support your employees by being sensitive to their needs and offering them assistance when they need it, they will repay you with not only hard work but with their loyalty. People are unlikely to go looking for new jobs if they feel respected, appreciated, challenged, and nurtured in their current positions. Even if yours is a large organization, make your employees feel like owners by having a voice in major decisions, working directly with clients, or owning stock in the company.

I enjoyed talking with Mal Warwick, coauthor of the book *Values-Driven Business*, on my radio show, and he told me the story of Gary Erickson, founder of the Berkeley, California, company, Clif Bar. Erickson founded the energy-bar company with his wife in the early nineties. "The company thrived," said Warwick, "because Gary and his wife built it around their personal values of appreciating their employees not as workers but virtually as partners. They shared the benefits that came from their business by instituting environmental policies at a very early stage that made their employees feel good and helped them gain extra market share because they were a company that was really doing good in the world. By the late nineties the company was thriving, and sales were more than $1 million. Gary and his then–business partner received an offer for the company of $120 million. Now Gary could have just walked away, as his partner wanted to do, with $60 million in his pocket, and said good-bye to his employees and his company. But at the final hour, he decided to reject the offer. He's still paying off his partner, but the company is in his hands. He's continued to expand the environmentally positive programs they instituted. They have an active program of supporting worthy nonprofit organizations, such as the Breast Cancer Fund, not just with money but by giving their employees the opportunity to volunteer by using the company's facilities and its promotional efforts to support the work of nonprofits. The employees feel like owners."

Wall Street Journal columnist Sue Shellenbarger, who writes regularly about employment issues, recently devoted a column to the idea of creating a great workplace and the importance of truly engaged employees to the companies they work for and to customers as well. She wrote, "A growing body of research is finally proving what advocates of workplace quality have known for decades: that the human beings who execute the goals of business are more than just cogs in a wheel. Truly engaging them can have an almost magical effect on the bottom line." Shellenbarger noted that in a study of approximately 300 companies by Hewitt Associates in Lincoln, Illinois, improved employee engagement preceded improvements in company financial performance. Even in the companies posting below-average profits, a rise in employee attitudes tended to precede a profit turnaround.

Maintain a Motivated Environment Work to maintain employee enthusiasm in your workplace. Check in constantly with workers to see if they have everything they need to do their jobs. You need to give them a voice and to actively listen when they speak, and you need to clearly communicate your expectations. The longer somebody is in a position, the harder it often is to keep her motivated. Yet this longtime employee may be one of your most valuable workers. She knows the work and is a repository of company history.

My guest Derrick Neufeld from the business school at the University of Western Ontario believes that in order for employees to want to move up in an organization, they need to be led by a manager who sets a strong example of looking at the big picture rather than focusing exclusively on short-term goals. "If we're not leading by example, if we're not stimulating the people in the organization to really step out and to start managing and lead in new ways, I think we may get stuck in very short-term thinking. We're thinking about what is being produced today, but not necessarily the longer-term picture of what we're going to produce as a company a year from now unless we trust our employees, and we stimulate and create a culture where we're all focused on the long-term picture."

Look around your shop and pick out the employees you hope will still be on the job in five years. Then make sure they're challenged.

Provide Learning and Growth Opportunities

When you help an employee improve existing skills or learn new ones, not only are you helping and motivating that person, but you are also helping your organization. Invest in employee training programs, and encourage and pay for your staff to take work-related classes. Lend moral support to an employee who wants to go to business school at night or learn a new trade. Workers who feel their jobs are creative and interesting tend to work the hardest. Terry Bacon said on my show, "Good managers need to be able to give people responsibilities and let them do their work. The number-one thing that people want from their manager is to feel that they're trusted. I work with many managers who micromanage, and they hover over employees, giving them nothing but criticism. If they talk to them at all, it's to criticize something. It really comes down to letting people do their jobs. Challenge them, don't make them do mundane work all the time, but give them something that is deeply satisfying to them from a professional standpoint. Show them that you're willing to work hard, too. I was surprised that eighty percent of the people I surveyed said that it's very important to them to see that their manager has a very strong work ethic."

It's critical to encourage and train supervisors to be on the lookout for employees who have the potential to grow in more than a linear fashion. Give them techniques to nurture and harvest their abilities and potential.

Develop Incentives Employers must develop innovative ways to retain good employees. Think of the old carrot and stick. What can you dangle out there that will make your staff want to keep working for you even when the money is tight? Is there something other than cold hard cash or stock that will help motivate employees to continue to enjoy their work and stay productive? Maybe you can bring in lunch once a week or offer health-club memberships as employee incentives. That lunch may seem like a small gesture, but it means more than the sandwiches you serve—it's the statement of appreciation that counts. Flex-time is another noncash form of remuneration that can be appealing and important to your valued employees.

Award Performance Bonuses Instead of Raises If you can't afford or rationalize an immediate raise to one of your best workers, consider a performance bonus. Glenn Shepard told me he prefers performance bonuses at the end of the year rather than raises, which unrealistically escalate a worker's sense of entitlement. Shepard's theory is that "everything should come as close to merit-based pay as possible. It's based on a very simple principle of psychology, not of economics, and that is if you reward good behavior and punish bad behavior people will behave well. But if they're rewarded without having to earn the reward they have no incentive to work hard or to do what you want them to do."

It's hard to argue with that.

Offer Training, Mentorship, and Coaching One of the best ways to reward longtime employees who are consistently strong performers is to offer them more challenges. By providing the chance for them to sharpen or learn new skills, whether by following a mentor, taking a class or a seminar, or being coached in specific areas, your workers grow stronger by continuing to develop their careers and their abilities. Mentoring can help younger workers understand different rules and regulations within an organization and foster the transfer of knowledge. Ask more mature employees about who helped them to succeed, and that will help them understand the importance of mentoring someone. Technology is changing at such a rapid pace; simply by keeping employees up-to-date on the latest computer and telecommunications equipment, you can help them to build their knowledge and expertise in this critical area.

Bring in
Outside Training

If yours is a small operation, you probably don't have your own training department. There are plenty of outside resources—such as career coaches and training companies—skilled in helping employees meet and exceed not only their organization's goals but their own as well. Bringing in an outside expert for a one-day in-house training session can be an invaluable employee-retention tool. A career counselor can also be a strategic resource

❝ ❞   Advice for employees: Learn what you need.

Most of us think we know what we want, but too few of us manage to figure out what we really need. Remember Mick Jagger's advice that we can't always get what we want, but if we try, we just might find that we get what we need. I doubt he was referring to office politics or workload when he crooned "Satisfaction," but the lesson applies to your workplace. If you simply lust after an idealized sense of what your workplace and workday should be, you'll likely be disappointed. If, instead, you make a short list of what you really, really need to make your everyday work experiences satisfying, you may find that you can create an environment that may not be ideal but certainly becomes tolerable. With such a list, you have the initial tools to approach your boss and your coworkers, and to help yourself make those desired changes.

for managers to rely on when work performance, attitude, or behavior in the workplace become problematic. Career counselors are trained and educated to help workers tackle difficult work-related issues and achieve their highest career goals.

Set Goals   Can you imagine playing soccer if you couldn't see the goal? Or playing basketball if there were no hoop? For many employees, it's difficult to work hard on a consistent basis without a specific, attainable goal in sight. Not just a project goal, but a set of goals set out by the organization that everyone can strive for, from top to bottom. Goals should be motivating, agreed upon, realistic, results oriented, and timely. They should be flexible enough to change based on the customers' changing needs and demands. In addition, each worker should have a set of personal career goals or objectives.

Discussing employee potential during our interview, Susan Gebelein said, "In thinking about employees' potential, you want to review how their performance is now. You want to look at what kind of potential they have, and then you want to look at what kind of roles are they ready for. There are a variety of different assessment processes that you can use to pick up different kinds of data to get that information." Simple questionnaires can be a swift and easy tool to gather such data on your work force.

Hold Employees   Your employees must be held accountable for their work
Accountable   product. That seems so simple and obvious, but you'd be shocked (or maybe not if there's a slacker "working" next to you) how prevalent shoddy work habits are in America today. Attacking the lazy and the sloppy is one reason goal setting and vision sharing are so important. If an employee or a team agrees upon clear objectives and timelines, it will be easy to see if someone isn't keeping

up or is letting down the rest of the team. Put goals and objectives in writing and ask your employees to sign off on important, time-sensitive projects.

Tom Markert, author of *You Can't Win a Fight with Your Boss*, offers this bit of advice that goes for workers as well as bosses: "You're not going to get ahead in any company today in any part of the world unless you're delivering results. If you're not achieving your objectives year in and year out, you're simply not going to get ahead. There are a lot of really good people out there, and companies will reward those people first and foremost who are delivering their objectives. That rule is called 'putting in the hours.' And I think it's an important one. The world isn't vanilla anymore, and you've got to be able to adjust your style and your tactics when you're dealing with different kinds of people, and you've got to make sure you're doing the kinds of things your boss expects you to do."

Putting in the hours isn't just warming the chair; it's getting the work done well.

Foster Collaborative Teamwork

In my experience many of the most successful companies found their success through fostering a work culture based on collaboration and teamwork. When a group of diverse people from different backgrounds and experiences come together to solve problems and share ideas, the end result is creative and rewarding, and team members are satisfied. In a teamwork environment, strategic planning, decisions, and actions all function more efficiently when approached collaboratively. To help build teamwork, bosses and managers should let workers know that teamwork is the company norm. They should model teamwork in their own interactions with each other and the rest of the organization. Use work teams to solve real issues and to improve real work projects. Strong teamwork needs to be rewarded, celebrated, and publicized companywide.

Mix It Up Supervisors must be able to mix and match different relationships in the workplace. Frequently a stale or stalled worker will perk up when she starts reporting to a different manager. Someone who is feeling under challenged may benefit greatly by working with a different team. Don't wait to change the reporting structure in your organization until someone gets promoted. Mix up your teams—with plenty of advance warning and buy-in from all concerned—from time to time. Let your employees suggest different work relationships and collaborative teams, and take them up on their suggestions. Your workers will grow from this experience.

Delegate and Step Back Once you've picked your teams and made your assignments, just like the coach of a winning football team, you need to step back and let your padded and helmeted employees do what they do best. That doesn't mean you don't huddle with them between plays, and, of course, you choose the quarterback. You can make sure your workers do excellent work by delegating projects and duties to the most qualified people for the task at hand. Delegating means giving others the chore and the chance to do something that you might normally do yourself but know they are capable of doing. When you delegate, you give your employees the power to make decisions and work closely with coworkers and supervisors. This, in turn, gives them a sense of control and entitlement. They will know they have earned your trust and respect.

Give Workers a Real Voice I had the pleasure of interviewing David Sirota, chairman emeritus of the Sirota Survey Intelligence and coauthor of the book, *The Enthusiastic Employee: How Companies Profit by Giving Workers What They Want.* Sirota has more than thirty years' experience dealing with workplace behavior, and he told me there's a strong correlation between enthusiastic employees—not indifferent or occasionally happy but truly enthusiastic employees—

and how they are treated within an organization. Sirota believes companies profit by giving workers what they want.

"Through our research," Sirota told me, "we identified three major goals of employees. The first we call equity, or to be treated fairly." This includes pay and benefits. "The second we call achievement, and primarily it's for employees to be proud of what they do and proud of the organization for which they do it." The third he calls camaraderie. "It's very, very important to people at the workplace to have coworkers with whom they cooperate, who are friendly, who they enjoy working with. If these three goals are satisfied, that's when you have an enthusiastic work force."

Sirota stressed that job security is especially important to employees, and it is critical to treat them fairly, like people not like expendable or interchangeable objects. "We're talking about people who are really enthusiastic about their work, enthusiastic about their employer, really engaged, and trying to do more than what they were hired to do; the people who go out of their way," Sirota said, and he's found that only about 15 percent of the companies he's studied can be classified as having enthusiastic work forces. That's a miserable track record for American business. We can do better; we must do better. And improvement can start with you.

Sirota made the point that there is an equation in business between how the customer is treated and how the employees are treated. "There is a very strong relationship between the two. We have all kinds of data to show the relationship between how you treat people and their morale or their enthusiasm and the overall performance of the business." In today's harsh business climate, with downsizing, outsourcing, and benefits slashing, how you treat your workers is of utmost importance.

Use your employees as the experts they are to help you identify opportunities to save money and become more efficient. They know the business intimately; they know where the waste is located, where the slippage and leakage is occurring.

Extend the Honeymoon

There's nothing like the first six months of a new job. Once you figure out who everyone is and what your position entails, you throw yourself into your work with enthusiasm. You want to show your new boss that she was smart to have picked you. You want to fit into the workplace culture and make friends. You're careful not to make mistakes, come in late, or do anything else wrong. This is the honeymoon stage of employment.

New hires are eager to please and ready for a challenge. Unless something really goes wrong, an employee is unlikely to become disgruntled during this phase. How can you extend the honeymoon so the worker continues both to enjoy her job and to produce high-quality work? Get to know her. Watch how she interacts with colleagues and managers and make changes where it seems as if there may be a bad fit. Make sure she is included in meetings and team-building exercises. Just as we have to keep the customer satisfied on an ongoing basis, so must we keep our employees happy.

Show Recognition and Approval

Have you ever been inside a business where Employee of the Month plaques and pictures fill the wall? Did you think, "Jeez, how corny is that?" Or maybe this is a description of your own workplace. If it is, you're on to something. Employees value recognition and appreciation more than anything else. So what if having an employee of the month is corny? Most employees love to be honored and recognized, not only by their boss but also by their peers and the public. Other ways to show recognition for employee efforts is to build a little fun into the organization's agenda. Take the team out for lunch or dinner, a ballgame, golf or hiking, or a trip to an amusement park. Start a coed softball or basketball league. Employees may be pleased with a day or an afternoon at a local spa. Make these regular outings so employees not only have an incentive to do their best but have something fun to anticipate together.

Bad news is inevitable in the business world. Whether it's a round of layoffs, poor stock performance, or a reduction in benefits, it's no fun to be the bearer of unpleasant news. Layoffs are tough not just on those employees who are let go but also on those who stay. Sometimes remaining workers experience a kind of survivor's guilt, and that can devastate morale.

My guest, Louis Uchitelle, who writes for the *New York Times* and is the author of *The Disposable American: Layoffs and Their Consequences*, watched outsourcing and globalization result in massive layoffs. This downsizing, he's convinced, is motivated mostly by corporate lust for a greater profit margin. "Most layoffs occur because they have become the easiest means of reducing labor costs. But layoffs result in a lot of unmeasured costs, particularly psychological damage. Most people who suffer layoffs aren't unemployed for very long—they get other jobs—but layoffs damage your mental health by telling you that you don't have value. We reinforce it as a nation by telling people, look, it's just a matter of education and retraining. You're in a job that doesn't have value to our global economy, our high-tech industry, and you need to get yourself educated and retrained. People try to do that, and then they don't get jobs that pay as well as the jobs they lost, and society says, it's not our fault, it's your fault."

You can mitigate the pain. If you have to lay people off, tell the employees affected by the layoffs first. If you have a human resources department or an employee assistance program, rely on them to help you through the process. Pay close attention to your remaining employees. Keep them abreast of any other changes involving budgets, pay cuts, or additional bad news. Make sure the information circulating around the workplace is accurate; this is a time when rumors race. Bring your staff into brainstorming meetings; give them a voice in departmental decisions. This will help them regain a sense of control.

How to Give Stress-Free Performance Appraisals For most people, just the words *performance appraisal* conjure acute anxiety, whether they're on the giving or receiving end of the evaluation. My guest Sharon Armstrong recognized this stress factor in the workplace and wrote the book *Stress-Free Performance Appraisals* to try to help. She contends that if handled right by following some simple, logical techniques, performance appraisals can indeed be free of stress.

Planning and Preparation One of the first tips Armstrong mentioned during our interview was the importance of planning for the performance appraisal. Develop a standard for performance reviews that specifies the time interval over which the employee is being evaluated, specifics about the job and the skills needed to do it, and a section for action items that address any improvements the employee will be expected to make. Get to know your worker and try to create an environment that will engage and motivate that person to stay in close communication with you. Armstrong says it's all based on logic, "Really, that just means talking all the time so that when the time comes for the appraisal meeting, it's just culminating or summarizing all of those other discussions. And of course don't have your performance appraisal on the same day as the holiday party!"

No Surprises Armstrong also made the point that an employee shouldn't be surprised or taken aback during a performance appraisal. "It's part of the manager's job to make

No Layoffs at Southwest

The September 11 attacks decimated the U.S. airline industry for quite some time. People were afraid to fly, passenger counts dropped off sharply, and every airline lost money. Major airlines cut flights, and many sent close to 20 percent of their work force packing. Yet some of the airlines were able to bounce back successfully. What accounted for the resilience of the airlines that weathered the crisis and came out ahead?

Let's take the case of Southwest Airlines versus US Airways. Southwest was founded in the 1970s with the mission to deliver the highest quality of customer service matched by a strong dedication to the support and well-being of its workers at every level—and all that for bargain fares. The company's core values focus on employee and customer care. In the tumultuous days that followed September 11, Southwest Airlines was the only U.S. airline not to lay off staff. It managed this feat because it had the lowest costs and the strongest balance sheet. Rather than layoffs, the airline revised its growth plans, delayed new plane deliveries, and instituted cost-saving measures that did not include pink slips. Southwest's CEO at the time, James F. Parker, told *BusinessWeek*, "We are willing to suffer some damage, even to our stock price, to protect the jobs of our people." Not only did Southwest refuse to lay off people after September 11, 2001, but its stock recovered much faster than other airlines, and it was the only one that remained profitable immediately after the disaster.

On the other hand, US Airways, another low-cost carrier, racked up the highest number of layoffs in the industry after September 11—a 24 percent reduction in staff compared to an average of 16 percent. The airline's stock took a nosedive from around $40 per share in January 2001 to just over $6 a share twelve months later. US Airways' revenues dropped, its expenses continued, and the airline dipped into its cash reserves. The organization eliminated planes and facilities in the months after September 11, perhaps taking advantage of the crisis to restructure and downsize as it tried to stay in business.

At Southwest no one lost their job, and at US Airways, 11,000 jobs were eliminated. Who came out on top?

Today Southwest Airlines is continuing to make money and still has some of the lowest fares in the nation. Its wages are also among the lowest. But the airline makes stock options widely available so that all of its employees can partake in the company's success. Southwest's executives receive pay increases that are no bigger, proportionally, to what other workers get. The company's consistent no-layoff policy discourages its managers from hiring too many new people when the industry is doing well. Most important, Southwest's employee morale is high. The people who work for the airline feel they are treated well and fairly, so in turn they treat their customers the same way. In fact, at Southwest, the customer is not always right. The company policy is to back its people.

US Airways, however, has suffered since September 11, filing and finally emerging from two rounds of Chapter 11 bankruptcy. The airline suffered highly publicized wage cuts and furloughs, creating heightened anxiety among its work force, so much so, in fact, that airline union leaders have used the terms *stressed out, loss of faith,* and *angry and frustrated* to describe the collective mood of its workers. A *Consumer Reports* survey of 23,000 of its readers, which came out in June 2007, ranked US Airways as the worst airline based on customer satisfaction.

What do I conclude from the comparison of these two similar organizations with very different issues and images? At Southwest, there is a built-in commitment to the employees in good times and bad, and the airline has never wavered from its core values. That kept morale high among its staff, and a positive, satisfied work force meant satisfied, contented customers. US Airways was quick to resort to layoffs and restructuring, paying little attention to the impact this had on its workers. The airline has continued to struggle since 2001 and, as the *Consumer Reports* survey found, is best known for its poor customer service. It's easy to see how this applies to every businessperson out there: Pay attention to your employees. Treat them like human beings, not pawns in a game. Look at layoffs as a last resort. Ask your workers for their help in coming up with creative ways to cope with a crisis. Satisfied employees make for satisfied clients or customers. ∎

sure that it isn't a surprise. The manager should have been talking about performance appraisals and performance evaluation from the start of the employment cycle, planning goals and then having a number of mini-meetings and conversations so the employee will be aware of how he or she is being assessed. Often that doesn't happen because managers aren't comfortable in this process." Remember, any performance issues that will be discussed in the evaluation should have been addressed as soon as they came up, not saved for the appraisal meeting.

Starting the Meeting

Always start a performance appraisal in a professional way. Schedule the first performance review for six months after the employee starts work, and let the worker know you have scheduled the meeting. It's important for a supervisor to go into the meeting well prepared and with a positive attitude. Engage the employee in the conversation; you shouldn't do all the talking. Work toward an atmosphere of trust and the sharing of ideas and opinions.

Give Behavioral Examples of Performance

Too many bosses make the mistake of being vague during performance evaluations. It doesn't work to say, "You know, Tom, you really need to work on your attitude." What does that mean to an employee? It's much better to be prepared, to be able to provide good and specific examples that justify the rating. Don't just say, "You're doing your job well." Instead offer an example: "I really like what you did last March when you saved our inventory after the explosion on the assembly line by calling the fire department while everyone else was just running for the exits." Point out three specific activities that the person did (good or bad), which can serve as talking points and open up a thoughtful discussion.

Avoid "Recency"

In my discussion with Sharon Armstrong about the mistakes supervisors make during performance appraisals, she brought up something she calls "recency." She defined it this way. "It's when you get distracted by something irritating that happened two weeks ago before you sit down with the employee, and that's all you can remember. It becomes bigger than life, and you don't have a tendency to look over the entire evaluation cycle." "Recency" can be a two-edged sword. Say reviews are scheduled for December (a poor choice because of the distractions of the holidays). Work could kick in with enthusiasm by September, as employees hope bosses forget problems dating from January to August. More simply put, if you know you'll be rewarded in January with a big bonus, you'll probably work hardest in the fall, just before the review period. But in the spring and summer, there may be little incentive to work hard when the bonus seems so far away.

"People do tend to think about what happened recently," Armstrong pointed out, "especially if they're not keeping good notes throughout the cycle. A variation of recency is called the halo effect. One particular behavior or action that someone shows in their job takes on a bigger-than-life status on the part of the employer. So the whole rating is as good as the result of that one thing. We need to be aware of these all-too-common pitfalls. Anything that distorts reality, favorably or unfavorably, should be avoided."

Encourage Back-and-Forth Discussion   A fair and productive performance appraisal should be a two-way street, a conversation between the employer and employee. The employee should be an active participant in the evaluation. There should be some good back-and-forth discussion throughout the meeting. A lot of organizations use self-assessments, which help workers bring up things during a performance appraisal that a supervisor may have forgotten. This kind of evaluation gives the employee a chance to talk things over calmly with the employer, appraising herself and the organization—often to the benefit of the manager and the company.

Listen   Be prepared for the performance review with an agenda and points to cover, but leave room for active listening. The evaluation isn't just about what you want to yell at the poor captive worker sitting on the hot seat facing the Third Degree. Nor is it only about what you think needs to change on his part. It's also about how he feels—it's about his observations and opinions about his job, his department, and—yes—about how you're doing as his boss.

If the Employee   No matter how prepared you may be, you will prob-
Explodes!   ably run into a situation where an employee goes a little nuts during his or her performance evaluation. What do you do when a worker wigs out during a performance appraisal? Expert Sharon Armstrong says, "I've had this happen in a performance meeting where the employee just kind of goes berserk and takes no responsibility for their behavior. And you know what I do if I'm a supervisor in that situation? I terminate that meeting immediately. It's not the type of setting where you want to try to discuss performance, and you set up ground rules for the next time. If it gets to the point where it's too extreme, then the employee might need to separate from the employer. It might not be a good fit. I think it's even dicier when an employee is faced with a boss who is hard to predict and flies off the handle. I think we've all been in situations where we haven't left jobs, we've left bosses."

This is a prime example of the two-way street and another situation where it's important to keep your HR and legal departments involved to minimize the risk to the company, to other employees, and to yourself.

Set a Tone   One way to avoid a confrontational or unpleasant
of Mutual Goal   performance review is by setting a tone of mutual goal
Setting and   setting and problem solving. During our interview Arm-
Problem Solving   strong insisted, "Mutual goal setting should be discussed along with what the department is going be doing, and that is hopefully aligned with the organization's strategic

plan and the value the employee has to add." Part of a positive outlook is focusing on what the worker can bring to the table, not on her flaws or faults.

Establish a Forward-Looking Tone

Armstrong believes that rather than spending the bulk of the time reviewing the past, supervisors should devote a good chunk of a performance evaluation to looking ahead. "It's important to get the employee excited about what's coming up," she counsels. "It's not about spending a lot of time looking back, spend a portion of the time looking forward." Looking at new goals and how workers can participate in meeting them can be a real motivator.

Closing the Meeting

Just as you start the performance appraisal in a professional manner, you should close the meeting the same way. Make sure you give the employee plenty of time to voice her thoughts and opinions, review what was discussed, and schedule a time to check in for a progress report. Ask the employee to sign a copy of her evaluation, signifying that she has read and understood it. Most such forms have a space in which employees can add comments.

Follow-up

When you set specific goals with your employee during her review, it's important to follow up on what was discussed. Those regular "mini-meetings" will help both you and your employee stay in touch and focused on the goals established during the performance appraisal.

Armstrong pointed out that most managers are not that skilled when it comes to giving performance appraisals. "One challenge companies have," she said, "is that they expect managers to be able to do performance appraisals kind of naturally. They don't give them the system or training. I asked managers what makes appraisals so difficult. They told me they were never taught how [to do them], it makes them uncomfortable, they're afraid it's going to be misunderstood, they don't have the time, the situation isn't that serious, they don't want to make a big deal of it. All these excuses. The managers weren't held accountable for doing feedback throughout the year and having a good performance appraisal discussion. I think that has to change. I think companies have the responsibility to make sure they're setting up good systems."

Lessons Learned   Remember, a good boss should be like a good therapist. Good therapists listen to their patients; they respect and honor their differences and their quirks, and they make themselves available when their patients need them. The best therapists offer support, encouragement, and physical and spiritual guidance. They provide a sounding board for their patients as they struggle with life's big and small issues. When a patient is in crisis mode, good therapists work to help their patient meet the challenges head-on, providing advice, coaching, and, of course, active listening to help individuals live up to their full potential.

Everything I've mentioned can also be applied to good bosses. No, you don't have to literally offer counseling to your employees, but since you provide them with the paycheck that allows them to do those things, in a way you do. And you should support, educate, and listen to your workers in the way therapists do their patients. Employees thrive and succeed when they get the attention and recognition they crave. Again, listen to your employees, work to understand them, don't judge them because they are different from you, and make sure you nurture them along in their careers.

Summary: FICTION: Because you're the boss you can come into work
A Harmonious   in a bad mood and vent or be grouchy; it's one of the
Work   perks of being a supervisor.
Environment   FACT: As a boss, you need to manage your moods, put your emotions aside, and set a positive tone in the workplace. You are a role model, not an exception.

FICTION: Since something is bound to go wrong, you shouldn't trust anyone in your company.

FACT: If you have faith in your employees and demonstrate it, especially during a crisis, they will be more confident and more likely to perform better.

FICTION: If an employee has a "look" or style that you don't approve of, it is okay to tell them to change.

FACT: If a worker has tattoos, pink hair, or some other style that you don't like, as long as it does not affect their work and is not inappropriate, you should temper your personal preferences and let the employee be.

FICTION: Once you've hired good people, you don't need to worry about their career goals or learn about their interests outside work.

FACT: By getting to know your employees, in the workplace and a little bit about their hobbies or interests, you are treating them as individuals not objects, and showing them you care, which is critical in growing great employees.

FICTION: There is no correlation between how your organization treats its workers and how they act toward your customers.

FACT: It has been proven that employees who feel valued and appreciated provide customers with a higher level of service.

FICTION: It is much better to pay annual raises, even if you can't afford to, than to rate employees on their performance.

FACT: Performance bonuses are more motivating than raises.

FICTION: Awarding workers with Employee of the Month plaques or taking the whole department out to a ballgame is gimmicky and not appreciated by employees.

FACT: Employees value appreciation and recognition for their hard work and achievements almost more than they do their paychecks.

FICTION: If your company is losing money, it is smart to lay off employees.

FACT: Layoffs should be your last resort if your organization is in trouble. It is better to come up with other cost-saving measures that won't result in plummeting employee morale.

FICTION: In a performance appraisal, the supervisor should do all the talking.

FACT: A stress-free performance evaluation should involve a back-and-forth discussion between employer and employee, with mutual problem solving and goal setting.

mental hygiene in the face of disgruntled employees

A Foundation of Mental Hygiene

I often use the term *mental hygiene* on my radio show, and I can't stress its importance with regard to dealing with disgruntled employees in the workplace. Good mental hygiene, or mental health, is all about balance, and it is essential for both personal happiness and business success. Healthy mental hygiene in a boss plays a significant role when dealing with troubled employees. That's true whether the origins of the disgruntled attitude and actions are part of a personal problem or are related to the workplace. If you enjoy functional maturity, you are in a healthy position to discuss workplace problems and to take remedial supportive action to minimize it. Mental hygiene is a blend of inner reality, or inner psyche, and external environment—as well as mental and emotional maturity.

Good mental hygiene comes from self-awareness, along with your interactions with the other people in your life. So—no matter how angry, disappointed, or disillusioned you may become—never cut yourself off from friends and family. People close to you can often provide the reality check you need to see where you're at and to bring light to those things you can't see for yourself when you're too close to a problematic situation.

As a boss, I can honestly say that there have been times when I've struggled to keep my own mental hygiene in balance. When one man starts a company as an entrepreneur in a garage and that business grows into a big company, one of the biggest problems he'll have—especially creative, energetic types who like to build and have great vision—is that he doesn't necessarily come equipped with management capabilities. So a person like that—someone like me—has to learn when to step out of the way on a day-to-day basis and hand control over to someone who's competent and not a yes man. I have trouble doing that, as do many other leaders. But if we can take that step back, if we can keep our mental hygiene intact and our egos in check, then our organizations will be more likely to flourish.

Stay Aware of Your Feelings

Of course it's important for supervisors and managers to be attuned to their employees' feelings. If a worker feels undervalued and unappreciated, it is more likely that he will become disgruntled. And one unhappy employee is like that proverbial rotten apple in a barrel; it can spoil the whole bunch. As a boss you need to be aware of your feelings, too. Whether it's due to work-related stress or personal problems, if you feel out-of-control or overwhelmed and you let your own negative emotions invade the workplace, you're asking for trouble.

There's a popular term these days: *living in the moment.* What that means is trying not to always look ahead to the future, anticipating what's coming next, but instead focusing on the here and now. You have to shut out all the "buts" and "what-ifs" and just deal with the present to live in the moment. This is critical in dealing with your feelings as a supervisor. Listen to your employees and coworkers, and then listen to yourself. Focus on your thoughts and emotions in that moment. Are you excited, annoyed, frustrated, or relieved? Try to identify what you feel and then step back and ask yourself why you feel this way. Is it because of something that someone did or said, or are your feelings tangled up in another place that really has nothing to do with the situation at hand? There's a very strong correlation between self-awareness and the perception others have of you. If you have a healthy, reasonably accurate view of yourself and your impact on others, they will perceive you to be in a healthier mental state. This means they're more likely to relate to you in a positive, constructive way.

Listen to Your Gut Feelings about Employees

When people talk about trusting their gut feelings, do you think that's fine if you're talking about who's going to win the baseball game, but it doesn't apply to business? You couldn't be more wrong. Many of the most successful people in the business world survive mostly by trusting their instincts, especially when it comes to employees. Intuition is a primal part of the human brain, and since sometimes it starts with a queasy feeling in the stomach, people tend to call it their gut reaction.

Say you're sitting across from a prospective employee. Her resume looks great, she has experience in your organization's line of work, she went to a good college, and she's articulate and charming. Yet something doesn't feel right. You can't put your finger on it, but there's something about this person that makes you feel like she isn't the right person for the job, despite her qualifications. Maybe you hire her anyway, wondering why you should trust some random feeling. Well, that gut reaction, that intuition, is probably trying to tell you that there is some reason this person won't be a good fit. Maybe you should interview a few more people before you make such an important decision.

As a manager, you need to trust your gut feelings about employees. If you've worked with someone who's disgruntled, you've gone through everything you can to try to help this person, matched him or her up with the right supervisor and tasks, discussed areas of improvement, documented every discussion, and your gut is telling you it just isn't going to work out, then it probably won't. And it would be better not to prolong the inevitable and just let the person go. On the flip side, maybe there's a quiet but dedicated worker who your instincts tell you would make a great supervisor. Again, go with your gut and offer that person a challenge. Let the employee prove what he can do. If your instincts are correct, you'll wind up with a good new manager and probably a happier employee.

The Impact on Your Self-Esteem

It's unpleasant to find out that you have a disgruntled employee in your workplace. No one likes to hear that an employee is unhappy, angry, constantly complaining, or possibly looking for a new job. I've discussed lots of devices to handle all the different kinds of disgruntled employees you may encounter. But the one thing you shouldn't do is take it personally when an employee isn't a good fit or you have to let her go. Yes, it feels terrible. And it may make you feel like a bad boss. But you cannot let what is essentially a good business decision wreak havoc with your self-esteem. It's very easy to say, "Oh, I must be a really awful boss, maybe an awful person, because I had to fire that person or write up a harsh disciplinary letter. That guy must hate my guts right now, and what if he can't find a new job? How could I have even hired him in the first place?"

If you let yourself go down this path of self-doubt and self-pity, you're going to feel bad. I'm not saying it's wrong to be disturbed by coping with disenchanted workers or having to fire people. It's tough no matter what the reason. But if you've done everything in your power to try to make things right, and the person is still unhappy or you have to let them go, take your time to feel terrible, and then move on. Don't let one incident ruin your self-esteem. If it becomes a pattern and you're losing employees right and left, then yes, you might be doing something wrong. But the whole point of this book is that dealing with disgruntled workers is part of being in business, and running a business is not for the weak. You have to develop a bit of a thick skin and learn not to let small failures affect your overall self-esteem.

Guilt and Anger

Two emotions that everyone experiences, especially managers and supervisors, are guilt and anger, and they often go hand-in-hand with changes in the workplace. Although they are commonplace emotions you need to learn how to experience them without letting them overtake you.

If you have disgruntled employees, you might very well get angry, and anger is one of the more complicated negative emotions that human beings experience. It's a natural reaction, and yet you can't lash out at whomever or whatever is making you feel angry. Don't let your anger get the better of you. You can express your anger in a way that doesn't hurt others and that allows you to release some of it before it starts taking a physical toll on you. Repressed anger is not only unpleasant; it's dangerous and can lead to high blood pressure, headaches, digestive problems, and other physical woes.

Think about why you're angry. Focus on your feelings. Are you angry because an employee has let you down by not performing well or a former worker is slandering or defaming you or your organization? These are legitimate reasons to be upset. Then work on not reacting right away. Maybe you need to physically remove yourself from the situation—take a breather. Go hit some golf balls or play the Whack-a-Mole game at an arcade.

Can you channel the anger into some more productive action? If an employee is underperforming, schedule a meeting to talk with that person. Document all the ways he is not meeting agreed-upon goals. If an ex-worker is a problem, talk with your human resources department or an outside consultant, even a lawyer. You will probably find that simply by taking action, some of your anger will dissipate.

Guilt is also a subtly destructive emotion. Just as I've discussed survivor's guilt experienced by employees who still have their jobs after a layoff, supervisors and managers often feel guilty after they've disciplined or fired someone, even if it was clearly the right thing to do. But guilt is also an unproductive emotion. It eats away at your self-esteem and can immobilize you, rendering you incapable of moving forward. Review the situation that's making you feel guilty. Reassure yourself that you did the right thing. Don't isolate yourself. Talk with a trusted colleague or with a professional who can validate your feelings and help you remember that you acted appropriately. Just as unexpressed anger can eat away at you mentally and physically, so can unrelieved guilt.

Self-Blame　Self-blame is a lot like guilt. If you let it take over, it can make you question your decisions as a manger. In times of transition, especially during organization-wide budget cutbacks or layoffs, or even the firing of one employee, managers tend to blame themselves. As a manager, you might think it's your fault. I pushed the person too hard. Or, I should have seen the layoffs coming and warned my staff. This kind of negative thinking does no good; in fact, it is as harmful as guilt or anger. What's done is done, to use an old cliché. You can't change facts. If you've had to lay off employees or let go of someone who wasn't a good fit with your team, you most assuredly had good reasons. You can't take back what happened. As long as you were respectful of your employees' feelings, took the time to listen and help them as best you could, you need to move on. Look forward, look at the bigger picture, and resolve to make better hiring or budget decisions from now on. Don't deny your negative emotions, but don't wallow in them either. Trust your own instincts, your gut feelings, and your business experience in making the right decisions. Yes, we all make mistakes. But no one has ever become more successful by succumbing to self-blame.

Worry and Stress There really is no such thing as a stress-free workplace. No matter whether you're running a huge corporation or a tiny start-up, if you're a restaurant manager, a roofer, or an accountant, at some time or another you're going to encounter stress and anxiety on the job, especially because at work you interact with coworkers, supervisors, vendors, clients—a whole mélange of different people every day. The stress and worry you experience is often related to your relationship with coworkers. When there is a disgruntled employee spreading gossip around the office or whining about assignments, or you've got a micromanaging boss breathing down your neck, you're going to feel stress, and stress affects each of us in different ways. Some people experience stress as a kind of constant, nagging anxiety, and others experience physical symptoms such as headaches or an upset stomach.

Since we know that stress is a given, what can we do to cope with it? Like managing your moods, in times of stress, it's key to concentrate on doing your job to the best of your ability and not get caught up in the rumor mill or others' negativity. Treat your workers and coworkers with respect and empathy, and take the time to develop good relationships with them.

A feeling of being out of control can cause stress, and anxiety. Being on top of everything is not possible, and by attempting to do so you will stress yourself and others. Prioritize your tasks and tackle them one at a time. If you're having trouble with a disgruntled employee, review the situation before you schedule a meeting. Go over in your head what you're going to say. During the conversation, listen to the worker before speaking. Work toward a tone of mutual problem solving. Confrontations are very stressful for some people, but you will feel better if you are prepared. Don't attack an employee on a personal level, and don't take professional criticism personally either.

Dysfunction and Disgruntlement as Social Phenomena

Lest you think that disgruntled employees are somehow unique to your workplace, it's important to put all of this in an overall social context. Today's political and social atmosphere contributes a good deal to unhappiness in the workplace.

CNN personality Lou Dobbs joined me on my radio show soon after his book *War on the Middle Class* was published. For Dobbs, it seems understandable that disgruntled employees plague workplaces, and he told me he blames much of corporate America for a government he sees business controlling.

"One of the expressions no one likes to hear is class warfare," said Dobbs. "But precisely that is what we're witnessing. The middle class in this country is the foundation of our nation. The American dream resides in our middle class." According to Dobbs, there is an obvious key to creating a strong middle class. "Public education is a great equalizer in our society. I'm a product of public education. I was born poor and I was raised poor, both of my parents worked, and had it not been for at least six public school teachers my life would have been quite different. I feel obligated to make people aware of what's happening to our public education system, what's happening to our middle class."

As to the cause of this erosion of the middle class, Dobbs is specific regarding his opinion. He points to "mad trade policies and truly, truly immoral business practices," and "political parties that have turned their backs on the largest group of voters in the country—the middle class."

His words remind me of the work of economic historians such as Joseph Schumpeter who posit that capitalism breeds the seeds of its own destruction. Major corporations depend on the middle class to support them by buying their products and when their company policies decimate the public's buying power business suffers.

Dobbs agreed and pointed to his cast of villains: "Importing illegal alien labor and exploiting that illegal labor, exporting middle-class jobs, destroying the manufacturing base of this country."

No question that the crisis faced by America's threatened middle class exacerbates the stress for employees and increases the likelihood of employees becoming disgruntled.

During our conversation, Dobbs insisted the U.S. government is "dysfunctional." He pointed to airport security and other post–September 11, 2001, Homeland Security Department expenditures as examples. The government, he said, "is not accomplishing the ends to which it was created. We are witnessing the expenditures of billions and billions of dollars in this country for which there is no return whatsoever. People are justifying their existence by pointing to the billions of dollars being wasted as if that were a reason for their existence. It is pathetic. And the national news media I think bears great responsibility for letting this charade be perpetuated."

Dobbs and I agreed that to fix the system—and hence to minimize the disgruntled employee syndrome—the greed of some capitalists must be moderated by government regulation. Dobbs, a skillful communicator of course, said it well. "There's no greater believer in free enterprise democracy than me. There's no greater believer in capitalism than me. There's also no one who's more adamantly opposed to unfettered capitalism than I am. To think [unfettered capitalism] is a philosophy is really nothing more than a rationalization for an absence of social responsibility."

Amen to that is my response.

Nurture Yourself: A Review of the Basics

In my first book, *The Dysfunctional Workplace*, I devote a section to self-nurturing, and I'll revisit it now. To me, self-nurturing is just another more touchy-feely term for mental hygiene. You might have guessed that touchy-feely is not my style, but still, self-nurturing is a valuable tool we all need to learn how to use, whether we're dealing with a dysfunctional workplace or a disgruntled employee. Self-nurturing is all about taking care of your own needs first. Unlike a child whose parents are watching out for him, making sure that he is nourished and that his physical and emotional needs are being met, adults need to be aware of their own needs. As a boss, you need this kind of self-awareness. If you stop taking care of yourself, let stress get the better of you, forget to eat properly, or engage in other kinds of mental hygiene neglect, your actions will affect not only you but your employees and the rest of your organization.

In addition to being aware of your need for nurture and healthy habits, during times of stress or disillusionment, don't pull back from your support network. There should always be trusted friends and family on whom you can rely for support. Think of it like emotional chicken soup. No matter how bad you feel, that bowl of steaming hot, comforting soup always helps, and so does talking with the special people in your life. You may think you're handling a crisis at work just fine, but your spouse or your child or your friend can see the worry and stress eating away at you. Listen to them. If they tell you to take some time off, relax, refocus your thinking temporarily—let them guide you. Just as a child relies on his or her parents to stay safe and nourished, so must you sometimes rely on others, even if you hate, as I do, to admit it.

Physical and Mental Well-Being

More and more companies these days are installing fitness centers, paying for employee gym memberships, and encouraging employees to sign up for classes such as yoga,

Pilates, and indoor cycling. This is all part of the work/life balance that we should seek for ourselves. There is a lot of truth in the idea that to be healthy mentally you have to take care of your physical health: your body. Probably the best way to combat workplace stress and negative thinking is exercise. The wonderful thing is that there are so many different kinds to choose from. It doesn't matter whether you train for a marathon, take walks after dinner, play tennis or squash with a buddy, or dance the tango—keeping yourself active will keep you better able to fight off disease and better able to deal with whatever nightmares come your way at work.

The other side of physical nurturing comes from nourishment, literally. We all know obesity is on the rise in this country, and a lot of it has to do with the typical American diet. Even if you are thin as a rail, if you're starting your day with a triple-mocha coffee drink and a doughnut, eating a burger for lunch, and polishing off a high-fat dinner supplemented by a couple of cocktails at night, you're not performing at your best. You're putting yourself at risk for ugly conditions like heart disease, diabetes, and cancer, not to mention obesity. If you think you don't have time to change your diet (or your exercise habits), find someone to help you. There are nutritionists, fitness coaches, and even Web sites that, for a small fee, will help you put together a healthful diet and exercise plan that works for you, no matter how busy you are. Think of it this way: aren't you encouraging your kids to eat healthfully and to stay active? The same advice applies to you.

It's also important to get enough sleep. Americans are suffering an epidemic of sleep deprivation, and much of it is self-inflicted. Most of us need at least seven or eight hours of uninterrupted sleep each night, yet few are getting it. We're staying up later and later, trying to catch up on work, relationships, TV, Internet networking, even video games, in the wee hours. Do yourself a favor: go to bed! It's been proven that people who are sleep deprived cannot concentrate or perform at work as well as those who are rested.

In my first book, I suggest journal writing as a self-nurturing technique. This may seem like a very touchy-feely thing to do, but it can really relax the mind. And maybe you'll end up with a bestselling memoir! By putting your thoughts in writing, you can think about your experiences and your emotions with some clarity. On paper, you can clarify and analyze your feelings and maybe jot down some goals or ideas that you're not yet ready to share at work. Journal writing offers the potential to put you in touch with yourself.

Take a Break Slow down and take breaks when things just get too crazy. It's easy to think, well, I'm in charge so I just need to keep working and pushing myself to solve all the problems and try to make everybody happy. That just doesn't work. The more overwhelmed you get, the less you'll be able to think clearly and make good decisions. Taking a breather and slowing down is a much healthier approach to coping with workplace stress and difficult employees. Take breaks. Maybe you just let someone go. Or maybe a performance appraisal didn't go well, and the employee exploded in your office. Unless you have a critical meeting or appointment, take five minutes and go outside. Talk a brisk walk around the block or through the parking lot. If the weather is bad, find a quiet room where you can sit and take some deep breaths. Try to calm yourself with some positive reinforcement, such as saying internally, *I can handle this. The team will work it out. Every problem has a solution.* Some people meditate or do a few stretches. What's important is to physically and mentally remove yourself from the workplace and catch your breath. Regular breaks throughout the day help refocus your energy where it's most needed.

Keep Yourself Motivated

"Today is the first day of the rest of your life." Yeah, I know, it may sound old and tired. But its meaning is obviously as true as true gets. Maintaining a positive attitude in the workplace goes for all employees, including supervisors and managers. In the face of a troubled economy and worries about everything from violence to terrorism at work, it is critical for you, as a boss, to stay motivated so that you can lead by example. How can you keep your staff motivated and energized if you're feeling burned-out? Remember that motivation comes from within; it comes from your mindset, your mood, and your energy level. If you are stalled in your career, you need to find a way to make life interesting again. Keep your eyes open for new challenges, opportunities, and responsibilities that will get your creative juices flowing. Some people are inspired by reading about great leaders, athletes, and businesspeople who have achieved success in their fields. Others stay motivated by developing strong relationships with peers and colleagues or by keeping in touch with a mentor. Still others take classes or workshops to fine-tune existing skills or build new skill sets. As you lead employees in meeting your organization's goals and objectives, don't forget your own goals. By reaching for them, you will inspire people to grow as well.

The "Flow" of Work

When people are happy in the workplace, and they are adjusted to work that they're doing, they're usually proud of the organization and its public persona. Even if you have what some may consider a menial job—say, you're a bus boy at a restaurant or a garbage collector—it's possible to do things well. You can strive for more efficiency and to develop a flow and rhythm to your work so you can enjoy what you're doing, create new methods, new techniques, new challenges, and be involved in the moment as you're working.

This idea of creativity and "flow" is a favorite of Mihaly Csikszentmihalyi, professor of Psychology and Management at the Drucker School of Management at Claremont University and author of the bestselling book, *Flow: The Psychology of Optimal Experience*. Dr. Csikszentmihalyi was a guest on my show, and he explained his theory on the correlation between self-actualization and well-being, a relationship that he has studied around the world for forty years.

"I have been intrigued, Peter," Dr. Csikszentmihalyi said, "ever since I was ten years old by how strange it is that many people who had a lot of money and power and status were really very unhappy. And how you could find people who were almost invisible in society and poor yet had a smile on their faces; they were helpful and had energy and enthusiasm. So I began to study artists, musicians, and athletes and other people over the last forty years, and I found one key to make people have a really good life. It's the ability to concentrate on what I call flow, which is immersion in a task that they're doing, kind of like complete concentration. This comes from art, music, athletics. But what was most interesting to me is how often it comes from work. Despite all the bad rap that work gets, in many cases even for assembly line people and for clerical and service workers, it can be a very exciting situation. I make the case that if you are responsible for other employees, either as a supervisor, a manager, or a CEO, that part of your responsibility, and also what will make your organization more profitable, is to make conditions for flow more readily available in your company."

When I asked Csikszentmihalyi how a manager goes about creating these conditions in the workplace, he didn't hesitate. "When the worker is clear as to what they have to do, moment by moment, not just at the end of the year, and he or she knows how to do the work piece by piece, they can see how it will add value to the company. They're not distracted by not knowing what you want to do further down the line. The clear goal is essential. Good feedback is essential. You have to know how well you're doing, either because someone tells you, or because you have a measurement built into the job that tells you whether you are actually achieving your goals. The other important component is that the task should be well matched to your ability. So, clear goals, immediate feedback, and matching your challenge and skills are essential. And then you want a situation where you don't get distracted, where you don't have too many interruptions or changes in goals."

Some jobs are better suited for producing flow than others. Yet, as Dr. Csikszentmihalyi says, even assembly-line work can be arranged so that rather than it being mindless, robotic, and repetitive, workers can be placed and moved on the line so that their performance matches the task, and they can be shifted from easier to more demanding tasks as time goes on so they continue to be productive and feel rewarded by the work.

Mihaly Csikszentmihalyi stresses that people can practice self-help in the workplace even if they're not getting the right kind of leadership, so they wind up with more job satisfaction. In his studies around the world, he has found that it is human nature, even in a multicultural setting, that when people are self-actualizing, they are much better adjusted than if they are not, and money makes less of a difference to job satisfaction than many think. Those people "in the flow" experience a state of well-being when they're totally engaged and when they feel they can make a difference. It's almost a Zen-like scenario, and endorphins or feel-good hormones kick in to trigger physiological responses.

When I asked him about these physical changes, Csikszentmihalyi told me, "It's hard to measure this neurology, but there are different endorphins at work: For example, you get flow from playing chess or you get flow from parachuting out of airplanes, and they are very different

activities. The feeling is still remarkably similar, but different parts of the brain get involved, and different hormones
may be at work. The brain is involved in everything we
do, but the important thing is to develop control over
your own attention so that you can produce this feeling
by yourself, and then the brain and the endorphins will
kick in. The brain knows what you want to do, and when
you are in a situation where you are interested in focusing, the brain will allow you to concentrate."

One of the hallmarks of flow is forgetting about time
and place. That's why even the lowest-paid workers who
do the grunt work of the company can still experience
this feeling. After my conversation with Dr. Csikszentmihalyi, I am more convinced than ever that while there
will always be disgruntled employees in every workplace,
the tools and definitions in this book will help managers achieve "flow" in their own workplaces, making them
and their employees happier, if not as ecstatic as a chess
champion or a skydiver.

The Disgruntled Employee: A Fact of Life in Today's Workplace

Remember, whether you are a boss or work for one, there
are always disgruntled employees in every workplace, big
or small. There are a myriad of reasons workers are dissatisfied. Some of them feel they aren't being recognized
for their efforts and want more acknowledgement and
approval from their bosses. Others are burned-out, stale,
and stalled, ready to move on but unsure how to do it.
Still others have all kinds of emotional baggage they've
brought into the workplace from negative personalities
to raging egos to being depressed or ill. Plenty complain
about micromanaging, controlling bosses and supervisors.
No matter what the cause, we all have to learn to deal
with the people at work who just don't want to be there.
We must be experienced, trained, aware "psychologists"
in the workplace in order to detect and mediate problems
when they come up.

If you're a supervisor, your task is difficult, and there's no sugarcoating just how hard it is to manage other people as well as your own moods and emotions. You have to maintain control of your mindset and feelings, and rely on logic and facts to make decisions regarding difficult workers. You need to be empathic and understanding. Showing your employees you care about their needs is as important as how much you pay them. Yet you can't be too lenient or your workers will walk all over you.

Learn to read the signs of the different types of disgruntled employees. Someone who's moody and withdrawn may have personal issues or may just be bored. One who is cynical and criticizes everyone and everything may be terribly insecure and need to report to a different supervisor, or get professional help. Take the time to get to know your employees, and it will be easier to figure out what makes them tick.

When you're meeting with a worker, block out all of those extraneous thoughts floating around in your head, and really, truly listen to what she has to say. You may be shocked at how differently you both look at the same issue. Each meeting that you have with an employee should be a session of mutual goal setting and problem solving. No one likes to be lectured. Listen to what the other person is saying—and this goes for your personal life as well—before you respond. Don't jump in with a prescribed solution; it may the complete opposite of what the employee needs.

Besides recognition, employees seek fairness in the workplace. Strive to quell rumors and gossip. Make a point of sharing company goals and missions with all employees. Explain each position with all of its responsibilities, in writing, and reward your workers for a job well done. Take time for a little fun, even during tough economic times. Treat your employees to special meals, outings, and training to keep skills fresh. Make sure your staff knows you value them above all else at work.

And don't forget to take care of yourself. If people are your greatest asset, remember, you are a person, too. If there is no one above you in the organization to applaud your achievement and success, reward yourself. Take a vacation with family or a friend. Don't be a workaholic. Don't let stress and anxiety take over your life. You owe it to yourself to embrace a healthy and balanced lifestyle, and you are setting an example for your employees. You are the positive role model. It's a heavy burden, but if you do it right, it just feels natural, like the way you want to live.

Some Final Tips on Maintaining a Positive Workplace

Cultivating a positive, nondisgruntled workplace is a continuing task.

- Be prepared to have a flexible mindset. Let go of your negative opinions about workers and focus on each of them as an individual who can bring something of value to your business.
- Communicate clearly what you expect from your employees, and make sure they have everything they need to do their jobs. Remember that as they grow in their positions and the company changes, their needs and goals will change.
- Share the organization's overall mission, values, and vision with all of your employees from top to bottom.
- Constantly ask for feedback from your workers. Be willing to listen to criticism, and make changes and improvements in the way that you do your job.
- Offer training and skills development whenever possible. Don't let workers get bored or stale; make sure they find their jobs interesting and challenging.
- Acknowledge and reward employees as often as you can, even if it's just a plaque on the wall or a lunch outside the office. Remember that recognition for all that they do is of utmost importance to most workers.

- Stay positive and focused on the long-term goals not only of the company but also of your employees. Work with them to continue to develop skills, and elicit their input for how to make yours a better organization.
- And never forget the Fun Factor!

appendix

Following are excerpts from Peter Morris's interviews with the Business Shrink's guests who are cited in the text of this book.

THE disgruntled EMPLOYEE

Peter Morris, the Business Shrink, talks to colleagues:

Barbara Ehrenreich »

Author of *Bait and Switch: The (Futile) Pursuit of the American Dream* and *Nickel and Dimed: On (Not) Getting By in America*

PETER MORRIS: Share with us your conclusions after studying the plight of the well-educated, well-behaved white-collar job force and what they thought they were getting and what they really get.

BARBARA EHRENREICH: I got into this because following the publication of *Nickel and Dimed: On (Not) Getting By in America* I got so many letters from people who are in really bad situations: no money, facing eviction, medical debts, and no insurance. I began to notice that a lot of these letters were coming from people who were educated—college degrees, sometimes Masters degrees. People who had held decent paying white-collar corporate jobs at one point and then lost those jobs in a layoff. In some cases they just sank forever out of the middle class. So that got me curious and concerned. As a way of investigating I went out to search for a white collar job myself and to see what the world of job searching is like for white-collar folks.

PM: What did you experience?

BE: I had set a rule for myself that I would do everything possible, that I would do my best. I would utilize coaches, I would go to networking events, I would read business advice books—whatever was out there, I tried it.

One thing that is very striking when you interact with these supposed helpers is that there's a culture of blaming the victim; you're always being told that you can get anywhere, you can achieve anything simply through your attitude, simply through your personality, simply through beaming out positive messages to the universe.

PM: How did you position yourself in terms of the job that you were looking for? Or did you change what you were looking for in each interview?

BE: No. I was consistently looking for a PR job because that's something that a lot of journalists end up doing. I wanted to look for a job that I knew that I could do well at. So I had a fake resume but the skills advertised in that resume are real.

PM: And you were disappointed because the coaches were saying just have the right attitude, as if that were enough.

BE: They also do useful things. They help you spiff up your resume but at quite a cost. You spend about $200 an hour for a career coach. I went to as many possible kinds of networking situations as I could both with other job seekers and getting out among employed business people. After ten months . . . well, I won't tell you how it ended up because I don't want to ruin the book for you. But you sure don't get a lot.

PM: Did you apply nationally or just in one city?

BE: Nationally. That was another part of my framework; that I would go anywhere for an interview or for a job, if it were offered.

I don't think my experience is that unusual, because I certainly met a lot of jobseekers who'd been looking for one year or more and who had far more contacts than I did and real resumes, not fake ones, and had experience in the corporate world, which I lacked. Right now, 44 percent of the long-term unemployed in the United States are white-collar people.

First people who've lost their jobs just try to cut back on expenses and job search as diligently as they can. They may have to sell their house. They may have to auction their goods off on eBay. They keep on trying but eventually they probably say, "Well, I'm going to have to take any job." And then you're talking at seven, eight, nine dollars an hour at a place like Wal-Mart or another big-box store.

PM: Perhaps the bait and switch mentioned in your title started over the last twenty years as the new generation grew up and paid for high-priced education and were fed false expectations of what a job and an education will get you.

BE: I think you're right, Peter. Business is the most popular major on American college campuses. It's not because people love this subject so much compared to say poetry

or philosophy, but because the promise is there of a
secure income, possibly even wealth.

Something has really changed in the last decade and
a half in this country; corporate jobs offer very little stability anymore.

We haven't talked enough in this country about the
psychological consequences of that. Here you do everything right; you play by the rules, you conform and
dress in manner and go get the right degrees and you do
a good job, that's no guarantee of anything.

We have in this country very little by way of social
supports for people who lose their jobs or fall into pov-
erty. We don't have universal health insurance.

PM: Share with us two or three other manifestly absent social
supports that you think if they were installed through
public pressure, legislation, or writings of people like
you who really have a great following that would make
a difference?

BE: Universal health insurance is an obvious thing. It might
have made sense thirty years ago even to tie one's health
insurance to one's job, but when people just have so
many more jobs, thing are different. You can't have
something as basic as health insurance attached to jobs.
Another thing we need is much more generous and
long-term kinds of unemployment compensation. Right
now it runs out in most states after six months.

PM: That makes a lot of sense. I think that one of the important things is that we understand the economics of these
structural changes. Contrary to popular conception,
they're not just costs that don't have a return on investment. They have a return on investment to the individuals and to society. And if people bother to quantify them
they'd find out that that kind of universal health insurance actually would probably be a dividend to society,
even economically.

Ben Dattner »

Expert on psychological profiling in the workplace

PETER MORRIS: The psychological test is getting more pervasive all the time in the workplace.

BEN DATTNER: Absolutely. I think as companies realize that people are their only enduring source of competitive advantage, they're realizing that in order to compete they really have to pick trained staff and the right people.

PM: According to what you've said, a lot of the people who administer these tests are misapplying them. Why is that?

BD: There are two major uses for these kinds of tests. The first one is for selection, both into companies and then once within companies into higher level or different roles. The second use for these tests is in order to assess and develop employees, to develop their capabilities. These tests are increasingly popular for both uses. But companies often don't know what the proper use for these tests are, either for selection or development.

PM: It seems to me that the real benefit lies in the second-level tests that help integrate people for their highest and best use in the corporate society.

BD: That's very true. I think it's important to keep in mind that these tests not only assess intellectual ability, but they also assess personality fit.

PM: As you well know, intellectual ability and the assessment of the intellect is just at the beginning of the frontiers of science. Most scientists will tell you that we know very little about the intellect and so consequently the thing that we're probably better capable of assessing is human interaction and problem solving: how do people deal with stress, how do they deal with pressure from above, peer pressure, how do they deal with crises, how do they deal with competition and conflict?

BD: Exactly right.

PM: I notice in your background, Ben, that your doctoral dissertation studied the relationship between narcissism and fairness in the workplace. Can you talk about that?

BD: Narcissism is something that unfortunately is a pervasive part of organizations. And as much as we like to believe some of the latest thinking and latest bestsellers about emotional intelligence or the triumph of humility in the workplace, unfortunately all of us know organizations and very successful executives who display extreme narcissistic tendencies.

PM: And that tends to get in the way of team spirit, corporate core values and culture, and can lead to a demoralized work force who are not recognized in their own right for their contribution.

BD: Absolutely. Narcissism isn't necessarily all bad. Narcissism can be good under the right circumstances, and if managed in the correct way, narcissists can be skilled communicators, they can be brilliant visionaries, they can be brilliant technologists and financial professionals. So it's important not to rule them out simply because they may not be the best people to work on a team or the most fun people to share a suite of offices with.

PM: I agree that a narcissist can often be the brilliant leader around which a company can be built. I distinguish between what I call a "vertical leader" and a "horizontal leader." A vertical leader is one who may be more attuned to hierarchy and to motivation and to rank and to order and to boundaries and to cooperation and flow of work. Where a horizontal leader can be brilliant as well as narcissistic because he leads by example.

BD: Absolutely. Unfortunately narcissists often surround themselves with executives who confirm their visions of the world and who are not bold enough to push back.

It also depends on circumstances. Somebody who's very effective at founding an organization from an entrepreneurial perspective might not be nearly as effective when more influence and bureaucratic systems and structures need to be put in place.

PM: Conversely, if a narcissist maintains a positive self-image, the people working with the narcissist are able to be supportive and feel like they're in a good environment.

BD: Exactly. If you believe that you work for a powerful, brilliant, charismatic leader, that also makes you feel more valued because you're part of a high status organization.

Narcissists split the world into people who are great and people who are unworthy. He or she might be extremely supportive and even caring to the people in the in-group and quite outrageous and exploitative to the people in the out-group.

PM: Tell us a little bit about cases where a different result in the psychological test can result from whether it's looked at from a personality side or from a contextual side.

BD: That often happens. For example I'm an executive coach. I'm often brought in by a manager who says his employee needs coaching. The employee's problem is that he doesn't work well on a team, he's not assertive enough, he's not organized enough. Before we start this coaching process I'll suggest I interview people, just to try to get a read on what's going on. Often what you can find out is that the employee is being accused of not being assertive enough because the boss is domineering or bulldozes the employee and doesn't give him or her an opportunity to be assertive.

A much better predictor of how somebody's going to act is the role that the person performs in the organization rather than his or her personality. Certainly personality attributes lead all of us to find our ways to professions where there's a fit between some of our natural preferences and the demands of the job. However, research shows that when people move from research and development into sales for example, suddenly they become much more extroverted even if their natural preference is not to be extroverted.

David Sirota »

Author of *The Enthusiastic Employee:
How Companies Profit by Giving Workers What They Want*

PETER MORRIS: It's a provocative title your book has: how companies will profit by giving the workers what they want. And of course that sounds counterintuitive doesn't it?

DAVID SIROTA: Sounds loony. In fact, it sounds like the road to bankruptcy, but it's a path to business success.

PM: What are these factors of worker motivation? Can you give examples of these factors being applied successfully?

DS: Sure. Through our research we identified three major goals of employees. The first we call equity: to be treated fairly, paid benefits and so on. The second we call achievement and it focuses on being proud of what they do and proud of the organization. And third, camaraderie; this is very, very important to people at the workplace who have coworkers with whom they cooperate, who are friendly, with whom they enjoy working. When those three goals are satisfied you have an enthusiastic work force.

Let's take equity, to be treated fairly. A key element of that is job security. What's happened over the last two or three decades as a reaction to paternalistic management of the past is that to meet highly competitive conditions, employers have begun to treat workers almost as interchangeable objects. I don't mean that they're cruel. But this is treating workers almost indifferently. The sentiment is, we owe nothing more to you than that paycheck. Loyalty doesn't count.

A consequence of that is indifferent employees. The reason I chose that word "enthusiastic" for my titles is we're not just talking about happiness here, we're talking about people who are really enthusiastic about their work, enthusiastic about their employer, really engaged and trying to do more than what they were hired to do, the people who go out of their way.

I just finished some work with the Mayo Clinic. In many, many healthcare organizations you find all kinds of difficulties in the treatment of people. A lot of that has to do with the work force. The assumption of the Mayo Clinic is that the way patients are treated will depend on how their employees are treated. So they do all kinds of things for their employees. For example, if they have surplus employees and new technology, they just don't lay people off; first they try to find other work for them in the institution.

PM: That's very good. And it's important to make sure people are recognized for their work, that they're challenged, that they're mentored.

DS: And that they're working for a company of which they can be proud. A company that achieves. Not just achieves in a financial sense, but produces a quality product. The majority of workers don't want to produce garbage.

PM: On the camaraderie side I assume that there are a series of interactions both on the business side and the social side?

DS: Very much so in these organizations. About fifteen percent of the companies of the organizations that we have studied I would classify as having enthusiastic work forces. So it's not a large number.

PM: What about some of the powerfully productive companies like Microsoft and Google, which are famous for team structure?

DS: They're very team oriented. Take Southwest Airlines. You see how passengers are treated on a Southwest Airlines flight compared to other airlines. They are treated enthusiastically by enthusiastic employees. Employees in fact who are treated that way, the way I've described, by the organization.

That's what I mean. Give workers what they want— and by and large workers are quite reasonable in what they want. When you ask people are you satisfied with your pay, if they feel that they're paid competitively they say, yes, I'm satisfied with my pay.

We have all kinds of data in our book to show the relationship between how you treat people, and the overall performance of the business. We have for example the relationship between stock market performance and the treatment of people and their morale. And there's a very, very strong correlation.

PM: David, clear up one inconsistency for me, please. You said there's only fifteen percent of the companies that have an enthusiastic work force but it sounds like a larger percentage of companies have generally good morale.

DS: I'd say there are four levels of morale: enthusiasm, which I've just described, people who really care about an organization, feel it's a great place; moderately satisfied is the second level; indifference is the third level; and anger is the fourth level. Unfortunately only a small percentage of companies have enthusiastic work forces and outstanding business performance.

PM: What about indifferent employees?

DS: An indifferent employee does the work you asked him to do. Doesn't do more. What happens, of course, is that indifferent employees can treat customers indifferently.

PM: David, in understanding what it takes to have an enthusiastic or even moderately satisfied work force, we've discussed equity, achievement, and the camaraderie. How do people maintain that relationship with their companies in today's world of outsourcing, slashing benefits, and other globalization trends?

DS: That's a very good question. Is this practical in today's world? Let's go back to the job security issue. The point of that is not that you can guarantee lifetime employment to people. If there are good business reasons to downsize in some way, workers want to know that their needs are somewhere high on the list of what management considers in making those decisions.

PM: Sometimes harsh realities set in and sometimes disappointments are inevitable. But if the communication is sincere and bilateral and meaningful, there are tradeoffs, and efforts are made; then at least that cushions the blow and the relationship can be maintained.

DS: Absolutely. When there's a good business case and you communicate it clearly to people. The overall majority of people are reasonable and they understand business and business conditions.

PM: Your book shows that the key question is not how to motivate employees, but how to sustain the motivation employees naturally bring to their jobs.

DS: Right. That's a very important point. When you divide our data by how long people have worked there, you find morale at the beginning of employment is very high in every company.

PM: The honeymoon stage.

DS: Yes, but in those fifteen percent the honeymoon lasts throughout their career.

Derrick Neufeld»

Professor at the Business School
of the University of Western Ontario

PETER MORRIS: You point out the companies are having to grapple with the issues of workers working from off-site and the consequences of this in terms of how to monitor time and productivity.

DERRICK NEUFELD: Yeah, I've done a fair bit of research in this area. I think the compelling reasons for wanting to work at home or work remotely are there in spades. Companies see potential benefits in terms of saving money, saving time, having more satisfied employees, and employees find it also very enticing in terms of having flexibility and the ability to spend more time with their family.

PM: There are a number of industries that have used this quite beneficially: telemarketing industries, airlines reservations . . . you could probably come up with a hundred more.

DN: Sure. This is nothing new in terms of management theory, is it? We all know that the enlightened manager is not one who watches the employee minute by minute. Rather, he sets some objectives with the individual, and the idea is let's look at the quality and productivity at the end of the week or the month or the project.

PM: Some companies are always comparing employees who are telecommuting to employees who are in the office. I wonder, if they're making those comparisons all the time then why don't they just evaluate productivity, quantity and quality and deliverables?

DN: I think a lot of times what happens at the senior levels of larger organizations is the senior folks take a look at the metrics, the balance sheet of whether telework makes sense, and they conclude yes it does. They put together a fantastic program, and on paper it all looks great. But by the time it dribbles down through the ranks of the organization and hits the level of middle management something else happens. At that level the

manager may say, no. Because is Bob going to be trust-
worthy if I let him work from home? I don't know if
he's going to get his work done. I better keep him here
so that I can watch his output.

PM: I think also we need to be aware of what situations are
suited to telecommuting and which aren't. In certain
jobs, especially middle level and above, there is no substitute for at least some regularized time frame of physical contact and physical appearance.

DN: Yeah, that water cooler kind of inner action can kind
of disappear. In fact I think the most successful telecommuting programs out there are the ones where the
person is at home or off campus for maybe one to three
days per week, but is still, every week, she is still spending a day or two, at least, at the office. Your other point
about what situations and what personalities are suitable
is something that requires a lot of thought. Not letting
certain folks go home because this wouldn't likely work
for them very well can make sense. They've got young
kids at home or they live in a tiny apartment, and they
don't have the room to really spread out.

PM: I think a lot more work needs to be done in figuring
out the type of assignments that lend themselves to this
off-campus work and telecommuting and the type of
manager who's most able to maximize the output and
to monitor the situation.

DN: Exactly. If we're not leading by example, if we're not
stimulating the people at the next level in the organization to really step out and to start managing and lead in
new ways, we may get kind of stuck in very short-term
thinking.

Glenn Shepard »

Author of *How to Manage Problem Employees* and
How to Make Performance Evaluations Really Work

PETER MORRIS: Welcome Glenn. Tell us, how do you manage a disgruntled employee?

GLENN SHEPARD: The first thing that I do is hold the manager accountable. Too many managers today are scared of confronting problem employees, and they make the situation worse when they do that.

PM: How should they confront a problem employee?

GS: Attack the issue when it's still a molehill instead of a mountain and don't avoid or ignore the little problems. For example the employee who constantly comes to work five minutes late—that's not the problem, that's a symptom that you have a problem employee who doesn't respect the boundaries.

PM: When the employee doesn't heed the warnings, what do you do?

GS: You hold them accountable. The big problem we have today with such low unemployment is that managers are scared to death they're going to lose an employee if they actually hold them accountable.

PM: But it's also easier to reach out and network for other candidates, easier than it was in the past when information wasn't so targeted and abundant.

GS: What I always tell managers is, as long as you're being reasonable you don't run off good employees that way. In fact, it's allowing the bad employee to get away with murder that will cause you to lose the other good employees, who'll go look for a better run organization to work for.

PM: I think that people are anxious more today than ever before because everything is so unsettled and changing fast. But that's certainly not a reason for an employee to not have boundaries and not to be professional.

GS: I agree a hundred percent. We see companies laying off thousands of people but you can find a job somewhere if you really want to work today.

PM: Can you give examples of a firm that's successfully implemented your advice?

GS: Yes. Yesterday I spoke to a conference for a company that employs registered nurses. RNs are in high demand right now. This company goes into the homes of patients who are in their latter years, so they employ lots of nurses. One lady from Missouri who is a nurse manager had attended my seminar a couple years ago. She just got all fired up and went back, she got rid of some problem employees, and she laid down the law. She said yesterday, you know, it's like a whole new organization. People want to work for us now because I finally stepped up to the plate and became the manager I needed to be.

PM: Well that means then that some heads have to roll often in order to set the precedent.

GS: I hope that the heads don't roll, but that's up to the employee not the manager. When a manager comes in and says, okay, there's a new sheriff in town. You can't come to work late. You can't just call in sick. You're going to have to play by the rules. People either shape up or they ship out, it's their call.

PM: We live in such a litigious environment that sometimes people are also afraid of disciplining an unruly or disgruntled employee or an underperforming one because of fear of legal reprisal.

GS: That's something that managers should keep in mind. Make sure that you document everything you do, and be able to prove that you were fair and consistent in how you treated people. That's the only defense you can have in today's litigious environment. But by not disciplining or holding problem employees accountable you could also have legal problems.

PM: If you have a tough conversation, isn't it often good to have someone else in the room?

GS: Absolutely. Some companies have policies that managers cannot even have conversations until they have a witness, especially concerning sexual harassment.

PM: I would think in any evaluations that could lead to tough consequences it's good to have somebody else there.

GS: Absolutely. And this is why it's so important for managers to be proactive. On performance evaluations, you can't be a softie who's scared to give someone low scores if that's what they deserve. We shouldn't wait until it becomes a disciplinary conversation to confront the employee.

PM: Now, Glenn, you characterize the different generations and their attitudes in the workplace. You call the generation born right after World War II the "silent generation"; people who were born between 1925 and 1946.

GS: Yes.

PM: They valued discipline, duty, delay gratification, loyalty. Then the Baby Boomers were born between 1947 and 1959. They rebel against family life and value self-gratification. Now Gen X, Generation X, from 1962 to 1984, they're cynical and they don't work for work itself. Would you say they resent working after normal hours?

GS: They see staying after five o'clock as a sign of weakness or inefficiency. Baby boomers sometimes see the employee who hits the door at five o'clock as disloyal.

PM: And then Generation Next, who are now twenty-three years old or so, you say that they are the "I want it now" generation?

GS: Sure, because they've grown up with instant gratification over the Internet or anything else. So they're having a tough time adapting to the work world.

PM: Is that going to be a tough group to discipline?

GS: Well, the good part about that group is they're not as rebellious and independent as some of their predecessors. On the other hand, they have a group-think mentality. For example, there was a study that was released in *USA Today* last week that says 44 percent of the people who responded don't think that how they dress affects their job and their promotions.

PM: That's a Silicon Valley attribute, isn't it?

GS: Very much so, which unfortunately applies everywhere in America. You see people showing up for job interviews wearing flip-flops now.

PM: You prefer performance bonuses at the end of the year rather than raises that escalate people's sense of entitlement unrealistically, don't you?

GS: Absolutely. Everything should be as close to merit-base pay as possible. It's based on a very simple principle of psychology: If you reward good behavior and punish bad behavior people will behave well.

Lou Dobbs »

CNN commentator, author of *War on the Middle Class:
How the Government, Big Business, and Special Interest Groups Are
Waging War on the American Dream and How to Fight Back*

PETER MORRIS: I'm fascinated by what you've written in the *War on the Middle Class*.

LOU DOBBS: Both political parties, as I write in the book, are under the sway and domain of corporate America right now. You really cannot be a partisan and be aligned with one party and be correct, in my judgment, about the national interests and the common good.

PM: You can't be a problem solver if you're an ideologue. Tell me what's the premise of your book.

LD: Straightforwardly, there's a war against our middle class. This is class warfare. Warren Buffet said that "this is outright class warfare, and my class is winning." It's absolutely true. The middle class in this country is the foundation of our nation. The American dream resides in our middle class. And public education is a great equalizer in our society. I'm a product of public education. I can tell you straightforwardly I was born poor and I was raised poor, both of my parents work, and had it not been for at least six public school teachers my life would have been quite different. I feel obligated to ensure as best I can that people are aware of what's happening to our public education system, what's happening to our middle class, whether it be mad trade policies and truly immoral business practices, or whether it be political parties that have turned their backs on the largest group of voters in the country—the middle class.

PM: I don't want to put words in your mouth, but what I'm hearing is that these major corporations which depend on the middle class to support them by buying their product, are pressing down on them at the same time.

LD: Absolutely. Importing, illegal alien labor and exploiting that illegal labor, exporting middle-class jobs, destroying the manufacturing base of this country.

PM: Let's address how to restrict or limit inflow of immigrant labor and what does that mean. Lou, you're not saying you want to kick out the people who are here. It sounds as if more you want to reduce the inflow.

LD: No, actually I don't even want to do that. It is a partisan game that's being played in Washington, this so-called comprehensive immigration reform. It is nothing more than a fig leaf for further inaction and avoidance of policy decisions. You have literally hundreds of thousands of people marching on May 1. Illegal aliens and their supporters demanding rights. That crystallizes as clearly as it can in anyone's mind the fact that we have policy upside down in this country. We cannot reform immigration law, Peter, if we cannot control immigration. And we cannot control immigration if we do not control our borders and our ports. Until we secure our borders and are in charge of our ports and capable of inspecting cargo, 95 percent of which is now un-inspected, we are whistling in the dark.

PM: But how do we secure our borders in a cost-effective way and in a humane way?

LD: We're spending $30 billion plus on a homeland security department that neither is inspecting cargo nor securing our borders. Homeland security, we have to agree, is nothing but a sham. We have to secure that border. That means whether it's boots on the ground, whether it's fences, we have to control our borders. And we have to control our ports. Otherwise this government continues to perpetrate a fraud on the American people.

The fact is that we're letting public relations and perception be the watchwords of government administration. Our government is dysfunctional. It's not accomplishing the ends to which it was created. Ah, we are witnessing the expenditures of billions and billions of dollars in this country.

PM: For no return.

LD: For which there is no return whatsoever.

The national news media, by the way, I think bears great responsibility for letting this charade be perpetuated.

Eight major media corporations control most of the media in this country, whether on the Internet or whether in television or radio. We have allowed ourselves to be relegated to he says/she says journalism rather than digging for the facts and for the truth. We've been overwhelmed in this country by the orthodoxies and the elites who manipulate them. That sounds Orwellian, and frankly the environment we find ourselves in is frighteningly Orwellian.

PM: When Henry Ford was around and we were egalitarian, we used mass production and mass marketing to create a middle class, and now we're the ones with the huge gap between the rich and the poor.

LD: Exactly. Henry Ford paid his employees when he began his assembly lines two and a half times more than the prevailing wage. Asked why he did this, Henry Ford said, "Because I want my employees to be able to buy the products they create." What an idea! Meanwhile we have watched wages stagnate in this country for thirty years.

PM: Lou I think the real bottom line here is that because of globalization some of these major international multinational corporations are basically arbitraging away from our worker base . . .

LD: Absolutely.

PM: . . . using outsourced cheaper labor, using benefits of capital gain and other manipulations to increase their profit while not engaging the middle class reciprocally in job opportunities and in benefits.

LD: You're exactly right. The Trade Adjustment Act provides for training on jobs lost to international trade. The fact is there isn't enough money available from that program to train anywhere near the number of people who've lost their jobs or have been regulated to far lower paying jobs when they did lose them to outsourcing and to international trade.

The other issue is, what in the world are we training people for? This economy generated 22 million jobs during the 1990s. And we immediately lost 5 million as this new century began. We did so not because American workers were less productive, less intelligent, but rather because we adopted new business practices that were absolutely deleterious to the middle class. The war on the middle class starts with trade policy. Because it's our border. It begins with illegal immigration. It then goes to our public education system, which is the great equalizer for this society. These companies are not investing in their communities or their employees. The fact is we put our middle class in direct competition with the cheapest labor in the world. No amount of training, no amount of education can change the world for them if we permit that.

You do not have to have a college degree in this country to enjoy the American dream. The Constitution begins, "We the people . . ." We are a nation dedicated to equality, equal educational opportunity, and equal economic opportunity. Not everyone will succeed. Not everyone will get lucky. But everyone should have the same opportunity to develop their God-given gifts, to work hard and to achieve the American dream.

PM: What are some of the things to do to be more protective of the middle class?

LD: We should be following the same trade policies as our trading partners. Our trade policies should be reciprocal, they should be mutual, and they should be balanced. The fact that we have not followed a balanced trading relationship for thirty consecutive years is, is bankrupting the nation.

Become an Independent. Become unaffiliated and push back against these political parties that are spending $2 billion to lobby 536 people in Washington, D.C.

I lay out a number of solutions in *War on the Middle Class* to education, to the issue of healthcare. But public education first and foremost requires a national policy.

PM: What I think is fascinating about your approach is that we're living in a world with too many choices. Crises are what I call disseminated. We're anesthetized by a million pinpricks. Right now it's one hit, one nick here, a nick there, you go to education, you look at taxes, you look at trade, you look at unemployment, you look at the lack of a comprehensive plan to provide healthcare for Americans . . .

LD: Right.

PM: . . . and each one of them you can debate and then have attention deficit disorder and go to the next one. But nobody's putting the whole thing together. You're attempting to put the thing into one context.

LD: And in *War on the Middle Class* I try to do exactly that. And based on early response I think I've done fairly well. It's not just a book with me it's a manifesto.

Louis Uchitelle»

PETER MORRIS: I wanted to ask you before we begin, in your definition of layoffs does that include firing on the merits or is this more like tightening the belt?

LOUIS UCHITELLE: This is not firing on the merits; that's always been part of the system and that will go on as it always has. People can be fired because they don't measure up. This is about a phenomenon that's about thirty years old that's just layoffs for business reasons. Many of them are not justified, and that's the problem.

PM: My guess is there may be five to seven percent of that number that would be disguised firings on the merits.

LU: Maybe I shouldn't use the words "not justified." I should say unnecessary or beyond what's necessary. We so acquiesce to layoffs that we've gone beyond what's necessary. As for the numbers, the government reports on worker displacement, as they call it. It comes out to about 4 percent of the nation's fulltime workers every year. That's what we can count. If you counted in the disguised layoffs that often come in the form of forced retirements, buyouts, forcing people to shift to an outsourcing company, then you get up to about 7 percent of fulltime workers every year. That's a big percentage.

PM: That certainly is. In your mind are all of the layoffs a function of the outsourcing and the globalization or is this a trend that goes beyond all of that?

LU: The portion of the layoffs attributable to companies going overseas is a small part of it. I would say that most of it is taking place because it has become the easiest means of reducing labor costs. But what we have then is a lot of unmeasured costs, particularly psychological damage. What you're telling people in effect is that they don't have value.

I began to run into that as I did my reporting for this book. I went to psychiatrists and psychologists, and they said, yes, we see it all the time, this damage to self-esteem. Never mind the unemployment part of it. Most people who are laid off aren't unemployed for very long; they get other jobs. It's the damage to your mental health by being told that you don't have value. We reinforce it by telling people, look, it's just a matter of education and retraining. You're in a job that doesn't have value to our global economy, our high-tech economy. Get yourself educated and retrained. People do that or try to do it, and then they don't get jobs that pay as well as the jobs they lost. Society says, it's your fault, it's not our fault. You didn't do the retraining right or you didn't go to the right place.

PM: What should be done about this problem? Sounds like a pernicious negative cycle.

LU: My book is an attempt to point out that we once were a country that built job security over a number of decades. Management itself was a big part of the construction of job security. It worked very well starting in the late nineteenth century. The government then came in during the Depression and furthered job security with labor laws. Unions came in to supplement it. But it was a uniquely American form of job security that worked for both management and labor. There were plenty of strikes and disputes, but when the strikes were over the jobs were still there.

All that was broken. We went step by step, from 1977 to 1997, dismantling this system. In the process we forgot what existed. What I hope to do with this book is to reawaken in people a sense of alternatives and therefore a debate.

That's not to stop layoffs. We do live in a much different world than we did in the sixties and our earlier history. But it is to limit layoffs. Instead of laying off ten people, you could have gotten by with laying off seven people. Boeing for example working with its plant workers in Seattle, said to them during one contract negotiation, look, we might have to cut labor costs, but before we do it, we agree to let you, the workers, figure out another way to reduce that labor cost. And the workers often did find ways to do it.

The most efficient companies in this country often turn out to be the companies that do not engage in layoffs.

Mal Warwick »

Author of *Values-Driven Business*

PETER MORRIS: I often say it's great to be able to do good and make good at the same time. I think that's the dream of many of us entrepreneurs as well as corporate executives but sometimes it's easier said than done. What's your formula for making those two goals coexist peacefully and synergistically in a company?

MAL WARWICK: Well it's not a formula exactly but I think it is an approach. We very consciously chose the title *Values-Driven Business* for our book because the approach requires that you take stock at the outset of what your values are, what's most important to you in the world. Take into account how you can live a life that promises to give you fulfillment through your business and exercise those values in the process.

PM: What's a good example of a business that's achieved that?

MW: Let me talk about a little company in Berkeley, California, called Clif Bar. It was founded back in the early nineties by a very enthusiastic and accomplished mountain biker, named Gary Erickson. Gary was out biking one day and he was stoking up with energy bars and he was just at the breaking point. They were so distasteful to him, he said there's got to be a better way.

He went home, and he and his wife went into his mother's kitchen. They got to work, and for months they fooled around with recipes in that kitchen until they came up with a good-tasting energy bar that was nutritious and had all the natural goodness that he thought was very important to make the product appealing to thousands of people who need extra bursts of energy.

The company thrived because Gary and his wife built it around their personal values of appreciating their employees, not as workers but virtually as partners: by sharing the benefits that came from the business, by instituting environmental polices that made their employees feel good and help gain them extra market share because they were a company that was really doing good in the world. By the late nineties the company was thriving. Sales over $100 million.

Gary and his then-partner received an offer for the company of $120 million. Now, Gary could have just walked away, as his partner wanted to do, with $60 million in his pocket and said good-bye to his employees and to his company. But at the final hour he decided to say no to the offer. He's still paying off his partner. But the company is in his hands. He's running it. He's continued to expand the environmentally positive programs that they've instituted. They've built a new facility with a tremendous gym and fitness facility. They have an active program of supporting worthy nonprofit organizations such as the Breast Cancer Fund. Not just with money, although they do give a lot of money, but also by using the opportunity to recruit their employees for volunteer opportunities and by using the company's facilities and its promotional efforts to support the work of that and a number of other worthy nonprofit organizations.

PM: That's a great example. How do we preserve this?

MW: Well, you've certainly put your finger on what is probably the leading issue in the community of companies that attempt to practice socially responsible business. There was the sale recently of The Body Shop. Anita Roddick's company was founded in the mid-seventies and was one of the early icons in the socially responsible business movement. The Body Shop was sold to L'Oreal, a French company, and there is considerable speculation in the British business press that the French and the English once again will prove that they can't get along with each other and that the merger will not succeed. But at any rate that's the direction that has gone. And just a couple of weeks ago Tom's of Maine, an even earlier example of the venturesome and innovative efforts to bring values to bear in running a business, was sold to Colgate-Palmolive.

Martin Yate»

Author of *Knock 'Em Dead: The Ultimate Job Search Guide*

PETER MORRIS: Good to have you with us. What are these practical tips for landing a killer job?

MARTIN YATE: You have a book in front of you that's over 300 pages, that's in print all around the world in many different languages, that we've been adding to for twenty-one years. So it's a whole encyclopedia of tactics depending on your situation.

PM: A subset of what you're involved with is disgruntled employees who want to change jobs.

MY: I've had a career coaching practice for many years, and I have people coming to me all the time. They want to change jobs, and they want to get a promotion because no one appreciates them there and they're not growing. Now, sometimes that is true, and in the real world we do move if we've been in a job for a number of years and we haven't had significant pay increases, significant promotions. Chances are we have been stereotyped, categorized, and pigeonholed. Sometimes a change helps. But sometimes we don't have to make the move. I think everyone listening tonight recognizes that in their department, their company, there's always an inner circle and an outer circle. And we all know which part of that circle we belong to. If we're part of the outer circle maybe we want to try to get at the inner circle before making the decision to move. It might save having to make the move.

PM: What are some of the areas that get employees disgruntled and what are some of the ways to deal with them?

MY: There's as many days in the year as the ways we can get disgruntled. I think very often employees can feel left out of things: there are some people who get the plum assignments, who get the special projects, who get the biggest raises, who get the promotions. Those are the guys who are in the inner circle.

Think of an analogy: A fire starts in the corner of the office. There's ten of us in the department, one guy calls the fire department and one the security. Another guy gets the sand bucket. Another guy gets the extinguisher. Two more stand and point and say, hey, look guys, there's a fire in the corner of the office. And the other four say, hey, let's take off and have a break while those idiots put out the fire.

If you're not one of the ones who is making a difference with your presence it's probably through making the wrong alliances that you became part of that outer circle. So it's not going to help you to change jobs, because you can wind up in the outer circle at the new job.

What we need to do is say, hey, wait a minute. Maybe I can change some things I do. Maybe I can get to be a member of this inner circle in which case I'll be doing better with this company. I've got a better chance of growing here.

PM: So sometimes we have to take responsibility for our own plight and do something about it within the company that we're at.

MY: We live in a world where we really have to take responsibility for ourselves. Many of us grew up in a world where it was find a job, start at the bottom, hang on with ten fingers, ten toes, and if you lose a finger, hang on with nine because you're going to be rewarded with a growing career and long-term employment. We know that's not the truth anymore. We stay on jobs about four years. We're off somewhere in the middle of about a half century work life, and we're going to have three or more distinct careers in that time. That's nine job changes within careers, three major job changes. Boy, I've *got* to take responsibility for things.

PM: When the idea of going into the inner circle comes to mind, I think of two very distinct aspects of that: one is providing the right work product in front of the right supervisors, peers, team; and the other part of it, which relates to the social aspect. If some people aren't very social, can they still get into the inner circle?

MY: I think that there are politics in every company in every industry. But politics and being a member of the inner circle does not expand to doing brown nose things. The people who really make things happen in a company aren't always the people who have the time to do the schmoozing.

PM: Well that's reassuring.

MY: Networking is very important in this modern world. And people talk about networking very glibly. But here's a piece of advice that will help. It's probably the best thing anyone listening tonight can do for their career, apart from buying *Knock 'em Dead*. That's to become connected to your profession. Take out a membership in a professional association.

You get to go to the monthly meetings and meet and know and be known by the best-connected, most committed people in your profession in your area. When you are getting ready to make a change in your career, you've got the membership database or membership directory.

PM: That's a very good point. In the era of these frequent employee turnovers how do employers best retain good people?

MY: First rule of management, last rule of management, is get work done through others. Which means if you don't hire them effectively in the first place you will never manage them productively in the second place, and the good people won't stay with you.

Mihaly Csikszentmihalyi »

Professor of Psychology and Management at the Drucker School of
Management, Claremont Graduate University

PETER MORRIS: I can't tell you how many people I've spoken
to over the last couple of years on my radio show who
attempt to prove positive correlation between wealth
and happiness. I constantly put your teachings in front
of them. You really have pioneered in understanding the
correlation between self-actualization and well-being.
And that has probably broader implications today for
society and for health and for the work force interna-
tionally than ever before. Perhaps you could share that
with the audience.

MIHALY CSIKSZENTMIHALYI: Well it is, Peter. I mean I have been
intrigued for many years, ever since I was ten years old,
by how strange it was that many people who had a lot
of money, power, prestige, and status were very unhappy.
I've also been intrigued by how you could find people
who were almost invisible in society and poor who had
a smile on their faces. They were helpful, and they had
energy and enthusiasm. So I got to wonder about what
makes people able to derive enjoyment from their life
without necessarily having to accumulate a lot of material benefits and rewards. I studied the artists, I studied
musicians and athletes, and then slowly many, many
other kinds of people over the last forty years. I found
that one key to what made people really have a good
life is an ability to experience what I call flow. Flow is
immersion in what they're doing, complete concentration in a task they're doing. This comes from music, art,
athletics. But what's more interesting to me is how often
it comes from work—people can find this total commitment to some task at work. Often when people come
home they feel more depressed and kind of aimless and
purposeless because they think that at home things are
kind of automatically good but they aren't—unless you
make home life exciting and interesting.

Despite the bad rap that work gets, even for assembly-line people, for clerical and service people, it can be

a very exciting situation. In my book I make the case that if you are responsible for other workers under you, either as a supervisor, a manager, or a CEO, that part of your responsibility is to make conditions for expanse and flow more readily available in your company.

PM: How does one create more flow or more condition for flow to be expressed in work?

MC: Bits and pieces of what we found have been known for a long time by people. If the worker is very clear as to what they have to do moment by moment, not just kind of at the end of the year, you have added much value to the company. That clear goal is essential. Good feedback is essential. You have to know how well you're doing either because somebody tells you or because you have a metric built into the job that tells you whether you are actually achieving your goals.

The task should not be above what you can do or below what you can do but should be well matched to your ability. If you want to enjoy your job, you try to make it more complex or less complex. Make the demands not too high or too low on your skills and your ability. So clear goals, immediate feedback, matching your challenge and skills are essential.

One of the worst kinds of misunderstanding I think you find at work is to think that a smart worker is one who does as little as possible and is able to get away with as much as possible and invest as little of herself in the job as possible. But that prescription is almost sure to make you both bored and disaffected with what you're doing.

PM: So how can we customize jobs on an assembly line or a factory with thousands of workers to make sure that each one of them is engaged in a flow?

MC: Some jobs are much better designed for producing flow. But there are many ways of organizing an assembly line. By now most of those old-fashioned lines have been made obsolescent by robots doing the most menial task or the most repetitive task. If you are on the assembly line and you're not put in a situation where you can really use your skills there are things you yourself can do to make your job more challenging—for example, by varying the speed in which you operate.

PM: That's exactly the point you stress in your book on flow, that people can practice self-help even if they're not getting the leadership that they should get.

MC: Yes.

PM: That increases productivity, and that increases a level of happiness and sense of well-being. You have studied around the world for the last thirty, forty years in different countries and different cultures and found that if people are self-actualizing themselves they're much better adjusted than if they're not. Money itself is not something that makes a difference.

What is it about the brain chemistry or the psychology of people that puts them in that state of well-being when they're totally engaged in something that they like and they feel that they can make a difference?

MC: There are endorphins that work when you are involved. Some people get flow from being scared, other people get flow more from being busy, using their brain and playing music or chess or something. These activities stimulate different parts of the brain. The important thing is to develop control over your own attention so that you can produce this feeling by yourself.

PM: Sometimes people can be so absorbed in what they do that they don't even notice their surroundings.

MC: Absolutely. That's one of the hallmarks of flow: You forget time, you forget the place. One of my students studied women with breast cancer and found they report much less pain when they're really involved in what they are doing.

We have gotten to the point that too many people
don't really enjoy their work, they don't enjoy their
family life, so they need all kinds of extrinsic ways
of stimulating themselves to too much: drugs, alco-
hol, extreme forms of entertainment. That is not very
healthy. I think we have to make sure that we build flow
into the kind of things that really matter.

PM: Positive stress flow can involve challenges but they are
positive challenges and they're positive stress as opposed
to negative stress.

MC: That's right.

Samuel Gosling »

Assistant Professor of Psychology at the University of Texas

PETER MORRIS: Tell us about your specialty. I notice that you have a number of intriguing interests and studies in Applied Psychology starting with relations between work space and people.

SAMUEL GOSLING: That's right. The work space is part of this broader idea that the environments that we craft around ourselves are rich with clues about what we're like. Not only does my research look at work space in offices and cubicles, we also look at things like people's bedrooms, their Web pages, their music collections, and so on.

PM: As a show that celebrates the intersect between business and psychology I should note that your work would not only help people look at other people and observe them through their spaces but it should help the people better understand who they are.

SG: Yeah, and understand the impressions they convey to other people, too.

PM: There's a very strong correlation between self-awareness and perception of yourself by others. If you have a healthy and reasonably accurate view of yourself and how you affect others and how you're perceived by others, you tend to be in a healthier mental state. Tell us some interesting points on what you've learned in your research.

SG: Well we've learned a number of things. We've learned that work space is a very rich environment with clues about people. There are a number of different mechanisms through which people leave traces of their personality in their spaces.

People often ask me, Can you learn a lot about someone from their work space or from meeting them? The answer's always, It depends on what you want to know.

PM: If one alters one's work space to create a better impression, will that have a salutary effect on the person's actions and thoughts as well?

SG: I think it may help a bit. But I think the more important point is that that's much harder to do than one
might think. I've been around a lot of people's offices
and a lot of people's bedrooms. One question I get a
lot is, Well surely before you sent your research team in,
surely the occupants just tidied up the place, so you're
not really learning about them at all, you're learning
about the impression they want to give you. Having
gone around to many offices one thing that becomes
very clear is there's a very big difference between a tidy
office and a tidied office. The power of personality leaves
its imprint on your spaces. You can't give the impression
of being a highly conscientious, organized, task-oriented person an hour before the assessment team comes
because you have to live that life. In order to have a
truly tidy place, a deeply tidy place, you have to live the
tidy life.

PM: What a lost opportunity it is in the recruitment and
interview process for jobs. Wouldn't it be good to have
the equivalent of a home visit at the candidate's current
office?

SG: I think it would, though I don't think, for example, that
you can learn a lot about how nice somebody is. But if
you're looking for someone who is time-focused, organized, and so on, then an office would be a very good
place to go.

PM: Can you match up certain tell-tale signs with certain
interests and values?

SG: Yes, you can. It's important to understand that there are
different ways that we leave our personalities on these
spaces.

The first one is the obvious one, what I call "identity
claims." This is where people make statements about
themselves to others. They put up a poster, which signals their values to others, or something like that. Then
there's self-directed identity claims that are a symbolic

expression of our feelings and values. We may, for example, have a pebble from the beach where we had our first kiss or something like that.

When you walk by someone's space it's not to get too hung up with any individual clue. We need to look for the overall pattern.

PM: Great point.

SG: One of the biggest signals of someone who is high on openness is these people tend to have very distinctive spaces. We saw a lot of those when we went around advertising offices. Those people tend to be creative, broad minded. Those people have distinctive things. It's hard to characterize them in terms of particular objects because what characterizes them is their uniqueness.

The next way to leave a mark on a space is what I call "behavioral residue." This is inadvertent reflections of who we are; these aren't deliberate statements. If you look at my office, it is full. The desk is full of papers, they're not in neat piles, and it's pretty chaotic. Now, those aren't there because I'm trying to send a deliberate signal to others about who I am. Those are the inadvertent residue of my behaviors. My bookshelf is disorganized because I don't put books back where they should be, and I don't line them up and so on. These are things that are just unintended consequences of our behaviors. That's a very good way of learning about people too, because you can see these traces of their behaviors, and of course personality ultimately is about behavior.

PM: That's well put. Well put. Does physical tidiness necessarily correlate to mental organization or does it tie more to physical organization, which may or may not relate to mental organization?

SG: I think it generally does. I think someone who has an organized desk—the books are in order, the pencils are sharpened, and they have spare stamps in the drawer and sufficient envelopes—those people are tidy, organized, those are people you would want to put in jobs where it was important to keep track of ideas and numbers and so on. If I was trying to find someone who would be an air traffic controller or who'd be an accountant, I would feel much better if I went into their office and the place was neat and tidy. Because they're not going to forget about the statement from December or they're not going to forget about the 747 coming in from Karachi. For other positions you may not need them to be high on that trait. You may want them to be more flexible with different rules for different sorts of jobs. So there isn't one trait that's good in all cases.

PM: That's interesting. I have a tax accountant who's brilliant in terms of tax treaties and nuances, and his office looks like W. C. Fields' office, papers go right up to the ceiling. But if you ask him to find something, he can go into the middle of a stack and pull out a single piece of paper. He's not physically organized, but he is mentally very organized.

SG: Maybe for what he does it's important to be creative and free thinking.

PM: Absolutely correct. Thank you very much.

Terry Bacon»

Author of *What People Want: A Manager's Guide to Building Relationships That Work*

PETER MORRIS: You offer a great solace to a manager who wants to have the employees that she is directing respect and even like her. You say that this can be accomplished without fraternizing. Just by learning how to treat employees like human beings. It sounds so obvious that there must be something revolutionary about it. Can you share with us your values on the subject?

TERRY BACON: I think it is obvious and when I was writing the book I felt a little silly giving some of the advice I gave because it seemed so self-evident. But the fact is, a lot of managers don't do it.

It's as simple as just calling people by name and treating them respectfully. What employees say they want in the workplace is not the holiday parties and the fun and frivolity. They say they want the manager to trust them, they want to feel challenged, they want to feel good about themselves, and they want to be appreciated for who they are and what they do. This is all pretty basic, but it does come down to the manager treating them like human beings instead of human resources and treating them sensitively and with respect.

PM: What are the best practices that managers can do to set the tone for a reciprocal and good relationship with his or her people?

TB: I think one of the first things is that they need to be able to give people responsibilities and let them go do their work. I said that the number one thing that people want from their manager is to feel that they're trusted. I work with so many managers who micromanage and hover over employees. If they talk to them at all it's to criticize something. It really comes down to letting people do their jobs. Challenge them, don't make them do mundane work all the time, but give them something that is deeply satisfying to them from a professional standpoint. Show them, too, that you're willing to work hard. I was surprised that 80 percent of the people

I surveyed said that it's very important to them to see that their manager has a very strong work ethic.

PM: That's all important. Can you give us some examples of manager negative moods that can affect employees?

TB: Well, everybody gets up on the wrong side of the bed sometimes. Sometimes you come in and you feel negative. What I tell managers is that you have to park that when you get into the office. You've got to try to set your moods aside and manage your relationships with employees so that they are positive. It's up to the manager to set a positive tone in the workplace, and I think if you do that, people will reciprocate. Of course not everybody will. Some people will take advantage of the boss no matter what. So my other piece of advice to managers is that you have to set boundaries.

PM: Such as what?

TB: For example, if somebody is sick, you should give them the day off. If they have a sick child or something, it's important to be humane and to allow them to take care of that. But if somebody starts taking advantage of it, you have to draw the line. As well, lots of people upwardly delegate. An employee will refuse to make a decision that he or she should make and force the manager to make it. Then they blame the manager if it goes wrong. One of the boundaries I recommend people set is to say, look, if it's your job you make the call, but you accept the responsibility for it.

PM: That's a key point. I find many people have trouble accepting responsibility for their actions or non-actions.

TB: Managers have to hire well. People like to feel confident and skilled, and I say, then hire competent, skilled people. If they don't do it, you really should let them go.

PM: Talk to me about disgruntled or unhappy employees in different situations. How should management cope with them? I understand that in your business life you were president/CEO of Lore International Institute, which is a global HR resource and consulting firm where you specialize in talent management executive education. You've also worked for companies like American Express, GE, Ford, Halliburton. In those situations you must come across disaffected or unruly or unhappy employees. What are some examples of how a manager deals with each type of disgruntled employee?

TB: If you have a lot of disgruntled employees it's a systemic problem. If there are conditions in the workplace that are causing that, you need to deal with it. If you have people leaving, do exit interviews and try to understand the reason they're leaving.

When you have individual disgruntled employees it's best to confront them with it; try to determine the source of the problem. If it is something you can deal with and they're a valued employee, then you probably should try to deal with that. Some people are just going to be unhappy no matter what you do. I tell people at Lore, we try to make this a great place to work but it's not for everybody. If this is a place where you can thrive, great, we want you. If it's not, you should go someplace else.

PM: As a manager you have to deal with these problems early on when they rear their head. You can't wait, put it under the rug, deny, delay, defer, because it only gets worse.

TB: Now that's right. It's like having something in your refrigerator that starts growing mold. You can't just ignore it; you need to get it out of there. If you have disgruntled employees they can spread.

PM: Terry, as you say, most employees aren't looking just for friends, fun, and intimate conversation with workplace peers. They want honesty, respect, clear communication, support, acceptance, cooperation, and trust. When they don't have that, they can be disgruntled. We've heard of examples in the press where people go postal and have shootings at factories, where people are hacking computers and so on. Can you give us some examples of how those situations occur and how they're dealt with?

TB: The situations occur for a variety of reasons. One of them recently happened in London. A Deutsche Bank employee named Helen Green sued the bank and won a $1.5 million judgment for harassment on the job. Harassment came primarily from other female employees, who did a number of stupid things, including boarding up her desk and losing her mail and taking her computer away when she had to work, things like that. It was the kind of behavior that the manager, who knew that it was going on, should have put a stop to it right away. This sort of thing happens more frequently than you might think.

PM: How did this picked-on employee end up in this situation?

TB: She came in and didn't develop relationships. There was a long-time clique that existed there, and she didn't fit in. She did not socialize with people. She preferred to go home after work.

On the other hand it shouldn't be up to an employee to have to socialize with the people they work with. My research showed that only about 7 percent of people go to work expecting to develop friendships with their co-workers. It's not necessarily why people go to work.

Certainly the manager of that group should have known what was going on. I think he did know what was going on and failed to act.

PM: And that's where the company became liable.

TB: The company became liable, absolutely, yeah. For a million and a half dollars, which is no small sum.

PM: Let's say you do work for a company, like Halliburton, that does business in dangerous areas. Halliburton employees drive a truck and make a hundred thousand, two hundred thousand dollars a year, and yet they become disgruntled. How do you manage people in tough workplace situations where they're getting combat pay, so to speak, yet they still seem to never be happy?

TB: Obviously that's an extreme situation. In situations like that the trade-offs for the employees are very explicit. It is a contract where they accept a certain amount of risk for the reward they're receiving.

When you have disgruntled employees it's best to try to understand the source of the issue. In a minority of cases it's going to be somebody who's chronically unhappy and they're just not going to be satisfied at all. But often it's a systemic issue or it's an issue with the manager.

I worked with one of the large automakers where an entire workgroup was unhappy, and it stemmed from the boss. This boss was a micromanager. She told people one thing then changed her mind later. What I had there were a hundred disgruntled employees, and all had the same reason.

PM: Assume the managers don't take swift action or they stand and let it happen, and then the employee wreaks havoc—either they hurt somebody on the job or they kill a few a people or they hack into the computer. Have there ever been cases where those companies have been called to task and found liable for allowing it to get that far?

TB: Absolutely, because the company bears responsibility for the safety of people in the workplace. If you fail to act on a situation and someone goes postal, companies absolutely have been found liable. You have a responsibility I think to ensure safety in the workplace, and that's why there's no substitute for very swift action if you sense that someone's reaching the brink. You have to take them off the line and deal with the situation very quickly.

PM: That's a very important point because it's now no longer an issue of an employee needing to leave or have his
or her job changed, but you're dealing with the lives of
other people, you're dealing with personal property, corporate property, and third-party customers.

What happens when a whole unit becomes
unhappy? You gave an example earlier where a hundred
people were unhappy about the same thing. Does that
spread like wildfire where there's a couple of people
who are unhappy, management ignores it, then they go
to each other and form their own support group?

TB: That's exactly what happened in this case. A lot of people were unhappy and of course they talk to each other.
They're in the meetings together, they see what's going
on, they see how their peers are treated or mistreated.
People in a case like that get bunker mentality. They
hunker down. You have very suboptimal performance
from this group, and that's where companies suffer most.
The greatest challenge for companies is that a whole
unit or a group of people will just shut down. They'll
start doing what's required but nothing more.

PM: Are you ever brought in when people in a group are
disgruntled and you have to have a certain amount of
emergency work to help level the situation before it
becomes totally dysfunctional?

TB: Yes. We are commonly called in in situations like that
where we really have to do a massive triage to overhaul
the whole thing.

PM: Can you give us an example of that?

TB: An example of it is actually an organization I'm working with now. It's a large nonprofit, and there are really
issues all around. The board hasn't been doing its job, the
executive director is an outstanding person and techni-
cally very competent but really lacks the management
skills to do what he should, the employees have a history

of delegating upward, forcing this executive director to make decisions and then blaming him for it when they don't work.

In a case like that, work with everybody throughout the chain; from the chairman of the board to the other board members to the executive director to the employees. In cases like that I just go right back to basics: let's establish a charter for each person that explains that person's roles and responsibilities and establish some measurements for how the organization's supposed to work.

PM: What I find to be the case in a lot of entrepreneurial companies is too much overlap, often there's too much flying by the seat of the pants. It's a good exercise every once in a while to have people put in writing what they think their job description is and what their mission is.

TB: One of the main symptoms of a lack of understanding of mission is when you hear people start saying, it's not my job. Usually for me that is a sign that you have some fairly serious issues just in defining the purpose of the organization and the roles of the people within it. There's no substitute for clarity in a case like that. You have to sit down and get people to rethink what they're doing and clarify their roles and responsibilities and their actions and communications with other people.

One thing that people expect in the workplace is fairness. If you've got a situation where some people are having to do the jobs of others and they see that these other people are being paid the same or in some cases even paid more . . . there's no easier or faster way to mess up a workplace.

index